OXFO LATIN COURSE

G000255074

TEACHER'S BOOK
PART III
SECOND EDITION

CONTENTS

MAURICE BALME & JAMES MORWOOD
OXFORD UNIVERSITY PRESS

Oxford University Press, Great Clarendon Street, Oxford OX2 6DP

Oxford New York

Athens Auckland Bangkok Bogotá Buenos Aires
Calcutta Cape Town Chennai Dar es Salaam Delhi
Florence Hong Kong Istanbul Karachi Kuala Lumpur
Madrid Melbourne Mexico City Mumbai Nairobi Paris
São Paulo Singapore Taipei Tokyo Toronto Warsaw

and associated companies in
Berlin Ibadan

Oxford is a trademark of Oxford University Press

© Oxford University Press 1997
Reprinted 1999

ISBN 0 19 912232 6
All rights reserved. This publication may not be reproduced,
stored in a retrieval system or transmitted, in any forms or
by any means, without the prior permission in writing of
Oxford University Press.
Within the UK, exceptions are allowed in respect of any fair
dealing for the purposes of research or private study, or
criticism or review, as permitted under the Copyright,
Designs and Patents Act, 1988, or in the case of reprographic
reproduction in accordance with the terms of licences issued
by the Copyright Licensing Agency. Enquiries concerning
reproduction outside those terms should be addressed to the
Rights Department, Oxford University Press, at the
address above.

Printed and bound in Great Britain by
Butler & Tanner Ltd, Frome and London

Introduction

We have made this revision of the Oxford Latin Course in response to many suggestions received from teachers in both Britain and the United States; we are extremely grateful for their encouraging and constructive response to our queries. While the basic principles of the course remain the same, we have introduced several changes.

What is different about the New Oxford Latin Course?

The biggest change we have made is to split the course into four parts instead of three. Part I uses only the present tense of the verb together with imperatives, present infinitive and the first three declensions. Part II completes the indicative tenses of the verb, active and passive, and introduces the 4th and 5th declensions. Part III immediately introduces the subjunctive and covers all common Latin syntax; it is inevitably longer than the first two parts and incorporates a fair amount of 'real' Latin in the later chapters. The final part is a straight reader of the same authors as those presented in the old Part III.

We have reduced the length of some of the stories, especially in Part I. In a reading course that relies partly on an inductive method, it is essential that students should read as much continuous Latin as possible. However, a reading course must reflect the fact that the time allowed for teaching Latin has now been cut to the bone.

In order to reflect a wider cross-section of Roman society we have given female figures a greater role in the course, for instance by sending Horatia to school with Quintus and by including the stories of Psyche and Cloelia (Part I) and by adding letters from Scintilla to Flaccus and Quintus (Part II). We have likewise increased the amount of narrative that deals with daily life.

The learning curve of grammar and syntax has been made more gentle. In all parts there are several chapters in which little or no new grammar is introduced, to give students a chance to catch their breath.

Another big change is that each book is now divided in two; the narratives, comprehension exercises and background essays come first; then, in the second half of each book, come the grammatical explanations and exercises. This has two advantages: first, the narratives present an uninterrupted story with social and historical comment in the essays; second, the presentation of the grammar is made clearer.

We have expanded the grammatical explanations to some extent, filling in some gaps (e.g. the vocative and the mixed conjugation are explained in their proper places). The fuller grammatical explanations may afford some difficulty to younger students; we suggest that teachers handle these as suits the age and ability of their students, perhaps by using less grammatical terminology.

We have added four new types of exercise: (1) the occasional short playlet, to encourage students to speak Latin aloud fluently and expressively; (2) *Respondē Latīnē* exercises, in which students are asked to answer questions on the narrative in Latin; (3) grammatical exercises concentrating on the different parts of the verb; (4) word-building exercises intended to increase students' vocabulary.

Much of the background material has been completely rewritten, partly in order to cover hitherto neglected aspects of the ancient world. We have also considerably increased the amount of primary source material in the essays, so that students may be encouraged to make a direct response to the activities and attitudes of the ancient world.

We have added an appendix to each part, which gives a longer passage (in Part III, several longer passages) of continuous Latin to encourage fluent reading.

The Teacher's Books now include an expanded commentary on points of language and background, translations of all narratives and exercises, as well as three attainment tests for each part. There is also an appendix on metre in the Teacher's Book for Part III.

The aims of the course

Our aims throughout the course have been for the student:
1 to develop, at an appropriate level, a competence in the language studied;
2 to read, understand, appreciate and make a personal response to some of the literature in the original language;
3 to acquire some understanding of the civilization within which the literature studied was produced;
4 to develop a sensitive and an analytical approach to language by seeing English in relation to a language of very different structure and by observing the influence of the ancient language on our own;
5 to develop the ability to observe, abstract and analyse information, paying due regard to evidence, and to develop a sympathetic awareness of others' motives and attitudes.

3

These admirable but ambitious aims match those of the GCSE National Criteria for Classical subjects in the UK. They are unlikely to be achieved unless, from the very start, our students read Latin not as a linguistic jigsaw but as a vehicle for conveying meaning to which they habitually make a personal response. We have tried to construct a narrative that will evoke such a response, at first at a simple level, but gradually becoming more sophisticated. As students develop some understanding of Roman culture and history through the Latin narrative, the illustrations and the background sections that conclude each chapter, and as Horace himself slowly emerges as a sympathetic character, they may respond intelligently to the actual poems embedded in the later stages of the narrative.

The structure of the course

Of the four parts into which the course is now divided, the first three provide an introduction to the language, culture and literature of the Romans. By the end of Part III basic grammar and syntax have been covered and the student should be ready to tackle unabridged texts. The final part is a reader, containing passages from Golden Age authors – Caesar, Cicero, Catullus, Virgil, Livy and Ovid.

The first three parts take the form of a narrative which tells the story of the life of the poet Horace. Part I covers his boyhood and schooling in Venusia, with digressions when his schoolmaster tells stories from the *Iliad* and *Aeneid*, to which are now added stories told by Scintilla and Flaccus to their children. In Part II Flaccus takes Horace to Rome to the school of Orbilius. He goes on to study under the rhetor Heliodorus and then proceeds to the Academy in Athens. This part ends with the murder of Cicero, the father of Quintus' friend Marcus. In Part III, with the arrival of Brutus in Athens, Quintus becomes involved in political events and joins the army of Brutus. After the defeat and death of Brutus, he returns to Italy; his parents have disappeared in the chaos of civil war, and he goes to Rome. We then trace his career as a poet and his friendship with Virgil, Maecenas and Augustus. Part III ends with the deaths of Maecenas and Horace himself.

Part I is fictional, its fictions adhering to the few facts we know. Part II, though containing a great deal of fiction, is structured round known facts. Part III sees Horace at the centre of world-shaking events and moves much closer to history; in this part we often quote from contemporary authors, including a fair amount of Horace's own poetry.

It is impossible to make sensible recommendations on how long to spend on each part, as there are so many variants – the number of periods allowed each week, the ability and age of the students, whether students have studied any other foreign language, etc. If the time factor means that any of the course must be omitted, we suggest that the fabellae are the least important features in respect of narrative coherence and it is probably they that should be sacrificed.

Why Horace?

The choice of Horace as the central character has several advantages. First, his life covers the end of the republic and the Augustan revolution, the period of the Golden Age of Latin literature, which is the reading target at which we aim; and since Horace was involved in these great events, students acquire some understanding of the historical background to this literature. Second, Horace was an exact contemporary of the younger Marcus Cicero, to whom, at the cost of some bare-faced fiction, we give a major role in the story; this enables us to introduce his famous father, the one man about whom we know at first hand even more than we know about Horace himself. Third, his friendship with Virgil enables us to prepare the way for the extracts from the *Aeneid* that appear in the final part. By the time students come to read extracts from Caesar, Cicero and Virgil, the authors will be old friends, or at least acquaintances, whose social and historical background is already familiar. The literature will not, we hope, seem remote and unreal but related to what they have already read and relevant to their own experience.

Lastly, Horace's stay at university in Athens enables us to sketch in some of the Greek background to Roman literature; without some knowledge of this Roman poetry simply does not make sense, for, as Horace himself says:

Graecia capta ferum victōrem cēpit et artēs
intulit agrestī Latiō.
Greece captured took its wild conqueror captive
and brought the arts to rustic Latium.
(*Epistles* 2.1.155–6)

And so we intend that everything in the course should contribute to the overriding aim of preparing students to read the literature of the Golden Age with sympathetic understanding and intelligent appreciation.

Linguistic principles

We have tried to combine the best features of the modern and the traditional methods of teaching Latin. From the modern method, as exemplified by the Cambridge Latin Course, we accept that the aim of any Latin course should be the acquisition of reading skill and that everything else, linguistically speaking, should be subordinate to this aim. Hence translation from English into Latin is used only as an adjunct, to practise grammatical forms and concepts;

for this purpose, we believe it has an important role in the early stages.

Second, we accept that the Latin language should be taught in a Roman context, so that understanding of the language and the culture proceed *pari passu*.

Third, we accept that the acquisition of reading skill is in part an inductive process; that is to say, the student learns from experiencing the language as an instrument conveying meaning, not simply by analysis. As a broad principle we believe that students should first read with understanding (and, if required, translate) and then study the grammar and syntax they have already met in context. We do not insist on a rigid application of this principle; if experience suggests that in some cases it is more helpful to do so, teachers may want to explain the grammar before reading the narrative. But it remains true that the first experience of new grammar and syntax always occurs before explanation, in the captions below the cartoons which introduce each chapter. Moreover, we believe that in fact students can, after understanding the cartoon captions, in nearly every chapter, go straight on to the narrative and read it with understanding.

Although we accept what we have called an 'inductive' approach, we also believe firmly in the necessity of learning vocabulary and grammar thoroughly. We do not hold that 'immersion' in the language will enable students to form a 'personal grammar', as we do in our native language. We tabulate all grammar in the traditional form, though the order in which we introduce it is not traditional.

We are well aware that for those brought up on the traditional method our approach may at times seem unsound, if not bizarre. It certainly takes courage for a teacher who has never tried it to plunge into this method of teaching the language. We can only say that it works in an extraordinary way and that it is much more entertaining for both teacher and taught than the traditional method; it results in quicker progress and holds the students' interest. Finally, if the grammar is properly learnt after the narrative is completed and the exercises are carefully done, the student will acquire as sound a grasp of the language as those brought up on a purely analytic approach and will eventually read Latin literature with more fluency and appreciation.

Teaching methods

Cartoon captions

Every chapter begins with cartoons, the captions of which introduce new linguistic points. Their meaning is intended to be self-evident and students should be able to read and understand them straight off with the help of the pictures. We suggest that you read them to your students and then ask them to read them aloud, paying attention to correct pronunciation. Understanding can then be tested either by question and answer in English or by translation.

After reading and understanding the captions, most students will be able to tackle the narrative with no further explanation until they come to study the grammar; they will in fact have have acquired an understanding of the new linguistic points inductively. In the text we do occasionally make explicit comment on new features. Teachers must judge whether more formal explanation is necessary before tackling the narrative but we do not on the whole consider it desirable. If students ask questions about the grammar you must answer them honestly, but with as little delay as possible.

Chapter vocabularies

We have put the chapter vocabularies before the narrative. We do not recommend that students should learn these vocabularies until after the narrative has been read (vocabulary sticks better if it has been encountered in a context), but their reading will be more fluent if they have first glanced through the lists of new words. We have kept these lists as short as possible in relation to our target; learning becomes easier as more words appear which are related to words already known.

We arrange the words under the headings: verbs, nouns, pronouns, adjectives, adverbs, prepositions, conjunctions. Students who are unfamiliar with the names of parts of speech will need some help with these terms, but teachers should not make too much of this. Students will soon come to understand them from experience.

Verbs are arranged alphabetically by conjugation – 1st, 2nd, 3rd, 4th, mixed;* nouns and adjectives by declensions – 1st, 2nd, 3rd, etc.

Glosses

Unknown words that do not appear in the vocabularies are glossed in the margin of the narrative passages and elsewhere, but when a word has appeared three times glossed, we cease to gloss it (e.g. **ecce!**, **valdē**). Some words, the meaning of which is clear from the context and English derivatives (e.g. **flamma** in a fire context), are intentionally omitted; their meaning must be 'guessed'. Such words do appear in the General vocabulary but we consider that such 'guessing' is an essential skill; students should not allow themselves to be held up by ignorance of a single word, the meaning of which is clear from the context.

Students will be prepared to pass over difficulties which are glossed but unexplained, so that, as we repeatedly say in the commentary, teachers need not be delayed by these difficulties; the essential grammar at any given stage is learnt chapter by chapter after reading the narrative.

---

* 1st, 2nd, 3rd, 3rd **-iō**, 4th (US)

Narrative passages

It is intended that the narratives should be treated orally and taken as fast as the ability of your students allows. If they are taken too slowly, boredom will result; if they are taken fast, fluency of understanding will follow. A foreign language should be learnt through the ear as well as through the eye. The narratives – indeed, all the Latin in the course – should be read aloud by the teacher and, as far as possible, also by students, before any translation is attempted; and it should be read fluently and expressively with correct pronunciation. Although this recommendation may seem time-consuming, the practice will in fact speed up progress and encourage fluent understanding, and it will discourage word-for-word silent translation, which is death to any appreciation of literature. Teachers may wish to tell their students that Latin writers designed their works to be read at recitals to audiences and so Latin literature cannot be fully appreciated unless it is read aloud. (A guide to pronunciation is included in the Students' Book Part I (pp. 6–7), and practice in correct pronunciation, especially of vowels and diphthongs, should be the first thing to be taught.)

We want our students ultimately to understand Latin in Latin without translating. Although translation is the quickest and easiest method of testing understanding, teachers should not always require translation of the whole of every narrative, but should sometimes ask comprehension questions on a paragraph as a variant method of testing. To begin with, we suggest that the narratives are taken paragraph by paragraph; first the teacher should read a paragraph aloud, then the students should read it aloud, each perhaps taking a sentence in turn. Then the teacher should test comprehension by translation or questions on the meaning, or a combination of both; questions are useful if the student stumbles. The whole process should move quickly; the students' aim should be to read and understand the Latin at almost the same speed as they read English. In a long narrative it is always possible for the teacher, after reading a paragraph in Latin aloud, to translate it to his students. This does no harm provided the students revise the whole narrative for homework.

The ultimate test of understanding the sense of a passage is for the teacher to read it aloud once or twice while the students do not look at the text, and then test their understanding by comprehension questions or by asking them to tell the story in their own words. As an occasional variant, this exercise is much enjoyed.

Pair work in producing a written translation can be useful, if teachers are willing to allow students to discuss the translation process, though there is a danger that the abler pupil may find himself or herself doing all the work.

Translation is a complex process, not identical with understanding. The acceptable translation must not only be accurate but must express the meaning in natural English. The structure and idiom of Latin is often so different from that of English that word-for-word translation is unacceptable. Students who from the start elicit meaning from whole sentences or paragraphs are more likely to succeed in translating naturally.

Respondē Latīnē exercises

In most chapters the narratives are immediately followed by questions in Latin to be answered in Latin. It is intended that these exercises should be done orally and quickly, and as soon as the narrative is completed. Students must answer with a complete sentence in correct Latin. Some teachers may find that these exercises are too hard for their students and may decide to omit them. We do not supply answers to the *Respondē Latīnē* exercises in the Teacher's Book to Part III.

Comprehension exercises

Most chapters end with a passage of Latin continuing the story, some of which students are asked to translate; on the rest questions are asked which test the students' understanding without translation. We attach considerable importance to these exercises. They encourage students to read and understand Latin in Latin, which is our ultimate aim. They should be done after the grammar and vocabulary have been learnt. If teachers treat the main narrative orally, they may wish to ask for written answers to these exercises; this will show how fully the students have absorbed new grammar and vocabulary. Most of the questions can be answered by a close understanding of the Latin but we introduce some open-ended questions which ask for a response to the content of the story – the beginning of a critical understanding.

Fābellae

There are two playlets in Part III. The purpose of these is to encourage students to read Latin aloud fluently and expressively. You should first read the passage, with different students taking different parts, and make sure it is thoroughly understood, either by translation or questions on the meaning. Then, if time allows, it should be acted by the students.

Extracts of Latin poetry

From chapter 41 onwards we introduce excerpts from the poetry of Horace and Virgil. The chapters are so arranged that the harder passages usually come in the 'comprehension' sections; teachers who are pushed for time or who find these too hard for their pupils could omit them without missing out on any essential linguistic information. But experience has shown that although these extracts of poetry occur earlier than would be expected in a traditional Latin course, students cope with them unexpectedly well and usually enjoy them. This is partly because they are introduced in a context, which, in the case of the Odes, is admittedly foisted on them but which helps to make them more easily intelligible than if they were presented in isolation.

An appendix to the Teacher's Book gives a brief account of the metres used in the poems quoted in Part III and suggestions on how to teach them, for teachers who choose to do so. We do not consider it essential to teach students scansion at this stage, but it is important that they should be able to read the poems aloud rhythmically; all ancient poetry was written for performance aloud and sound is of paramount importance.

Grammar and exercises

If the narrative is taken orally and fast, there is a danger that understanding may be vague or incomplete. The exercises, by concentrating on particular points, impose the rigour that is missing in a purely inductive approach. Exercises testing understanding are placed immediately after the grammatical explanation of each point and take various forms: straight translation of Latin sentences, completion exercises, exercises concentrating on verb forms, etc. Most chapters end with an exercise demanding translation of short English sentences into Latin; these are the final test of grammatical understanding and are very useful in the early stages. The exercises are time-consuming and teachers will want to do some, e.g. those on verb forms, orally and quickly.

We do not give a commentary on all the grammar and exercises of every chapter; the grammatical explanations given in the Students' Book are generally sufficient.

Instead of the word-building sections which were placed after the *Respondē Latīnē* questions in the previous parts, a P.S. is added to each chapter after the exercises; these are sometimes additional word-building exercises, sometimes inscriptions or epigrams. The latter introduce no new linguistic features but extend the student's experience of the Roman world. Teachers will have to decide whether they have time to do these exercises in chapters which are already quite long.

Sequence of grammar and syntax in Part III

Parts I and II covered most basic accidence except for the subjunctive. Students have had extensive practice in the common sentence patterns of Latin and should be understanding them with ease and fluency. Part III introduces the subjunctive in the first chapter and goes on to cover all basic Latin syntax in rapid succession. By the end of Part III students should be ready to read unadapted Latin texts such as the extracts in Appendix 1.

Chapter 34
The subjunctive mood
The present subjunctive
Clauses of purpose
The imperfect subjunctive

Chapter 35
Indirect command
The pluperfect subjunctive
Passive forms of the subjunctive

Chapter 36
Deponent verbs
The present infinitive passive
Passive imperatives

Chapter 37
The ablative absolute

Chapter 38
The future participle

Chapter 39
Indirect questions
The perfect subjunctive

Chapter 40
Further uses of the ablative
Semi-deponent verbs

Chapter 41
Indirect statement

Chapter 42
Review

Chapter 43
Consecutive (result) clauses

Chapter 44
Conditional clauses

Chapter 45
Uses of the subjunctive in main clauses

Chapter 46
Review

Chapter 47
The uses of **cum**
The uses of **dum**
The connecting relative

Chapter 48
Clauses of fearing

Chapter 49
Impersonal verbs
Intransitive verbs in the passive

Chapter 50
Gerunds

Chapter 51
Gerundives

Chapter 52
Gerundives of obligation

Chapter 53
The predicative dative
The relative with the subjunctive

Chapter 54
Review
Summary of the uses of **ut**

The background material

The background material which is placed at the end of every chapter is intended bit by bit to build up a rounded, if incomplete, picture of Rome in the first century BC. We hope that it will both encourage students to acquire some understanding of the civilization within which the literature studied was produced, and develop their ability to observe, abstract and analyse information, paying due regard to evidence, as well as a sympathetic awareness of others' motives and attitudes (GCSE aims 3 and 5 (UK)).

We have followed each essay with questions which we hope will stimulate further thought about the topics raised, especially in the matter of how the civilization of Horace's day relates to the contemporary world. Here, of course, the differences are as important as the similarities. The questions can usually be answered on the basis of the background essays, the Latin story and, of course, the students' own experience. The level of sophistication demanded by these questions varies, and you may wish to omit some if they are too naive or too difficult for your students.

Where a topic appears to have struck a particular chord further reading may be encouraged. Some books recommended for following up topics are:

J. P. V. D. Balsdon: *Life and Leisure in Ancient Rome,* Bodley Head.
J. Boardman, J. Griffin, O. Murray (eds): *The Oxford History of the Classical World,* Oxford.
J. Carcopino: *Daily Life in Ancient Rome,* Penguin.
T. Cornell, J. Matthews: *Atlas of the Roman World,* Phaidon.
O. A. W. Dilke: *The Ancient Romans: How They Lived and Worked,* David and Charles.
M. Hadas: *Imperial Rome,* Time–Life Books.
N. G. L. Hammond, H. H. Scullard (eds): *The Oxford Classical Dictionary,* 2nd edition, Oxford.
P. Jones, K. Sidwell (eds): *The World of Rome,* Cambridge.
U. E. Paoli: *Rome: Its People, Life and Customs,*

Longman, repr. Bristol Classical Press.
D. Taylor: *Cicero and Rome,* Macmillan, repr. Bristol Classical Press.
G. I. F. Tingay, J. Badcock: *These Were the Romans,* Hulton Educational.

Our own debt to all of the above in compiling the background sections has been considerable. All are useful sources for additional information on many of the topics, and in the chapter commentaries we have only recommended specific books for additional reading where no very obvious or accessible alternatives exist. We are particularly grateful to Peter Jones and Keith Sidwell for allowing us to see the manuscript of *The World of Rome* (now published); this has made a valuable contribution to our essays.

Illustrations

The photographic illustrations and reconstructions in the text form an integral part of the course and should be discussed. Comments on them are included in the Commentary below.

Commentary

Cover illustration: a mosaic from Pompeii of the first century AD. The subject of birds around a birdbath is a popular one in Roman mosaics, and is here varied by the inclusion of two exotic parrots and a predatory cat.

Title page illustration: see note on pp. 22–3 below.

As Horace becomes more closely involved in the political events that shook the Roman world from the time of Philippi onwards, it becomes necessary to give a fuller account of what is going on. In this Commentary, among other things, we provide notes on aspects of the historical background which are touched on in the Latin narratives. Teachers will have to decide how much of this information they want to pass on to their students. At the same time we have from his own poetry and other sources much fuller and more reliable information on the events of Horace's life. We frequently quote from or paraphrase his own words; where we paraphrase such passages in the students' book, we give the relevant quotations in this Commentary.

It may be convenient here to give a list of Horace's works and their approximate dates of publication:

Satires 1	35 BC
Epodes	30 BC
Satires 2	30 BC
Odes 1–3	23 BC
Epistles 1	20 BC
Carmen Saeculare	17 BC
Odes 4	13 BC
Epistles 2	13 BC
Ars Poetica	10 BC

Chapter 34

Educated Romans regularly visited the famous sites of Greece and Asia Minor (cf. Catullus 46.6 – on his return journey from serving on the staff of the governor of Bithynia he visited the sites of Asia Minor: *ad clārās Asiae volēmus urbēs* ('let us fly to the famous cities of Asia')). Pausanias (fl. AD 150) wrote a guidebook for tourists with detailed descriptions of the sites.

Of all the sites in mainland Greece the most famous was probably Delphi and we may guess that Horace would have visited it while he was studying in Athens.

Cartoon captions

These introduce simultaneously present and imperfect subjunctive in purpose clauses with **ut/nē** and one example of the jussive subjunctive (**festīnēmus**, caption 2). This seems a formidable jump, but in practice students do not find it difficult.

If they falter at caption 1, ask them, 'Why did Quintus and Pompeius visit Delphi?' Answer: 'To see the shrine of Apollo.' This gives a precise translation of the **ut** clause and shows that the clause expresses purpose.

Caption 2: the clue to the meaning of **festīnēmus** is **age**. Quintus says, 'Come on, let's hurry.' It makes no sense to say 'Come on, we are hurrying.' It might then be worth confirming that whereas **festīnāmus** = we are hurrying, **festīnēmus** = let us hurry.

After reading captions 3 and 4, which will now occasion no difficulty, you could go straight on to the narrative, or, if you prefer, you could pause to consolidate what they have learnt from the captions by having a first look at what is said about the subjunctive in the Grammar section (p. 127).

Vocabulary

anteā, **antequam** (the preposition **ante** has already been learnt): you should make sure that students understand the distinction between preposition, adverb and conjunction. You may have to give them examples, e.g.

> **Delphōs ante noctem advēnērunt.**
> **Delphōs nōn anteā vīserant.**
> **antequam Athēnīs discessērunt, amīcōs valēre iussērunt.**

Quīntus Delphōs vīsit

Delphōs: Delphi is one of the many place names which are plural in form; compare **Athēnae, Athēnārum**.

4–8 ut ... vidēret; ut ... vīsāmus: students may ask why the tenses of the subjunctive differ; if you suggest that they translate in the less common form of English used to express purpose (he decided to go ... that he might visit; do you want to come that you may visit), they will find that English uses a similar sequence of tenses. But if no questions are asked, you can leave discussion of this until you study the Grammar.

7 Pompēium: Pompeius is the friend with whom Horace served under Brutus at Philippi; see *Odes* 2.7: **ō ... Pompei, meōrum prīme sodālium** ('O Pompeius, the first of my comrades'). We know nothing about him except what we learn from this Ode and although he served after Philippi under Sextus Pompeius, son of the great Pompey, we have no reason to suppose that he was closely related to him.

9 iamdūdum cupiō: 'I have long wanted' (present of remaining effects).

11 eāmus: 'let us go'. Students will notice that the present subjunctive of **eō** is **eam, eās, eat** etc. The only other forms of **eō** (stem **i-**) which start **e-** are **eō, eunt** and oblique cases of the present participle (**euntis** etc.). If **eāmus** is understood in its context, this point may be explained later.

13–14 eōsque monuit ut ... spectārent: 'and advised them to look at ...'. Indirect command is introduced in the next chapter, but as both the construction and the usual form of translation (English infinitive) are the same as those of purpose clauses, this example is unlikely to cause difficulty. No comment is necessary at this stage.

20 subitō Delphōs prōspexērunt: the site of Delphi is spectacular. The village is perched on the edge of the lower slopes of Mount Parnassus, two thousand feet above the valley of the Pleistos which leads to the Gulf of Corinth. Above it rise the two great cliffs known as the Phaedriades, 'the Shining Ones'.

The sanctuary of Apollo is an elaborate complex. On passing through the main gates you entered on the Sacred Way which winds up towards the great temple. On either side of the Sacred Way stood votive offerings made by individuals and states in thanks to Apollo; many states had built treasuries, buildings like small temples, in which to store the offerings they had made; the best preserved of these is the treasury of the Athenians, built in 490 BC to commemorate the battle of Marathon and to store a tithe of the spoils from this battle. The Sacred Way ends at the great temple; this stands on a massive platform and measures 197 feet by 72, austerely Doric in style. Successive temples were destroyed by fire, earthquake and plundering, but they were always rebuilt until the last was left to decay after

the dissolution of the Delphic oracle by the emperor Theodosius in AD 385. Its present ruined state makes it impossible to know anything for certain about the *adytum* (the inner shrine), an underground chamber in which the Pythia delivered Apollo's oracles.

Above the temple was the theatre. Apollo was the patron god of music and poetry, and every fourth year the Pythian games were celebrated, at which there were competitions in music (instrumental and choral) and drama, and recitations in verse and prose. To these were later added athletic competitions; a stadium was built high above the theatre and chariot races were held down in the plain.

We strongly recommend that you should show your students slides of Delphi, which remains even in its ruined form the most impressive and numinous site in Greece.

25 nē nox ... incidat: 'lest night falls on us'; **nē** here expresses fear rather than purpose, but the difference in meaning is minimal and students are unlikely to be bothered by this.

26 advēnerimus: future perfect indicative.

30ff. ā fronte: in front of the temple doors stood the altar where the priests made sacrifices to Apollo. Here we envisage a group of suppliants waiting to consult the god. We learn from ancient sources that there was always a queue of people waiting, either individuals or representatives of states sent on a sacred embassy. Some states, in return for their generosity to Apollo, were granted the right of jumping the queue, but most had to wait their turn. Moreover, the oracle only performed once a month for nine months of the year (in the three winter months Apollo was absent from Delphi) and so pilgrims often had to wait a long time.

When the time came, the procedure was elaborate. The suppliant first purified himself by washing in the Castalian spring. He then offered sacrifices, usually a goat, and a pelanos, a cake made from flour and honey. If the omens were propitious, he was next admitted to a room above the *adytum*. When his turn came, he handed the priest his question written on a lead tablet.

By now the Pythia, the priestess who was Apollo's medium, had descended to the *adytum*. Plutarch, philosopher and biographer, who was a priest of Apollo at Delphi from AD 95, says of the Pythia: 'She must come from one of the most honest and respectable families who live nearby and must always have lived an irreproachable life. When she descends into the place of prophecy, she does not take with her any kind of skill or talent, as she was brought up in the house of poor peasants.' She was in fact simply the vehicle through which Apollo communicated with men. Before entering the *adytum* she had purified herself by washing in the Castalian spring and by drinking from another sacred spring, Cassotis. She entered the *adytum* accompanied by the *prophētēs*, her interpreter, dressed in a simple white robe and holding in her hand a branch of laurel, sacred to Apollo. She seated herself on the sacred tripod (a three-legged stool) and fell into a trance. When she started to speak, the *prophētēs* would record her words. It was he who gave Apollo's response to the suppliant, either verbally or written on a tablet.

Despite the accounts of Plutarch and Pausanias, there is much doubt about what actually happened. Modern scholars reject the traditions that the Pythia chewed laurel leaves to achieve inspiration or breathed in vapours from a chasm below the tripod (there never was such a chasm). Whatever the actual process of possession may have been, there is no doubt that the vast majority of the Greeks took the whole business very seriously and believed in the truth of Apollo's oracle.

If the rituals were not observed, things could go badly wrong. Plutarch tells of a disaster which occurred in his time. The preliminary sacrifice had not been propitious but the suppliant insisted on going ahead (*Moralia* 438b):

> The Pythia went down into the *adytum* unwillingly, they say, and half-heartedly; and at her first response it was at once clear from the harshness of her voice that she was not responding properly and was like a labouring ship, as if she was filled with a mighty and baleful spirit. Finally she became hysterical and with a frightful shriek rushed towards the exit and threw herself down, with the result that not only the members of the deputation, but also the *prophetes* Nicander and the cult officials present fled.

A few days later the Pythia died.

42 futūrus: this is the future participle of **esse**; future participles are explained in chapter 38 but they are introduced in the narrative earlier, glossed.

43 vātēs Apollinis: **vātēs** meant originally a prophet but came to mean a poet, since a poet was the mouthpiece or interpreter of the Muses. The word has religious overtones. Horace uses it of himself, especially in conjunction with Apollo, e.g. **quid dēdicātum poscit Apollinem/vātēs?** ('What does his prophet ask of Apollo at his (temple's) dedication?', *Odes* 1.31.1–2; Horace writes at the dedication of the new temple of Apollo on the Palatine on 9 October 28 BC).

44 fōns Castalius: in drinking from the Castalian spring Quintus dedicates himself to poetry, for those who drank from it were inspired by Apollo and the Muses.

Quīntus Pompēiusque ad Brūtum īre parant

3 ineuntī: dative of the present participle of **eō** (**iēns, euntis**).

11 Pīraeum: the Piraeus was the port of Athens, about four miles from the city centre.

15 ad Asiam: after leaving Athens in September 44 BC, Brutus had gone to Macedonia to consolidate his army and had crossed to Asia in March 43 BC.

itūra: future participle of **eō**; so also **nāvigātūrus** (line 18), the future participle of **nāvigō** = about to sail.

Grammar and exercises

The subjunctive mood
This chapter makes a considerable leap forward but is not too difficult provided students understand the concept of 'mood', which is best introduced by examples in English. English expresses different moods by using auxiliary verbs ('may', 'might', 'let us' etc.); Latin changes the mood by using different verb terminations.

Students will notice that Latin, apart from the imperative, has one form only for all the non-factual moods – the subjunctive. To save confusion we only introduce in this chapter the 'jussive' use of the subjunctive in main clauses (other uses are not introduced until chapter 45). The term jussive is used to include both third person commands (e.g. 'let him go') and exhortations in the first person (e.g. 'let us go'); it is also found occasionally in the second person instead of an imperative, e.g. **dēsinās ineptīre** = stop playing the fool.

Both the present and the imperfect subjunctive are easily learnt. In the present, the difference in mood is indicated by the change of vowel: in the 1st conjugation **a** in the indicative, **e** in the subjunctive; in the other three conjugations (and the mixed conjugation) **a** in the subjunctive. **sim**, the subjunctive of **sum**, must be carefully noted; the only verbs which have this form apart from **sum** and its compounds are: **velim, nōlim, mālim**.

The imperfect subjunctive (1st person sing.) is formed by adding **-m** to the present infinitive active (the only exception is **fīō**, which has present infinitive **fierī**, but imperfect subjunctive **fierem**).

Clauses of purpose
It may seem a bit much to introduce purpose (final) clauses in the same chapter as that in which the subjunctive first appears. But the fact is that once the subjunctive has been learnt, these clauses present no difficulty. In modern English we almost invariably use the infinitive to express purpose, but it is worth making sure that students are familiar with the older form of expressing purpose in English, 'so that/lest we may ...'

etc., since in this form English uses the subjunctive and observes sequence, e.g. 'We are coming so that we may help you'; 'We came so that we might help you.' You might ask students to translate some of the sentences in exercise 34.3 both ways.

The rules of the sequence of tenses are restated in connection with indirect commands on p. 131 and yet again in connection with indirect questions on p. 144.

Students may find the use of the reflexives **sē** and **suus** in subordinate clauses difficult at first, since English makes no distinction between the reflexive and non-reflexive use of 'he, him, his' etc., but they will find that in all forms of indirect speech or thought the reflexives refer back to the subject of the introductory verb; purpose is a thought in the head of the subject of the verb which introduces the purpose clause; it is therefore 'virtual indirect speech' or 'suboblique'.

Background: Delphi

Exploration here could centre on the question of whether there is any kind of truth in the Delphic oracle. As we have seen (commentary on the first passage above), the priestess of Apollo, the Pythia, would go into a trance and give a frequently incoherent response which would then be put into meaningful, though often somewhat riddling, verse by the god's priest. These priests would gain much experience in giving advice and would presumably aim to interpret the utterances of the possessed Pythia in helpful ways. Plutarch illustrates the range of personal problems put to Apollo in his list of questions. People ask 'if they shall be victorious, if they shall marry, if it is to their advantage to sail, to farm, to go abroad'. The priests could give good, commonsensical advice to such questions. Thus it may be unfair to dismiss the whole business as a superstitious charade. For an excellent discussion, see the essay by Simon Price (chapter 6) in P. E. Easterling and J. V. Muir (eds): *Greek Religion and Society*, Cambridge University Press, and JACT: *World of Athens*, Cambridge University Press, pp. 98–100.

Teachers may like to read their students a translation of Aeneas' encounter with the priestess of Apollo at Cumae, where the Trojan hero landed in Italy, at *Aeneid* 6.42–155. Here Virgil creates a terrifying mystical aura as the Sibyl utters her dreadful prophecy.

William Golding's posthumous novel, *The Double Tongue*, Faber & Faber, is a striking book about a priestess at the Delphic oracle in its declining years.

Good visual material on Delphi can be found on the Perseus CD-ROM which operates on a PC/Mac computer and is available in the UK from Yale University Press, 23 Pond Street, London NW3 2PN, tel. 0171-431-4422.

Sources

p. 10, para. 2: 'Here I intend ...': *Homeric Hymn to Apollo* 247–53.
para. 3: the oracle's reply to Croesus: Herodotus 1.53.
p. 11, para. 1: the 'wooden wall' prophecy: Herodotus 7.140–44.

Illustrations

p. 8 (left): the Shining Rocks, the two Phaedriades, which tower behind the temple, are so called because they reflect the light. They are 800–1,000 feet high.

(right): for the Castalian spring, see the final paragraph of the background essay. The ruins in the photograph are of Roman or Hellenistic date.

p. 10: the ruins are of the great Doric temple of Apollo built in 366–c. 329 BC. It was reduced to its foundations by earthquakes and spoliation, but one complete column and parts of others were re-erected during the restorations of 1939–41.

p. 11 (above): in this photograph, we look down over the sanctuary of Delphi past the temple of Apollo which opens out into a vast valley containing the largest olive grove in Greece.

(below): Greek states built treasuries at Delphi to house their offerings to Apollo. At the same time they aimed to make propaganda points, especially through the beauty and expense of their buildings. The Doric treasury of the Athenians was built soon after 490 BC with a tithe of the spoils of Marathon. It was reconstructed by the French in 1904–6.

Chapter 35

Cartoon captions

In these, commands are first given directly with the imperative and then in indirect form with **ut/nē**. They should present no difficulty.

Quīntus mīlitat

2 **Dēlum**: the tiny island of Delos at the centre of the Cyclades was the birthplace of Apollo. According to the myth, Leto, pregnant by Zeus, wandered all over Greece and the islands looking for a place where she could give birth to her child, 'but no land dared to make a dwelling for Phoebus Apollo' (*Homeric Hymn to Apollo*); eventually Delos consented to allow Leto to give birth there: 'casting her arms about a palm tree, while the earth laughed for joy beneath her knees, Leto gave birth to Apollo'. The island thus became a holy place where the Ionians gathered every year for a

festival in honour of the god. By the time Quintus visited it, it had also become a commercial centre for the slave trade; it is said that 40,000 slaves changed hands there every day.

4 rediisset: the subjunctive is used because the **dōnec** clause is part of the indirect command (Quintus said: **nōlī nāvem solvere dōnec redierim**). In indirect speech all verbs in subordinate clauses are in the subjunctive. This is the first example of the pluperfect subjunctive but it is followed in the next sentences by **cum ... exiisset**, **cum ... spectāvissent** and **cum ... rediissent**. A word of explanation of the forms may be necessary but should not delay you at this stage.

10 Ephesī: Ephesus was at this time the most important port on the coast of Asia Minor. Its surviving remains are very impressive.

14 centuriōnem: for an explanation of the military ranks occurring in this chapter (*centuriō, tribūnus mīlitum, lēgātus*), see the backgound essay.

21 imperātōrem: this title was only given to generals who had been hailed as imperator after a victory; Brutus had been thus hailed the previous year after a victory over a Thracian tribe (the Bessi), against whom he had conducted a campaign before crossing into Asia.

24 prūdentēs ... vidēminī et strēnuī: the passive of **videō** is used to mean 'I seem'; students may notice that it is followed by a complement in the nominative (see chapter 36).

28 lēgātus ... trīstis īnspexit: the commander of the legion is, not surprisingly, sceptical about the military potential of these university students. Such recruits were apt to be promoted rapidly to become *tribūnī mīlitum* and Caesar had found to his cost that in a crisis they sometimes compared unfavourably with the long-service professional soldiers.

31 Lūcīlium: for Lucilius, see note on line 1 of the passage below.

Lūcīlius Quīntum ad disciplīnam mīlitārem īnstituit

1 Lūcīlium: Lucilius is a historical figure, whose death at the hands of mutineers is described by Tacitus (*Annals* 1.23; see p. 182 of the Students' book). We take from Tacitus his nickname **cēdō alteram** etc. His murder took place in AD 14, so his introduction here is an anachronism.

3 cēdō alteram (vītem): cēdō is an archaic imperative form (compare **estō** = be!), meaning 'give here'. Its only forms are **cēdō** (singular) and **cette** (plural).

vītem: centurions carried a vine staff as the symbol of their office, with which they belaboured the backs of errant soldiers.

3–4 cum ... frēgerat: 'whenever he had broken'; **cum** = 'whenever' is followed by the pluperfect indicative – see commentary on the Grammar section below.

As students have just been told that in past time **cum** is followed by the subjunctive, they may ask about this; if they do, you will have to explain, but if possible pass over it at this stage.

6 tēla ... gladiō: on the weapons of the Roman soldier, see the background essay.

opera: opus can mean a work of any kind, e.g. a work of literature, but in military contexts it is used particularly of fortifications.

19–20 quid facere dēbeātis: dēbeātis is subjunctive because the clause is an indirect question (see chapter 39). There is no need to explain this unless students ask about it; they will probably understand and translate without hesitation.

24–5 fīētis ... dignī: fīō = 'I become' takes a complement in the nominative (like **sum** and **videor**).

Grammar and exercises

Indirect command
This presents no difficulty, since the construction is the same as that of purpose clauses. In introducing indirect command you should remind students that **iubeō** (I order) and **vetō** (I forbid, I order not to) take the infinitive, as in English; but all other verbs introducing an indirect command or request are followed by **ut/nē**.

In exercise 35.1.5 **persuāsī** is followed by **ut dūcat**: it must therefore be a true perfect, 'have persuaded', as in the example above.

cum = when
The usages of **cum** are complex and they are dealt with more fully in chapter 47. In early Latin **cum** = 'when' took the indicative in all tenses, past, present and future, like other temporal conjunctions. But from Caesar onwards it is used with the imperfect or pluperfect subjunctive in past time, by the indicative in present and future time.

There are various exceptions to this rule, of which the commonest are:
1 the inverse **cum**, where the **cum** clause follows the main clause and the verb is in the indicative, e.g.
nox iam aderat cum domum rediērunt.
Night was already coming when they returned home.
Students are already familiar with this use.
2 iterative **cum**, i.e. **cum** = 'whenever', with pluperfect indicative, e.g.
cum vītem frēgerat, alteram ac rūrsus aliam poscēbat.
Whenever he had broken his vine staff, he asked for another and again yet another.
You may have to comment on this usage but don't delay over it.

Grammarians tie themselves into knots trying to explain why **cum** should have come to take the subjective; your students must just accept it as a fact.

Passive forms of the subjunctive
These are easily learnt, since in the present and imperfect, active person endings are simply changed to passive forms, as in the indicative; and in the pluperfect, the indicative (**parātus eram**) is changed to the corresponding imperfect subjunctive (**parātus essem**). Students will probably recognize them without any prompting.

Background: The Roman army – 1

This background section is largely informational in content. To the questions at the end could be added another: What do your pupils think of the Roman soldier's life? It sounds decidedly grim, but the low pay was doubled by Julius Caesar in 59 BC (Suetonius: *Divus Julius* 26.3) and there may have been considerable appeal in getting away from the life of a farmer to more exotic locations and in gaining plunder and the prestige of a successful campaign. Livy (42.34) tells of a former centurion named Spurius Ligurius who, when well into his fifties, complained that centurions over fifty were excluded from service. (See P. Jones and K. Sidwell (eds): *The World of Rome*, Cambridge University Press, chapter 4.)

Two valuable books for further exploration of the background material in this and the following chapter are Peter Connolly: *Greece and Rome at War*, Macdonald, and Sir John Hackett (ed.): *Warfare in the Ancient World*, Sidgwick and Jackson.

Illustrations

p. 13: the stone lions of Delos stand beside the Sacred Way which led from the sanctuary of Apollo to the Sacred Lake. Carved from Naxos marble at the end of the seventh century BC, they are badly weathered. Five remain *in situ*; one more is positioned before the Arsenal in Venice.

p. 14: the Harbour Street at Ephesus dates from the fourth century BC. The harbour to which it led has now silted up. It was one of the few streets in the ancient world to have street lighting. According to a dubious tradition, St Paul, whose Christian teaching sparked off a serious demonstration here (Acts 19, 22ff.), was imprisoned on the hill to the left.

p. 17 (below): our illustration from Trajan's column shows a field dressing station. On the right, a dresser, holding a roll of bandage, attends an auxiliary with a wound in his thigh; in his pain, the soldier grits his teeth and clutches the rock he is sitting on. To the left, a medical officer examines a legionary soldier.

Chapter 36

Cartoon captions

It is essential to warn students that the verb forms in bold print are passive in form but active in meaning; there is no way they can induce or guess this from the context. It may indeed be a blow to their self-confidence to find, after they have learnt laboriously to distinguish between active and passive, that some common verbs appear to confuse the issue. (For more on deponent verbs, see the commentary on the Grammar section below.)

When your students come to study the list of deponent verbs in the Vocabulary, you will need to draw attention to the passive form of the present infinitive, which is dealt with explicitly in the Grammar section.

Scintilla dēspērat

1 **nūntiī peiōrēs**: by now it would have been known that Antony and Octavian were leading their armies against Brutus and Cassius.
4 **tabellārius**: **tabellāriī** were couriers hired by individuals or companies to carry letters to and from the provinces.
5 **signum**: 'seal'; letters would ususally be written on tablets (hence **tabellārius**) which were tied together and imprinted with a seal.
7–8 **quid passa es?**: 'What have you suffered?', but we would say, 'What has happened to you?'
11 **ō diem nigrum**: exclamations are in the accusative case.
15 **officium suum perficere dēbet**: Flaccus, though born a slave, is a patriotic Roman citizen and a staunch defender of the republic and the old republican virtues. Perhaps he was inclined towards Stoicism, which laid great stress on duties.
23ff. **Quīntus tamen imprūdens est ...**: Decimus is a prudent man, who chooses what appears to be the stronger side; to him the Liberators are assassins. He has a larger stake in the status quo than Flaccus and is not prepared to sacrifice it for 'liberty', to him no more than a name. His attitude results in a family schism. Such divisions must have been a common feature of the civil war at this time, and indeed of all civil wars.
36–7 **saeviet ... terrārum**: before Scintilla faints, her last words anticipate Virgil: *Georgics* 1.510: *saevit tōtō Mars impius orbe*.

Fābella: Quīntus Pompēiusque ad disciplīnam mīlitārem īnstituuntur

The playlet offers some light relief in the midst of the darkening shadows of civil war. It is linguistically easy and could be done quite quickly, but can be omitted without missing any new linguistic features.

13 ecce, hostēs in nōs prōgrediuntur: Lucilius is playing a war game. Pompeius is too stupid to understand this, or perhaps he is pretending not to, to annoy Lucilius.

35 dextrō pede: Roman soldiers marched off right foot first, whereas our soldiers start with the left.

Grammar and exercises

Deponent verbs

Latin deponents are verbs which have 'laid down' (**dēpōnere**) their active forms. A fair number of Latin deponent verbs have less common active forms, e.g. **comitō** besides **comitārī**, **assentiō** besides **assentior** etc. It is bound to be hard for students to understand why any verbs which are passive in form should be active in meaning; and unless some have studied Greek and understand that these verbs function like Greek middle verbs, you cannot offer them any explanation. They will just have to accept it as a peculiarity of the language. They must learn the list of deponent verbs with special care.

The present infinitive passive of 3rd and mixed conjugation verbs always causes trouble; you should draw special attention to this form.

Passive imperatives

These forms will hardly be met, as we say, except from deponent verbs. They are ambiguous in form, the singular being the same as the present active infinitive, and the plural being the same as the 2nd person plural of the present passive indicative; the context will be the guide to the meaning.

Exercise 36.6

In 2 'setting out' will be translated by a perfect participle, since the action of 'setting out' precedes that of 'we sailed.' But in 7 'going out' will be a present participle, since we met the commander at the time when he was going out. Latin is more precise in its use of tenses than English.

Background: The Roman army – 2

Siege (pp. 22–3): a poweful description of a successful siege by the Romans, that of Jerusalem by Titus in AD 70, is in Josephus (*The Jewish War* 21).

corōna cīvica (p. 23, para. 3): it was proposed that this should be awarded to Cicero for having saved Rome from Catiline's conspiracy (Aulus Gellius: 5.6); and the senate decreed that a civic crown should be hung from the top of Augustus' house (Cassius Dio: 53.16). A further topic for exploration could be the regard in which we hold military heroes today. How do we honour them?

For further reading, see background notes on chapter 35.

Illustrations

p. 20: in another scene from Trajan's column, a Roman commander and his legionaries look on from their camp as auxiliary troops battle with attacking Dacians. To the right, Roman troops prepare to repel an assault on their section of wall.

p. 23 (below): our illustration from Trajan's column shows the *testūdō* formation. The enemy are rushing back into their fortress, while the legionaries ascend the hill under the cover of their shields.

Chapter 37

Cartoon captions

Each of the captions contains an ablative absolute phrase. Students should be encouraged to translate them by English clauses ('when the sun was rising', 'when they had put on their arms' etc.). In reading and understanding Latin the ablative absolute may present little difficulty, but students will find it hard to use them correctly in translating from English into Latin.

Philippī

1 in Asiā: the Roman province of Asia covered the western and central parts of Turkey. Brutus had moved into Asia late in 43 BC and spent the following months in securing the province to his cause, raising money and reducing cities which opposed him.

2 plērīsque proeliīs: the most important of these actions was the reduction of the city of Xanthus in Lycia, south of Asia proper.

11 tribūnum mīlitum: we have made Quintus serve so far as an ordinary soldier (*mīles gregārius*); now he is suddenly promoted to be a *tribūnus mīlitum*. The *tribūnī mīlitum*, six to a legion, were young men from senatorial or equestrian families who in peace time were elected by the people, but no doubt in war the army commander could appoint soldiers to fill vacancies. Horace himself tells us that he served as a tribune; he says that people carp at him because he, a freedman's son, became a tribune: *quod mihi pārēret legiō Rōmāna tribūnō* (*Satires* 1.6.48). In fact, he says here that he commanded a legion as a tribune, and in the comprehensiō exercise we make him take over command of his legion when the legionary commander is killed in the first battle of Philippi.

13 ōrātiōnem habuit: the Latin idiom for 'made a speech'.

15 hērēdēs tyrannī: 'the heirs of the tyrant'; Octavian was literally the heir of Julius Caesar, the tyrant; Antony was competing to become the heir to his power.

18 meminerīmus: perfect subjunctive; **meminī** is a defective verb, i.e. it has only perfect stem tenses, and so the perfect subjunctive is used here (in a jussive sense), where an ordinary verb would have the present subjunctive.

23 Cassius eī obviam iit: Cassius joined Brutus with twelve legions at Sardis in August 42 BC, and the first battle of Philippi took place on 23 October.

26 prope Philippōs: Brutus' army had taken up a strong position blocking the advance of Antony and Octavian, who at once attacked, since they were short of supplies. In the first battle Cassius was routed and, hearing that Brutus had also been defeated, took his own life.

29 Mars anceps fuerat: literally, 'Mars (god of war) had been two-headed (i.e. undecided)'.

Brūtus vincitur

This passage describes the second battle of Philippi, which took place about three weeks later. After a hard fought engagement Antony broke Brutus' left wing and routed his forces. Brutus then committed suicide. Brutus' last words were a quotation from a lost Greek tragedy: 'Unhappy Virtue, you are, it seems, no more than a word, but I practised you as though you were a fact; but you were a slave to Fortune' (Dio: 47.49.2). Antony was deeply moved by the death of Brutus, who had once been his friend; he took off his purple cloak and threw it over Brutus' body (Plutarch: *Brutus*). The battle marked the final and irrevocable end of the republican cause: 'Henceforth nothing but a struggle of despots over the corpse of liberty' (R. Syme: *The Roman Revolution*, Oxford, p. 205).

4 proeliō exitiālī: Brutus describes the battle as **exitiālī** although it had been a draw, because casualties had been high and his friend and fellow-commander Cassius had died as a consequence of it. In fact the two battles of Philippi were the bloodiest of the whole civil war.

5 tē ipsum legiōnī praeficiō: the evidence for Horace's command of a legion is in *Satires* 1.6.48 (*quod mihi pārēret legiō Rōmānō tribūnō*). Horace does not say that he was promoted to be *lēgātus*, an appointment which could be made only by the senate, and we assume that he took over on the death of the *lēgātus* as a tribune.

The historical background, 42–31 BC

The events between the battle of Philippi and the battle of Actium are complex; we give a brief summary followed by a chronological chart, showing how the known events of Horace's life fit in.

After the battle of Philippi Octavian and Antony divided the Roman empire between them, ignoring Lepidus. Antony remained in the East to raise money

and consolidate control, Octavian returned to Italy. He had to disband 100,000 veterans; to provide for them, he took land from eighteen cities of Italy, including Venusia. This led to widespread discontent and violent resistance, encouraged by Antony's brother L. Antonius, who raised eight legions and occupied Rome. He was forced out of Rome and occupied Perugia, which was taken and sacked after a siege (winter 41/40 BC).

In spring 40 BC Antony returned to Italy from the East and when he was refused admittance to Brundisium, it looked as if there would be another civil war. This was averted through the diplomacy of Maecenas; an agreement (Treaty of Brundisium) was reached in October 40 BC by which the division of the empire was confirmed, Octavian to control all the West and Antony all the East; Lepidus was shipped off to Africa; the agreement was sealed by the marriage of Antony to Octavian's sister Octavia.

Meanwhile Sextus Pompeius, son of Pompey the Great, who had escaped after the battle of Philippi, carried on the struggle from Sicily, where he had been joined by numerous staunch republicans, including Marcus Cicero and Quintus' friend Pompeius. He had a large fleet and blockaded the coast of Italy. In 39 BC he met the Triumvirs at Misenum and made a treaty by which he was given a large command including Sicily; at the same time there was an amnesty, allowing the republicans who had fought with him to return to Rome. But he was soon at war with Octavian again and defeated him in two naval battles (38 BC). The following year Antony gave Octavian 120 ships (Treaty of Tarentum) and in 36 BC Agrippa defeated Pompeius at Naulochus. He was captured and executed in 35 BC. This marked the end of all republican resistance.

Despite the Treaty of Tarentum, the reconciliation between Octavian and Antony was shaky and a rupture became inevitable when Antony sent Octavia back to Rome and proceeded to join Cleopatra in Alexandria, acknowledging that he was father of the twins she had borne four years earlier. For the next two years while Octavian was consolidating his power in the West, Antony was involved in campaigns in Parthia and Armenia. When he returned to Alexandria in 33 BC, he formally divorced Octavia and married Cleopatra; as a wedding gift, he presented her and her children with most of the provinces of the eastern empire (the Donations of Alexandria). This gave Octavian the chance to unite Italy behind him in a war of propaganda in which Antony was represented as subservient to an eastern queen scheming to take over the Roman empire. When it was clear that Octavian was bent on war, three hundred senators left Rome to join Antony. The stage was set for the final round of the civil wars. In 32 BC the senate formally declared war on Cleopatra.

In summer 31 BC, leaving Maecenas in charge of

Italy, Octavian transported his army to Greece and after some months of manoeuvring encamped at Actium near to the camp of Antony. Agrippa, Augustus' general, won control by sea and Antony, whose forces were depleted by hunger, disease and desertions, was forced to offer battle by sea. The battle was fought on 2 September.

Chronological table

BC

42	Battles of Philippi (Oct, Nov)	
41	L. Antonius occupies Rome	
41/40	Siege of Perugia	?Horace returns to Italy*
40	Treaty of Brundisium; Antony marries Octavia	?Horace begins the *Epodes*; ?Virgil introduces Horace to Maecenas
39	Treaty of Misenum; amnesty	Marcus Cicero returns to Rome; Horace becomes *scrība quaestōrius**
38	Octavian at war with Sextus Pompeius; Maecenas' embassy to Antony	Horace begins *Satires* 1; Virgil's *Eclogues* published
37	Treaty of Tarentum; Triumvirate renewed	Virgil begins the *Georgics*
36	Agrippa defeats Sextus Pompeius	
35		Horace's *Satires* 1 published
33	Antony divorces Octavia and marries Cleopatra	?Maecenas gives Horace the Sabine farm
32	Rome declares war on Cleopatra	
31	Battle of Actium	
30	Antony and Cleopatra commit suicide at Alexandria	Horace's *Epodes* published

Grammar and exercises

The ablative absolute

This does not often present difficulty in reading Latin; once the principle has been explained, it is easily recognized. In exercise 37.2 we have put commas around the ablative absolute phrases, to show that they are independent of the structure of the rest of the sentence. Exercise 37.5 is probably the hardest exercise up to this point, since the English will not go straight into Latin; in every sentence the verbs are active in English but the Latin past participles are passive.

*The dates of Horace's return to Italy and his appointment as *scrība quaestōrius* are not known; Fraenkel (Horace, Oxford, p. 53) says he probably became *scrība quaestōrius* in 41 BC; we make it rather later.

Students should rephrase the English before translating, e.g. 'After greeting her mother ...' becomes 'Her mother having been greeted ...'.

In rephrasing the English in exercise 37.6, students will have to think whether they are using ordinary active verbs (with perfect participles passive in meaning) or deponent verbs (with perfect participles active in meaning).

In exercise 37.7, the ablative absolute phrases consisting of two nouns in the ablative are usually best translated by a clause, e.g. 'when Quintus was a boy', 'as the wind was following'; but English can also use a prepositional phrase, e.g. 'with a following wind', 'in the consulship of Pompey and Crassus', 'under the leadership of Brutus'.

Background: Brutus and Cassius

Exploration here could take the form of discussion of the characters of Brutus and Cassius. What do your pupils think of them? We may in fact have given an excessively idealized view of Brutus in our story and in this background passage. When Cicero was governor of Cilicia, he found to his disgust that Brutus was trying to wring interest at 48 per cent out of the people of Salamis in Cyprus, to whom he had made a substantial loan. (The traditional rate was 12 per cent.) His agent starved five of the local council to death. Caesar used to say of Brutus, *Quidquid vult, valdē vult* ('When Brutus wants something, he really wants it'). When seen in the context of the Salamis affair, these words have a sinister ring to them.

Even so, he surely possessed a fundamental integrity. Quintilian's comment on Brutus' philosophical writing may well have a wider application: *sciās eum sentīre quae dīcit* ('You can tell he means what he says').

The Shakespeare quotation (p. 28, para. 6) is from *Julius Caesar* (Act 5, scene 5).

lines 4–5: i.e. he alone was a member of the conspiracy because he was moved by a sincere belief that what he was doing was for the public good.

line 6: **gentle**: noble and magnanimous; **elements**: the Elizabethan view was that the four elements (earth, air, fire and water) made up the four humours of the body (phlegm, blood, melancholy and choler); these had to be perfectly balanced to create a physically and morally healthy man.

Shakespeare made considerable use of Sir Thomas North's translation of Plutarch's *Lives*, published in 1579. In the lines we have quoted he adapts the *Life of Brutus*: 'Antonius spake it openly divers times that he thought that of all of them that had slain Caesar there was none but Brutus only that was moved to do it as thinking the act commendable of itself; but that all the other conspirators did conspire his death for some private malice or envy that they otherwise did bear unto him.' Elsewhere in the *Life* Plutarch remarks that 'he was a marvellous lowly and gentle person ... was well-beloved of the people ... was rightly made and framed unto virtue'.

Illustrations

p. 25: this further scene from Trajan's column shows Roman soldiers setting off from camp. On tent poles over their left shoulders they are carrying a heavy load of kit, including a pack, a bottle for wine, and cooking pots.

p. 26: this relief is from the Arch of Constantine (AD 315) which was made up fragments from older monuments. The great historian Edward Gibbon described it as 'a melancholy proof of the decline of the arts, and a singular testimony of the meanest vanity'. However, situated next to the towering ruin of the Colosseum, it makes a powerful impression. The general is probably Hadrian.

p. 27: the acropolis of the town built for Octavian's sister Octavia after the defeat of Caesar's assassins in this area in 42 BC. The towers in the background are medieval.

p. 28: coins of Caesar, Cassius and Brutus (British Museum, London). Caesar wears a laurel wreath; the inscription reads CAESAR.DICT PERPETUO; by 15 February 44 BC, Caesar's title was *dictātor perpetuus* (dictator for ever). The inscription on the Cassius coin reads C CASSEI IMP. (of C. Cassius, the general); it dates from 42 BC. The Brutus coin dates from the same year and the inscription reads L PLAET CEST; above BRVT; to right IMP; one of Brutus' officers, Plaetorius Cestianus, issued this coin in honour of his general Brutus.

Chapter 38

Cartoon captions

The future participle is introduced in captions 2 and 4; examples of this part of the verb have been met before (and glossed) and students may recognize it.

Quīntus Athēnās fugit

Horace gives his own account of what happened to him after Philippi in *Epistles* 2.2.41–52; we quote the whole passage, which provides us with the skeleton of the following narrative. The passage begins with his education at Rome:

Rōmae nūtrīrī mihi contigit, atque docērī
īrātus Grāīs quantum nocuisset Achillēs.
adiēcēre bonae paulō plūs artis Athēnae,
scīlicet ut vellem curvō dīnōscere rēctum,
atque inter silvās Acadēmī quaerere vērum.
dūra sed ēmōvēre locō mē tempora grātō,
cīvīlisque rudem bellī tulit aestus in arma
Caesaris Augustī nōn respōnsūra lacertīs.
unde simul prīmum mē dīmīsēre Philippī,
dēcīsīs humilem pennīs inopemque paternī
et laris et fundī, paupertas impulit audāx
ut versūs facerem.

It was my good fortune to be reared in Rome and to be taught what harm Achilles in his anger did to the Greeks (i.e. he studied Greek literature at Orbilius' school). Good Athens gave me a little more skill, so that I wished to distinguish the straight from the crooked and to seek for truth amongst the woods of Academus (i.e. he studied moral philosophy and theory of knowledge at the Academy). But the harsh times tore me from the place I loved and the tide of civil war carried me, a novice, into arms which were to prove no match for the strength of Augustus Caesar. As soon as Philippi sent me off from war, humbled, with wings clipped and robbed of my ancestral home and farm, poverty which knows no shame drove me to write verses.

We do not in fact know when he returned to Italy and whether he was granted an official pardon. Octavian declared an amnesty in 39 BC (the Peace of Misenum), but Horace may have come back earlier and remained inconspicuous. This passage is the authority for the loss of his home and his father's farm.

We may safely assume that Flaccus' farm was part of the land confiscated from Venusia when Octavian was resettling the veterans. What happened to Flaccus himself and his mother, Horace never tells us, although he speaks of his father with such affection. We assume that his parents disappeared, like so many others, in the appalling upheavals of the times and died somewhere in poverty.

1–2 **scūtō abiectō**: this is suggested by *Odes* 2.7.10 (*relictā non bene parmulā*); but as a tribune and acting legionary commander, it is doubtful whether he would in fact have been carrying a shield and the passage should not be taken literally (see the commentary on the second passage of chapter 42, p. 25 below).

2 **campō**: **campus** is often used of a field of battle.

13 **prōdidissent ... vertissent**: the subjunctive is used because the clauses in which these verbs appear are part of Quintus' thoughts, i.e. they are virtually indirect, not direct, speech. This is unlikely to bother your students and you need not explain unless you are asked about it.

Strictly speaking the following sentences **imperātōre mortuō ... vēnerant** are also part of his thoughts and should be expressed in indirect speech, but we have departed from correct Latinity in order not to confuse students.

30 **ī cubitum: cubitum** is supine after a verb of motion, expressing purpose, literally, 'Go to lie down'.

Quīntus in Italiam redit

We have departed from our usual rubric in this exercise and ask students to read, understand and summarize the meaning in their own words. This is a useful and stimulating exercise which teachers could use on other passages if they wish.

10 **quārtō diē**: we allow four days for the journey from Piraeus to Brundisium, perhaps too little; when Cicero sailed from Patrae to Brundisium in 50 BC, the voyage took two nights and a day (*Ad Fam.* 16.9). Quintus had to sail right round the Peloponnese (there was no Corinth canal).

Grammar and exercises

The future participle
This has already featured in narratives and presents little difficulty once its form is known. Remind students that, like other participles, it is an adjective and must agree with the noun it belongs to.

You might ask them to form the three participles from an ordinary active verb and the three from a deponent verb and give their meanings, e.g.

capiō: **capiēns** present = taking
captus perfect = having been taken, taken
captūrus future = about to take

sequor: **sequēns** present = following
secūtus perfect = having followed
secūtūrus future = about to follow

Background: Octavian returns to Italy

Octavian was born on 23 September 63 BC. He was in Illyricum when Caesar was murdered in March 44 BC, and, after a brief hesitation, he returned to Italy. What were the feelings of this eighteen-year-old when he discovered on landing near Brundisium that Caesar's great-nephew had become Caesar's heir? Did he resolve then and there to become the most powerful man in the western world?

Caius Julius Caesar Octavianus (p. 33, para. 1): he took his adoptive father's name, and his previous name Octavius became an adjective, i.e. Octavianus. Thus his full name signified that he was the Caius Julius Caesar who had previously been called Octavius. He would

have expected to be called Caesar, but it has become customary for historians to refer to him as Octavian at this stage of his career to avoid confusion with his adoptive father.

Virgil's estate (p. 33, para. 6): we have followed the traditional view that Virgil, after losing his estate in the confiscations, won it back through a successful petition. Some modern scholars are less inclined to believe that *Eclogue* 1, from which this is inferred, is autobiographical: Virgil could in fact be conveying in a general way the consequences of the land confiscations.

Sources
p. 33, para. 1: 'Look at his name; then look at his age': Cicero: *Ad Atticum* 6.8.
p. 34, para. 2: 'Ours is the crowning era ...': Virgil: *Eclogues* 4.4–7, written in 40 BC.

Illustrations

p. 31: this view of the Acropolis of Athens is from the Mouseion hill. Above the great wall of the theatre of Herodes Atticus (left foreground) are the Propylaia and the small temple of Athena Nike. The Parthenon, the great temple to Athena, stands proudly atop the sanctuary, and in the right background is the steep Lykabettos hill.
p. 33 (above): this bust of Octavian, which makes much of his youthful good looks, is from Arles in France. The combed-forward hair is characteristic.
p. 34: Mother Earth sits holding children in her arms amid fruit, flowers and animals. To the right, a nymph has tamed the dragon on which she sits. At the bottom left a vase pours out its contents with a fine careless generosity. This relief from the Ara Pacis in Rome (13–9 BC) captures the spirit of Virgil's dream of another Golden Age.

Chapter 39

Cartoon captions

All four captions first give a direct question, which is then changed into an indirect question in parentheses. The meaning of the captions is unlikely to cause students any problems.

You may want to draw attention to the obvious fact that Latin, unlike English, uses the subjunctive in indirect questions. The reason for this will become clear later when students find that all clauses in indirect speech (except for indirect statement) have their verbs in the subjunctive.

Quīntus Venusiam revīsit

1–5 In the first paragraph all the indirect questions occur in primary sequence and in lines 1 and 2 we have perfect subjunctives: **acciderit** (you will need to explain this form, as it is identical with the future perfect indicative; cf. line 22, **abierint**) and **passa sit** (the deponent form will raise no problem).

8 adimere eīs cīvitātibus: 'to take away from those states'; **eīs cīvitātibus** is dative of the person concerned (or dative of disadvantage, as the old grammarians used to call it).

10 decemvirī: your students have met *triumvirī* and can guess *decemvirī*, a board of ten men. Octavian had a very invidious task in the resettlement of the veterans. All Italy was thrown into turmoil and there was terrible suffering amongst the dispossessed.

18–19 tōta Italia ... abductīs colōnīs: the old man's words echo Virgil: *Georgics* 1.505–7:

... fās versum atque nefās: tot bella per orbem,
tam multae scelerum faciēs, nōn ullus arātrō
dignus honōs, squālent abductīs arva colōnīs.

right and wrong are turned upside down: so many wars throughout the world, so many faces of wickedness, no honour worthy of the plough, the fields are filthy now the farmers have been expelled.

22 inventūrus sim: 'I am going to/I shall find'; this is the first example of the use of the future participle + subjunctive of **esse** to form a 'future subjunctive'. The meaning is obvious, but you may need to explain that Latin has no future subjunctive and uses this periphrasis to express futurity in indirect questions. We often use a similar periphrasis in English, e.g. 'I don't know what you are going to do.'

Quīntus parentēs suōs quaerit

1 decem abhinc annōs: 'ten years ago'; students may need reminding of this use of **abhinc**.

6 Capuam: Capua was the largest and most important town in Campania.

Gāius: Gaius featured in Part I of the course as the friend with whom Quintus used to go to the local school in Venusia.

16 Beneventum: this was a town on the Via Appia between Venusia and Capua.

Grammar and exercises

Indirect questions
Students must be clear that Latin, unlike English, uses the subjunctive in indirect questions and that the reflexives (**sē, suus**) refer to the subject of the leading verb, as in other forms of indirect speech.

They will have to learn the perfect subjunctive, which is not hard since the forms are the same as the future perfect indicative (except for the 1st person singular: **parāverō** in the future perfect indicative, **parāverim** in the perfect subjunctive, and the vowel lengths of the 1st and 2nd persons plural: **parāverimus**, **parāveritis** (indicative); **parāverīmus**, **parāverītis** (subjunctive)).

There is no future subjunctive in Latin (see note on line 22 of the first passage in this chapter).

We give the full rules for sequence, which may look a bit complicated but are really only common sense.

Background: The confiscations

The question at the end of the piece could evoke vivid responses to the tragedy of dispossession. The twentieth century has more examples of this to show than any other, and so it should be possible for students to empathize with the feelings we try to evoke in the narrative of these chapters.

Virgil's estate (p. 39, para. 1): see the note on the background section of chapter 38 (p. 19 above). 'It is unlikely that, with powerful friends like Pollio and Gallus, Vergil suffered any economic hardship as a result of the eviction ... Nevertheless the severing of links with his family home was clearly of emotional importance to him' (R. Coleman (ed.): *Vergil: Eclogues*, Cambridge University Press, p. 89).

The Virgil quotations are *Eclogues* 9.2–6 and 1.64–72, 74–8. In the second quotation 'bone-dry Africa' refers to the inland regions of Libya, not the coastal strip which was fertile and prosperous; 'Oxus' suggests the distant and inaccessible: it is not clear which river is referred to; 'fallow' is 'crop-land left fallow' (Coleman, note on 70–71).

Source
second question: *silent legēs ...*': Cicero: *Pro Milone* 4.11.

Illustrations

p. 36 (above): this is a view from Monte S. Angelo in Puglia in Southern Italy.

(middle): this marble statue of a poor Roman probably dates from the first century AD, and reflects the interest of the Romans in realism in their sculpture – as opposed to the frequently bland idealism of the Greeks. Thought to portray a fisherman, it has been restored in modern times. (British Museum, London)
p. 38: this triumphal arch of Parian marble was built across the Appian Way at Beneventum (now Benevento) in honour of the emperor Trajan (AD 114–16). It is 15 metres high with composite columns (i.e. combining the features of Doric, Ionic and

Corinthian capitals). At the top Roman consuls receive Trajan and Hadrian, and Jupiter offers the emperor his thunderbolt. At the middle level Trajan confers benefits on the Roman people. At the lower level we see Trajan's triumphant return after his German campaign. p. 40: this sixth-century AD mosaic of a goatherd milking is from the Mosaic Museum, which is in fact in the ruins of Justinian's palace, in Istanbul.

Chapter 40

Cartoon captions

Caption 3 introduces two semi-deponent verbs, one of which (**audeō**) they have already met in present stem tenses. You will have to explain what is happening here.

Vocabulary

fīō is used both as meaning 'I become' and as the passive of **faciō** = I am made. The present stem tenses are like those of **audiō** except for the infinitive, **fierī**, which is passive in form. The perfect stem tenses are supplied from **faciō**.

Quīntus amīcō veterī occurrit

9ff. **Apollō vīsus est ...**: Quintus' vision of Apollo is of course fictional. Horace's own explanation of why he took to writing poetry is very much more down to earth (*Epistles* 2.2.51–2):

... paupertās impulit audāx
ut versūs facerem

Shameless poverty drove me to write verses.

But he did claim that his inspiration came from Apollo (*Odes* 4.6.29–30):

spīritum Phoebus mihi, Phoebus artem
carminis nōmenque dedit poētae.

Phoebus Apollo gave me inspiration, Apollo gave me the art of song and the name of poet.

Poets often claimed to be under the protection of Apollo, god of poetry and music. Horace was a sceptic in religious matters, inclining towards the philosophy of Epicurus, who was a materialist, so what he says in the lines quoted above may be no more than a literary convention, but he does seem to have had a special feeling for Apollo.

14 **quō factō**: 'which having been done' = 'when he had done this'; students may need help with this use of the connecting relative, which is not explained until chapter 48.

19 **Marcum Cicerōnem**: Marcus Cicero joined Sextus Pompeius after Philippi but he returned to Italy and was pardoned after the amnesty of 39 BC. Marcus' subsequent career is not fully known, but he became consul in 30 BC and proconsul of Asia in 29–28 BC. When, and indeed whether, he went through the other steps in the *cursus honōrum*, we do not know.

30 **quaestor aerāriī**: there were two *quaestorēs urbānī* who were in charge of the Treasury (*aerārium*).

31 **scrība aerāriī**: Suetonius (*Vita Horatii*) says: *bellō Philippēnsī excitus ā Marcō Brūtō imperātōre tribūnus mīlitum meruit; victīsque partibus veniā impetrātā scrīptum quaestōrium comparāvit* ('involved in the campaign of Philippi by Marcus Brutus the general, he served as a military tribune; and when his side was defeated he obtained pardon and secured a clerkship to the quaestor'). The *scrībae quaestōriī* were important officials, usually of equestrian rank, permanent civil servants who assisted the quaestors, young men who held office for only a year, both in the management of public finances and in keeping the public records. Suetonius' word *comparāvit* suggests that Horace may have bought this office (modern scholars believe that Horace was not nearly as poor as he claims). In making Marcus Cicero present him with the job, we are again resorting to fiction.

33 **secundā hōrā**: the first hour was at dawn throughout the year.

41 **respōnsa magistrātibus reddēbat**: we give Horace the job of dealing with the public records rather than finance, for which he could scarcely have been well qualified. We do not know how long Horace worked at the Treasury; when he was given the Sabine farm (?33 BC), we may assume that he retired.

Quīntus ā senātōre malignō vexātur

This story is suggested by what Horace says himself (*Satires* 1.6.45–8):

nunc ad mē redeō lībertīnō patre nātum,
quem rōdunt omnēs lībertīnō patre nātum,
nunc quia sim tibi, Maecēnas, convictor; at ōlim
quod mihi pārēret legiō Rōmāna tribūnō.

Now I return to myself, the son of a father who was a freedman, whom all snipe at as a freedman's son, now because I am your friend, Maecenas, once because a Roman legion obeyed me as a tribune.

Horace would undoubtedly have had to put up with a great deal of snobbery as he ascended the social ladder, but judging from what he says himself, it left him unembittered, and in the end he was accepted by all from the emperor downwards.

3 **nōbilī genere nātus**: 'born of a noble family'; the *nōbilēs* were those whose family had held the

21

consulship, a small class which dominated the state and jealously guarded their exclusive claim to high office. In the last century of the republic only four *novī hominēs* (men whose families had not held the consulship) became consul, two of whom were Marius and Cicero.

Fābella

1–2 **Metellus ... Rūfus**: the Caecilii Metelli were one of the grandest families in Rome and were notoriously arrogant; since 250 BC every generation had produced one or more consuls. The early Roman poet Naevius (fl. 240 BC) had written: *fātō Metellī Rōmae fiunt cōnsulēs* ('the Metelli are fated to become consuls in Rome'); for this impertinence he was thrown into prison. The Metellus in this *fābella* might be Quintus Caecilius Metellus, consul in 57 BC. Servius Sulpicius Rufus was a member of another noble family; he was consul in 51 BC.

10 **respōnsa cēnsōria**: two censors were elected every five years to revise the citizen list; they had powers to strike off anyone guilty in their opinion of misdemeanour; this included the right to demote knights and senators. Their lists, the *respōnsa cēnsōria*, must have been among the documents most often consulted.

27–8 **numquam ... paenitēbit**: compare *Satires* 1.6.89 where, after describing how his father had looked after him in Rome, Horace says: *nīl mē paeniteat sānum patris huius* ('I would never be ashamed of such a father as long as I'm in my right mind'). See also the commentary on the second passage of chapter 43, line 29, below.

Grammar and exercises

Further uses of the ablative case

This section completes our explanation of the uses of the ablative case. The names of these uses are rather tiresome, e.g. 'ablative of measure of difference'; the vital thing is that students should recognize them in context. The only one which presents any difficulty is the ablative of price, which we present and exercise together with the genitive of value. These case uses are important; students often fail to recognize the genitive of value.

In exercise 40.1.2 **vīlī** is the ablative of the adjective **vīlis, -e** = cheap.

Semi-deponent verbs

Students will find these even more peculiar than deponent verbs; the only consolation is that these four (**fīō, audeō, gaudeō, soleō**) are the only semi-deponent verbs. The infinitive of **fīō** should be carefully learnt; it is a gross irregularity!

Background: Latin poetry

This thumbnail sketch of the development of Latin poetry is primarily intended to put Horace into a context which will help to make his poetry more easily intelligible. It is grossly oversimplified but it has still been impossible to keep out a lot of unfamiliar material, especially in the references to Greek poetry. Pupils should not be expected to learn all the facts given but it may help to prepare them for some of the unexpected features of ancient poetry.

The questions should provide a useful field for exploration, helping pupils to an awareness of genre and showing how continuously indebted to the ancient world our literary tradition has proved to be.

The influence of the Greek writers (p. 46, para. 3): not everybody approved of this: Cato the Elder wrote to his son, 'The Greek race is quite worthless and unteachable, and I speak as a prophet that when it gives us its literature, it will ruin everything' (Pliny: *Natural History* 29.13). The Romans tended to feel guilty about reading purely for pleasure: literature should be useful. See Horace: *Epistles* 2.1.161–3.

Catullus (p. 47, para. 2): it may be worth reading your pupils one of Catullus' poems in translation, e.g. 5. This will reinforce the points being made here. To a sophisticated group of pupils, it may also be worth remarking on how Catullus brought obscenity into the mainstream of European poetry. After him there is nothing that cannot be said.

Source

final para.: 'the poet who has mixed ...': *Ars Poetica* 343–4.

Illustrations

p. 42: this expressive statue shows Apollo in movement with his lyre. A Roman copy of a Greek bronze original, possibly by Praxiteles, the great sculptor of the fourth century BC, it balances an energetic sense of movement with a fine delicacy. (Museo Pio-Clementino, Vatican, Rome)

p. 43: the photograph shows the remains of the *tabulārium* at Rome, the building where the state archives were kept. It was designed in 78 BC. The podium and gallery are original. The upper storey was removed to make way for the medieval senatorial palace.

p. 44: this statue of a man wearing a toga and carrying a scroll, probably dating from the fourth century AD, was restored in the seventeenth century. The head, which dates from the first century AD, does not belong to the body.

p. 46: this fresco is from Pompeii and is now in the Museo Nazionale, Naples. The man (traditionally but incorrectly identified as Paquius Proculus since the house in which it was found had an election poster for Proculus painted on its front) carries a papyrus scroll. His wife holds a stylus to her lips and has in her left hand a two-leaved wooden tablet spread with wax. Her fingers and luminous eyes are painted with great delicacy. Her hair is dressed in a fashion popular about the middle of the first century AD.

Chapter 41

Cartoon captions

These give a series of direct statements which are immediately followed by the same statements in indirect form. Students are unlikely to have any difficulty in understanding and should be able to deduce how indirect statement is expressed in Latin.

Caption 2 introduces a perfect active infinitive, caption 3 a perfect passive and caption 4 a future active. These forms of the infinitive will be set out and learnt in the Grammar for this chapter. Their meaning may be clear to students from the context.

Quīntus carmina facit

The lines of verse quoted are from *Epodes* 2.1–28 (with omissions) and the concluding lines (67–70). The *Epodes* were composed between 41 and 31 BC and published in 30 BC. Metre: iambic trimeter followed by iambic dimeter (see Appendix):

bĕā|tŭs īl|lĕ, quī| prŏcŭl |nĕgō|tĭīs

ūt prīs|că gēns| mōrtā|lĭŭm

The Latin of these lines is very straightforward, but students may find difficulty (1) in the word order, especially the separation of adjectives from the nouns they agree with; (2) in the range of vocabulary; and (3) in the frequent omission of the verb **esse**.

We make this our first foray into Horace's poetry for several reasons:
1 The theme is likely to appeal. It reads at first as an 'escape' poem; the longing to get away from the troubles of city life to the innocent tranquillity of the country is common to us all. And when, at the end, the whole poem turns out to be ironical – the theme is being sent up – this is a good joke, easily appreciated.
2 The language is easy; there is not one subordinate clause. Provided students watch case endings carefully, they will quickly master the sense.
3 Its metre (regular iambics) is extremely simple; a reading aloud with correct quantities will quickly

enable students to feel this rhythm. There will be no need, at this stage, to go into elaborate metrical explanations.
4 In the next chapter Quintus is to meet Virgil, who is at this time composing the *Georgics*; the theme which Horace treats with urbane irony, Virgil treats with passionate seriousness.

14 faenore: *faenus* properly speaking means interest payable on money borrowed. Debt was rife in the late republic and the money-lender (*faenerātor*) was a notorious character; they charged exorbitant rates of interest, e.g. 48 per cent per annum.
15 mīles: this is in apposition to the subject 'he' (in the verb).
16 horret īrātum mare: i.e. as a sailor or merchant.
17 forum: this might mean literally 'the forum', but more probably it means, as often, 'public life' which took place in the forum.
18 potentiōrum: 'too powerful', or 'the more powerful'; Horace is thinking of the morning *salūtātiō*, when clients had to call on their patrons. Compare Virgil: *Georgics* 2.461–2, where Virgil is contrasting life in Rome with the tranquillity of country life; he starts:

> sī nōn ingentem foribus domus alta superbīs
> māne salūtantum tōtīs vomit aedibus undam

> If the house high with its proud doors does not spew forth a great wave of early morning callers from the whole house

19–28 The catalogue of the joys of the tranquil country life, for all its charm, is a literary commonplace of the time, which is echoed in the passage of the *Georgics* quoted above; Virgil also has cool valleys, lowing cattle and soft sleep under a tree. Or is Horace echoing Virgil? We do not know whether this Epode was written before this part of the *Georgics*.
30 iam, iam futūrus rūsticus: i.e. always on the point of retiring to the country.

When students have mastered the sense and are discussing the poem, there is one further point you might raise. The poem opens simply enough, stating a commonplace; but in the fourth line we have **solūtus omnī faenore**, a surprising addition in this context. The point of this does not become clear until in the concluding lines we find that Alfius is himself a *faenerātor*. The lines omitted return to a loving description of the joys of country life. This one line disconcerts the alert reader and is a warning that the poem is ironical.

The poem may be not only ironical but also ambivalent. Horace certainly mocks the aspirations of the money-lender, who does not really intend to leave Rome, since he is too set on making money. But Horace himself always had a longing to escape to the country (compare *ō rūs, quandō ego tē aspiciam*? (*Satires* 2.6.60); see chapter 53); and the description of the joys of country life is lovingly made and carries conviction. And so words which are ironical on the lips of Alfius perhaps express Horace's own heartfelt nostalgia.

Vergilius amīcitiam Quīntī petit

Virgil's *Eclogues* were all composed between 42 and 39 BC (except for the last which must be dated to 37 BC). They were an immediate success and brought him to the notice of Maecenas who admitted him to the closest circle of his friends. When Virgil met Horace we do not know but one may assume that it was soon after Horace's first poems were circulating. Virgil then introduced Horace to Maecenas (*Satires* 1.6.54–5):

> nūlla etenim mihi tē fors obtulit: optimus ōlim
> Vergilius, post hunc Vārus, dīxēre quid essem.

> For it was no chance that brought me in your way; good Virgil, and after him Varus, told you what I was.

The rest of the story of Horace's relations with Maecenas is told in subsequent chapters.

3 **tē diū quaerō**: 'I have been looking for you for a long time', present of remaining effects, used when an action begins in the past and continues up to the present. So also line 4 **diū cupiō** = I have long wanted to.

14–15 **poēma ... dē rēbus rūsticīs**: Virgil wrote the *Georgics* between 37 and 29 BC. Ostensibly a didactic poem on agriculture, modelled on Hesiod's *Works and Days*, it ranges far beyond this narrower theme, having a strong moral message on the virtues necessary to save the Roman world from destruction.

18–19 **ille negāvit ... recitātūrum esse**: Virgil was a perfectionist; it took him seven years to write the *Georgics* at an average rate of less than one line per day. Because the *Aeneid* was unfinished on his deathbed he asked that it should be destroyed, but Augustus countermanded these instructions and told Virgil's literary executors to publish it.

Grammar and exercises

Indirect statement

By the time students have read the cartoon captions and the narrative of this chapter they will be pretty familiar with the accusative and infinitive construction. It may be some help to point out that English occasionally uses a similar construction after some verbs, e.g. I believe him to be wise = I believe that he is wise; but English and Latin idiom differ so widely that a good deal of practice is necessary before students are really at home with the construction. You should make it clear that the accusative and infinitive construction is used to express

not only indirect statements but also thoughts, hopes, beliefs etc., as your students will understand from the list of verbs which can introduce it.

In presenting the full list of infinitives, particular attention should be given to **regī**, **capī** and **fore**.

negō: this is first used in exercise 41.3.5: **negāvērunt sē parentēs eius vīdisse** ('they denied that they had seen his parents'), but a more idiomatic translation would be: 'They said that they had not seen ...'. You should help your students here and point out that Latin never says **dīcō ... nōn**. Hence, in exercise 41.5.9 'said that he had never been' becomes in Latin 'denied that he had ever been ...'.

Background: Horace

Apart from the question at the end of the section, the obvious field for exploration is how far the poet of *Beātus ille*, now read by your pupils, corresponds with the poet here described. How sophisticated is that poem? How self-conscious is its use of the pastoral ideal?

Sources

p. 52, para. 2: Horace's claim to have naturalized Greek poetry: *Odes* 3.30.13–14.
p. 53, para. 3: Horace: *Odes* 3.30.1–6.

Illustrations

p. 50: this fresco of a pastoral scene centres around a statue of Priapus, god of gardens and fertility. Goats and cows graze contentedly amid a landscape which contains a number of rustic sanctuaries. (National Archaeological Museum, Naples)
p. 51 (above): a hoard of Roman coins. (Rheinisches Landesmuseum, Trier)
    (below): this portrait of Virgil is from the Codex Romanus, the fifth- or sixth-century edition of Virgil's works in the Vatican Library in Rome, which is one of the two earliest Virgil manuscripts. Note the box which contains the scrolls of his poetry and the lectern from which he recites it.
p. 52: this work by the great French seventeenth-century landscape painter Claude Lorraine captures the spirit of Virgil's *Georgics*, the poem he speaks of in this passage. (Barber Institute of Fine Arts, Birmingham)
p. 53: not one of the pyramids of Egypt to which Horace is clearly referring in the quotation at the end of the essay, but a pyramid built in Rome by a contemporary of the poet's, Gaius Cestius. This praetor, tribune of the plebs, and member of the seven-man team who were in charge of solemn banquets, died in 12 BC, and his ashes were placed in this pyramid. It is 27 metres high and stands on a base 22 metres square. An inscription states that it was built in 330 days. The

photograph is taken from the Protestant Cemetery in Rome where lie the poets John Keats and Percy Bysshe Shelley.

Chapter 42

Cartoon caption

The caption quotes the last line of Horace: *Odes* 2.7. Students will need help with its meaning: 'It is sweet for me to run mad as I've got back my friend.'

Pompēius ad patriam revenit

We know nothing about Horace's friend Pompeius except what we learn from *Odes* 2.7; it would be a fair assumption that he, like Marcus Cicero, returned to Rome after the amnesty of 39 BC.

2 **palātium**: the word properly means the Palatine hill; there was the house of Octavian, modest at this time, but spendidly rebuilt by subsequent emperors, which gave it the meaning of 'palace'.

8 **cēlāvisse ... cōnstituisse**: these verbs continue the indirect statements of Pompeius and so are in the infinitive. In continuous indirect speech the accusative (subject of the infinitive) is not usually repeated.

8–9 **Sextum Pompēium**: for Sextus Pompeius, see the commentary on the historical background to chapter 37, p. 16 above.

12–13 **Octāviānus veniam ... prōmīsisset**: Octavian freely granted amnesty to old enemies; in his efforts to unite all Italy behind him he practised a policy of *clēmentia*.

25–6 **quī ... carperent**: 'who might pick' = 'to pick'; the relative with the subjunctive can express purpose. It is glossed, but if students render **qui carperent** 'who picked', point out that the verb is in the subjunctive; they will then see that 'who might pick' expresses purpose.

Quīntus Pompēiī reditum carmine celebrat

Metre: Alcaics (see Appendix):

ō saēpĕ mēcūm | tēmpŭs ĭn ūl | tĭmŭm

dēdūctĕ Brūtō | mīlĭtīaē | dŭcĕ.

quīs tē rĕdōnāvīt Quĭrītĕm

dīs pătrīīs Ĭtălō | quĕ caēlō.

The Pompeius Ode (*Odes* 2.7) is not easy; with the help of the prose paraphrase which precedes it, students may be able to master it, but teachers who think it is too hard or that it will take up too much time can omit it without missing out on any new linguistic information.

Some might be content simply to master the paraphrase and leave the brighter students to attempt the original on their own. The principal difficulty lies in the word order, e.g. lines 1–5: **ō ... deducte ... Pompei**; English must take **ō Pompei** together. (The line numbers refer to those of the original poem, not the paraphrase.)

2 **Brūtō mīlitiae duce**: ablative absolute, 'when Brutus was leader of our warfare'.

7–8 **corōnātus**: a perfect passive participle used in a middle sense, 'having crowned'. This is a rare usage, imitated from Greek.

10 **relictā nōn bene parmulā**: to throw away one's shield was the ultimate cowardice; but as a tribune, Horace would probably not have had a shield, nor could the Roman's legionary shield (*scūtum*) possibly be equated with *parmula* (a little wicker shield). Horace is echoing an old tradition in which a succession of Greek poets lightheartedly accused themselves of cowardice. The first was Archilochus (7th century BC): 'One of the Saioi [his enemies] enjoys my shield, which against my will I left by a bush, an excellent weapon, but myself I saved. What do I care for that shield? Let it go, I will soon get another just as good' (Archilochus 6). All educated Romans would have recognized this echo and would no more have taken Horace literally than they would have believed that Mercury actually carried him to safety from the battlefield (a reminiscence of Homer: *Iliad* 3.380–82: Paris is about to fall to Menelaus, but 'Aphrodite snatched him out of the battle, easily, as a god can, and covered him in a thick mist and set him down in his sweet-smelling chamber').

11 **cum frācta virtūs (est)**: 'When the cause of Virtue was broken' or 'When brave men were broken'. Although Brutus claimed to have right on his side, the second rendering is perhaps easier, **virtus** being abstract for concrete.

minācēs: 'the threatening men' = 'those who had threatened'; Brutus' soldiers had been confident of victory.

12 **turpe** is best taken as an adverb = 'disgracefully', 'in dishonour' (for the form, compare **facile** = easily).

solum tetigēre mentō: 'touched the ground with their chins'; this could either mean 'they lay dead on the battlefield' or 'they prostrated themselves before their conquerors after defeat'; the latter is perhaps better, contrasting with **minācēs**.

17 **obligātam ... Iovī dapem**: 'the feast owed to Jupiter', i.e. a thank offering which Pompeius swore to make to Jupiter if he returned home safe.

In the verse and a half omitted, Horace gives orders for starting up the celebration – fill the cups with wine which brings forgetfulness (of past troubles), pour out the perfume (with which revellers always anointed themselves), make garlands to put on our heads, throw the dice to see who shall be the 'master of the drinking' (he would dictate how much should be drunk and how far the wine should be diluted) ... 'I shall revel as madly as the Thracians (notorious drunkards): now I've got my friend back, I am glad to go mad.'

The poem is shot through with deep affection and admiration for Pompeius. He is 'the first (i.e. the best) of his comrades', with whom he endured the ultimate danger in battle and enjoyed parties in times of leisure. He contrasts his own feeble behaviour with Pompeius' stern adherence to principle. Now he welcomes him back with all the resources at his command; he has even kept special casks of wine for the occasion and now he is ready to go mad with joy at his friend's return.

Grammar and exercises

No new grammar is introduced in this chapter. Exercises 42.2 and 42.3 give practice in all the constructions which have been learnt recently, including indirect commands, questions and statements.

In exercise 42.3.7 students may notice that both **cum cēna cōnfecta esset** and **cēnā cōnfectā** (ablative absolute) are correct, the second version being neater.

Background: Books

This background section is largely informational in content, and the comparison with books and book production in the modern world is the main area for exploration, as the questions below prompt.

It is also worth observing that while we are here dealing with private book reading, there were many recitals in Rome at which writers would give readings of their new works. See Pliny: *Letters* 1.13.

How expensive were books? Martial tells us that his first book sold for 5 *dēnāriī*. This is not a large sum, and most middle-class Roman citizens could afford books.

Libraries (final para.): Asinius Pollio set up the first public library in Rome in 39 BC. An example of a public library in the provinces is the one donated by Pliny the Younger to Comum (*Letters* 1.8).

Further reading: U. E. Paoli: *Rome: Its People, Life and Customs*, Longman, repr. Bristol, pp. 174–90; *The Cambridge History of Classical Literature*, Cambridge University Press, vol. 1, ed. P. E. Easterling and B. M. W. Knox, pp. 7–22, and vol. 2, ed. E. J. Kenney and M. V. Clausen, pp. 15–27; P. Jones and K. Sidwell (eds): *The World of Rome*, Cambridge University Press, chapter 9.1.

Illustrations

p. 54: the cartoon illustrating the party Quintus gave in honour of Pompeius' return is based closely on a wall painting from the *trīclīnium* of a house in Pompeii. It is the second of three related panels, which seem to show three successives stages in a dinner party. The first

shows a respectable scene, with the guests reclining fully clothed on their couches. In the second *furor* is setting in (see the last line of the Pompeius Ode: *receptō/dulce mihi furere est amīcō*). Dinner takes place in a garden under an awning. In the foreground is a table set with food and wine; on the right a boy approaches bringing more wine. On the left-hand couch a couple are stripped from the waist up; the woman raises a drinking horn to her mouth, the man embraces her with his right arm and holds a plate in his left hand. On the central couch reclines the host, who says: FACITIS. VOBIS. SVAVITER. EGO. CANTO ('Enjoy yourselves; I'm going to sing'). On the right reclines another couple, locked in an embrace; the man waves his right arm to his host and says: EST. ITA. VALEAS ('All right; good luck to you!').

FACITIS: this might be intended as an indicative ('you are enjoying yourselves') or, more likely, it is an error on the part of the artist, who intended to write FACIATIS (jussive subjunctive). Your students might be amused to learn that grammatical mistakes are not uncommon in inscriptions.

EGO CANTO: 'I'm singing'. The present tense is sometimes used in colloquial Latin to refer to the immediate future, as in English: 'Are you coming with me?'

The captions illustrate typical Roman writing; all in capitals, the words separated by dots, but no punctuation. Note that there is no letter **u**, so SVAVITER.

In the third panel there are musicians and nude dancing girls.

p. 56: this fine Mercury is the work of Benvenuto Cellini (1500–71). (Palazzo del Bargello, Florence)

p. 57: the manuscript, which dates from 20 BC, is the oldest Roman book in existence. The work of the poet Gallus, the four most legible lines read:

FATA MIHI CAESAR TUM ERVNT MEA DULCIA QUOM TV
MAXIMA ROMANAE PARS ERIT HISTORIAE
POSTQUE TUUM REDITUM MULTORUM TEMPLA DEORUM
FIXA LEGAM SPOLIEIS DEIVITIORA TUEIS

My fate, Caesar, will only then be sweet to me, when you are the most important part of Roman history,
and when after your return I read how the temples of many gods
have been made richer by your spoils fixed up in them.

The Caesar referred to is, of course, Octavian. The archaic spellings: **quom** = **cum**; **spolieīs** = **spoliīs**; **deivitiōra** = **dīvitiōra**; **tueīs** = **tuīs**.

p. 58: this enchanting fresco portrait of a young girl with a golden hair-net holding tablets and a stylus was discovered at Pompeii. Although it is popularly known as a portrait of Sappho, the poetess from Lesbos, it may be that the girl it portrays had no particular literary associations and that holding the stylus against the cheek was a popular pose: cf. the illustration on p. 46. (National Archaeological Museum, Naples)

Chapter 43

Cartoon captions

Captions 2, 3 and 4 introduce consecutive clauses. These present little difficulty, but you will need to prompt students over **adeō** (caption 2), which they have not learnt. English uses the indicative in consecutive clauses; it is not clear why Latin should use the subjunctive, seeing that the consequences expressed in the **ut** clause are usually facts.

Quīntus Maecēnātī commendātur

Although Maecenas was of noble birth, descended, as he claimed, from Etruscan kings, he chose not to enter politics but to remain a private knight (*eques prīvātus*). But he became the close friend and trusted counsellor of Augustus; he accompanied him on the Philippi campaign, undertook a diplomatic mission to Antony in 38 BC (see chapter 44) and he was left in charge of Rome and Italy when Octavian departed for the Actium campaign and on other occasions when Octavian was absent. He assumed a mask of luxurious indolence but was in fact a skilful diplomat and competent administrator, unfailingly loyal to his friends. Perhaps his greatest service to Augustus was as a patron of literature; he gathered round him a circle of poets, above all Virgil and Horace, whom he encouraged to write in support of the new regime.

Horace himself describes how Virgil introduced him to Maecenas and how Maecenas accepted him into the circle of his friends (see the second half of this chapter). Although they were related as patron to client, there is no doubt about the affection they felt for each other; this emerges clearly both from Horace's frequent references to Maecenas in the *Odes* and *Satires*, and from Maecenas' last request to Augustus in his will: *Horātiī Flaccī ut meī memor estō* ('Remember Horatius Flaccus as you do myself').

7 rēgibus Etruscīs ortum: 'sprung from Etruscan kings' (ablative of origin, compare line 23 **clārō patre nātum** = 'born from/son of a famous father'). Horace in *Odes* 3.29.1 hails Maecenas as *Tyrrhēna regum prōgeniēs* ('Etruscan descendant of kings', i.e. 'descended from Etruscan kings').

8 honōrēs: 'offices' rather than 'honours'.

10 Mūsās colēbat: 'he cultivated the Muses', i.e. he encouraged all forms of artistic endeavour; although the Muses are mentioned most often in connection with poetry, they were the deities who inspired all intellectual pursuits (there were nine Muses and in later times each had a particular function; thus Calliope was the Muse of heroic epic, Clio of history, Euterpe of flutes, Terpsichore of lyric poetry and dance etc.).

16 velim: 'I should like to' (potential subjunctive: see chapter 45).

29–30 negōtiīs ... revocātūrum esse: these sentences are part of what Virgil said and so are expressed in the accusative and infinitive construction of indirect statement; since the subject of the infinitives does not change, it is omitted.

Maecēnās Quīntum in amīcōrum numerum accipit

This passage replaces the usual comprehension exercise. The quotation is from *Satires* 1.6.45–78 (with omissions). The Satire's subject is snobbery; Horace has been praising Maecenas because, unlike others, he judges people by their merits, not their birth. Its metre is dactylic hexameter, the metre of all Horace's *Satires* and *Epistles* (see Appendix):

nūnc ād | mē rĕdĕ|ō līb|ērtīn|ō pătrĕ | nātum

2–3 dīcit Maecēnātem ... nōn sē contemnere: 'he says that Maecenas does not despise him.' Students may need prompting to recognize that the reflexive **sē** refers back to the subject of **dīcit** (Quintus).

8 nōn quia sim: quia = 'because' is normally followed by the indicative. The subjunctive is used here because the **quia** clause gives the reason from the point of view of those who are disparaging Horace; compare **quod ... pārēret** (line 9).

15 dūcō: 'I consider', an unexpected but not uncommon meaning of the verb.

17 nōn patre praeclārō ... vītā ... pectore: all three are ablatives of cause, 'not because of a famous father but because of ...'.

24–5 docendum artēs: 'to be taught the arts': the gerundive is passive but here has the object **artēs**; in the active **doceō** can take two direct objects, e.g. **iuvenem artēs doceō**; in the passive one of these may be retained, e.g. **iuvenis artēs docētur** = the young man is taught arts.

26 sēmet prōgnātōs: those born from himself = his own sons; **sēmet** is an emphatic form of **sē**.

29 prīncipī: 'the emperor'; this was the title by which Augustus preferred to be called; it has a civilian ring to it ('leading citizen'): he was trying to disguise the military basis of his power (see chapter 51).

patris ... numquam eum paenitēbat: 'he was never ashamed of his father'. You will need to comment on the use of the impersonal verb, literally: 'it never repented him of his father'. So far students have only met impersonal verbs which are easier to understand, e.g. **mihi placet** = it pleases me = I decide; **mihi licet** = it is lawful for me = I am allowed. (Impersonal verbs are explained in chapter 50.)

Horace's love for his father is one of his most endearing characteristics. This Satire continues: 'If no one can truly accuse me of greed or filth, if I am innocent and pure of heart (to blow my own trumpet), my father is responsible for this ... he kept me safe in Rome from all temptation. And he was not afraid that anyone would count it a failure on his part, if I had followed a modest profession as an auctioneer, or an auctioneer's agent, as he was himself; nor would I have complained: and for this all the more praise and gratitude is due to him. I would never be ashamed of such a father while I'm in my right mind.'

Grammar and exercises

Consecutive (result) clauses

These present no difficulty once it is understood that Latin uses the subjunctive while English uses the indicative. You should stress that the negative form is **ut ... nōn**, whereas in purpose clauses and indirect command negative clauses are introduced by **nē**.

Exercise 43.1

3 **tantī**: you may have to remind students that this is genitive of value = 'so highly'.

  accēperit: perfect subjunctive; in consecutive clauses sequence is not always observed; if the consequence is a single fact, the perfect subjunctive may be used in secondary sequence. This is unlikely to bother your students and perhaps you should not delay over it.

P.S.

Of all the thousands of Roman inscriptions which survive, funerary inscriptions must be the commonest and within a small compass they often express deep and touching emotion, like the first one quoted, in which the Roman centurion describes his little daughter as **animae innocentissimae** (a most innocent soul).

2 (Dessau 8529a): the tragic facts bear witness to the desolation of the mother; the only emotive words are the juxtaposed **pia cārae** (**pius** besides meaning 'dutiful', 'pious', often has the sense of 'loving'.)

3 (Dessau 8162): **nōn fuī, fuī, nōn sum, nōn dēsiderō**: 'I was not, I was, I am not, I feel no desires.'

4 (*CIL* 5.1636): the date of this inscription is unknown but it is unlikely to be earlier than AD 100, by which time Christianity was spreading throughout the Roman empire. Readers may recognize the language of Christianity: **iustōs et ēlectōs**: 'the just and elect'

(God's chosen people); **Martyrēs sānctī**: 'holy martyrs'. **habent** (line 6) looks like an error for **habēbunt** (**vīvent** is future); grammatical mistakes are not uncommon in funerary inscriptions put up by the less highly educated.

Background: Maecenas

A discussion of Maecenas' personality would be valuable here. How attractively does he come across? Do your pupils think it surprising that a man with a passionate interest in the arts should be a shrewd politician too? And if they are surprised, why?

Do we now think less highly of artistic productions which are intended to support a political regime?

We shall see evidence of Maecenas' generosity to Horace in chapter 46. Virgil had a fine house next to Maecenas' estate on the Esquiline hill. It seems probable that Maecenas gave him this.

As time went by, a coolness developed between Augustus and Maecenas. Suetonius (*Augustus* 66) and others say that Maecenas found out from Augustus of a plot to assassinate him (Augustus) led by the brother of Maecenas' wife Terentia. He informed Terentia of this, and she told her brother, who attempted – unsuccessfully – to escape. A love affair between Augustus and Maecenas' beautiful but difficult wife may have contributed to the coolness. However, when he died childless in 8 BC, Maecenas bequeathed his considerable property to his former friend.

Scribonia (p. 62, para. 2): Octavian married her in order to improve his relations with Sextus Pompeius, but the match was not a success. Octavian divorced her on the very day that she bore him a daughter.

From the tall tower of Maecenas' house on the Esquiline hill (p. 63, para. 3) the emperor Nero looked down on Rome as it burnt.

Further reading: there is an excellent essay on Maecenas by Stephen Harrison in *Omnibus* 7, pp. 18–20.

Sources

p. 62, para. 3: Horace says ...: *Satires* 1.5.29.
p. 63, para. 4: the story about Octavian is told by Cedrennus, the Byzantine historian; cf. Dio Cassius: 55.7.
first question: Octavian, Ajax and the sponge: Suetonius: *Augustus* 85.2.

Illustrations

p. 60: the painted walls of the luxury villa at Oplontis (see note on the picture on p. 91) are rich in their colour and characteristic of Roman wall painting in their *trompe l'oeil* effect.

p. 62 (above): this fresco of a fruit and flower garden is

from the Imperial Villa of Livia, the wife of Augustus, at Prima Porta near Rome. It was restored in 1952–3 just before falling into complete decay and is now in the Museo Nazionale at Rome. Bernard Berenson wrote: 'How dewy, how penetratingly fresh are grass and trees and flowers, how corruscating the fruit. Pomegranates as Renoir painted them. Bird songs charm one's ears. The distance remains magically impenetrable.'

(below): this bust of Maecenas is in the Museo Nuovo nel Palazzo dei Conservatori, Rome.
p. 63: the so-called auditorium of Maecenas dates from the reign of Augustus and was certainly in his gardens. The exact purpose of the building is uncertain, but the apse has tiered seats in a semi-circle, which would certainly be appropriate for an auditorium. It may be that Virgil and Horace read their poems here. In the niches are traces of red landscape paintings, but they cannot be seen in this photograph.

Chapter 44

Cartoon captions

Captions 1 and 3 contain future vivid conditional clauses with the indicative; these are already familiar to your students.

Captions 2 and 4 contain past 'contrary to fact' conditional clauses with the pluperfect subjunctive. This is a new linguistic feature. The context may well enable your students to understand them correctly straight away, but it will be worth pausing to consolidate their understanding of the use of the subjunctive in these conditional clauses.

Quīntus iter Brundisium facit

The passage is based on and quotes from *Satires* 1.5. In 38 BC Octavian was again involved in war with Sextus Pompeius and suffered two defeats by sea. That autumn he sent Maecenas on an embassy to Antony to ask for his help. Maecenas succeeded in effecting a reconciliation between Octavian and Antony, who met at Tarentum in spring 37 BC; the powers of the Triumviri were extended for another five years and Antony gave Octavian 120 ships. With his enlarged fleet, Octavian, after several setbacks, succeeded in finally defeating and eliminating Pompeius (battle of Naulochus, September 36 BC).

2 Vergilius aderit: Maecenas took with him a considerable train besides Virgil and Horace; apart from the diplomats who went on with him to Athens (Nerva Cocceius and Fonteius Capito, a friend of Antony), Varius Rufus, a leading poet, Plotius Tucca, who was later one of Virgil's literary executors, and the rhetor

Heliodorus accompanied him. He must have planned to enliven a tedious journey by the company of like-minded friends.

9–10 sī statim discēdāmus, nōn longē … prōgrediāmur: 'If we were to leave now, we would not get far.' Students will need help with this 'future less vivid' conditional; they are likely to translate it as an open conditional: 'If we start at once, we shall not get far.' Point out to them the difference in moods between this sentence and the following one, where we do have an open future conditional.

17 per canālem: the canal ran from Forum Appi to Anxur through the Pomptine marshes, a distance of about 40 miles. It enabled travellers to proceed at night and so save time and avoided a tiresome journey by foot or mule through the mosquito-infested marshes.

19 pedibus: 'on foot'. It is hard to believe that Maecenas or his companions in fact travelled on foot. They are more likely to have accomplished part of the journey by litter and part by riding mules or horses.

21–2 dum … traheret: dum = while (normally followed by the indicative), but here it is subordinate to the purpose clause **ut … possent** and so suboblique, i.e. it is part of a thought in their minds and so is in the subjunctive, following sequence (secondary). This is unlikely to bother your students and should not delay you.

24ff. *Satires* 1.5.1–41 (with omissions). Metre: dactylic hexameters.

24 Arīcia Rōmā: students may need help to see that **Arīcia** is subject (short final **a**), **Rōmā**, with **magnā** in agreement, ablative (long final **ā**). If they stumble, ask which word **magnā** agrees with.

25 Hēliodōrus: we know nothing of him apart from this reference. Many Greek rhetoricians taught at Rome.

26 inde Forum Appī: in colloquial Latin it is common to omit not only the verb 'to be', but also other verbs which can easily be suppplied from the context. Horace himself calls the *Satires sermōnēs* ('conversations') and often uses the language of ordinary conversation, fitting it to the complex hexameter metre with astonishing skill.

30 malī culicēs: the Pomptine marshes were notorious for their mosquitoes which carried malaria; numerous attempts were made to drain them but none succeeded until Mussolini took the job in hand in the 1930s.

31 āvertunt: 'turn aside' = 'prevent'.

34–5 missae pāstum retinācula mūlae … religat: a difficult sentence, mainly because of the word order; the object (**retinācula**) comes before the subject (**nauta piger**). A bit of old-fashioned analysis will probably be necessary; when students have seen that the skeleton of the sentence is 'the sailor ties the reins', the rest will fall into place.

pāstum is the supine of the verb **pāscō** = I graze;

the supine after a verb of motion expresses purpose; students have met more than once **ī cubitum** = go to lie down, go to bed.

36 nīl, a common contraction for **nihil** (included in the chapter vocabulary), is here used adverbially: 'not at all'.

43 Anxur (neuter): Anxur, also called Tarracina, lies near the coast on top of a high hill with white limestone cliffs. It was a considerable climb to get there.

54–5 tandem Brundisium advēnērunt: the whole journey from Rome to Brundisium was 366 miles and it took them about fifteen days. Brundisium with its magnificent natural harbour was the port commonly used for crossing to Greece.

Maecēnās Antōnium cum Octāviānō reconciliat

Instead of comprehension questions, students are asked to summarize this passage in English. It contains a good deal of information and summaries may not be short.

7 ut Antōniō convenīret: for Maecenas' embassy, see note introducing the previous passage.

13–14 uxōrem suam Octāviam: Antony had married Octavian's sister Octavia in 40 BC; it was a dynastic marriage to cement the alliance of the two leaders.

uxōrem suam ... Cleopātram ...: students may be put out by the absence of connecting particles between these clauses; Latin writers frequently omit connection between clauses which are parallel or contrasted, putting the contrasted words in emphatic first position (asyndeton).

14 Cleopātram: Cleopatra, the last monarch of Egypt descended from Alexander the Great's general Ptolemy, was in exile when Julius Caesar reached Egypt after defeating Pompey at Pharsalus (48 BC); she became his mistress to recover her throne and had a son by him. She followed him to Rome but returned to Egypt after his death.

Antony, who after Philippi controlled the eastern half of the Roman empire, summoned her to Tarsus in 41 BC. She became his mistress; he visited her in Alexandria, and after he left, she bore him twins, a boy and a girl. Seven years later, in 33 BC, Antony returned to Alexandria, divorced Octavia and married Cleopatra (see chapter 47). This finally determined that he and Octavian would fight it out for supremacy (see also the background essay, pp. 92–3).

The sentences for translation placed after the passage are intended to make sure that students have understood precisely the uses of the subjunctive in the conditional clauses.

Grammar and exercises

Conditional clauses

We have classified the types of conditional clauses under three headings:

1 'simple fact' or 'open' conditions in present or past time with the indicative.

2 'contrary to fact' or 'impossible' conditions in present or past time with the imperfect or pluperfect subjunctive.

3 Two types of future conditions: (a) 'vivid' with future/future perfect indicative (which have been used since chapter 27); (b) 'less vivid' with present subjunctive.

'Simple fact' or 'open' conditions with the indicative have been used freely since early in the course.

You might introduce your explanation of 'contrary to fact' conditionals by English examples, e.g. what is the difference in meaning between: 'If you did this, you were foolish' and 'If you had done this, you would have been foolish'? Students will then come to see that where English uses the conditional tenses ('would, would have'), Latin uses the subjunctive.

The use of tenses in 'contrary to fact' conditional clauses is apt to cause difficulty. There is no problem about the pluperfect subjunctive referring to past time. The difficulty is that the imperfect subjunctive is used to refer to present time.

With regard to 'future less vivid' conditionals, in which the present subjunctive is used to represent future time, you might want to point out that the present subjunctive in main clauses always refers to future time, e.g. 'let us go', 'we may go' etc.

There is further difficulty; English tense usage in conditional clauses is not precise, e.g. 'If father were here, he would advise us.' By sense this refers to present time, but its form could equally well refer to future time, e.g. 'If we set out at once (= if we were to set out), we would arrive ...'. This will probably cause few problems in understanding and translating Latin, which is what matters, but may present difficulty in translating from English into Latin; in exercise 44.3 we have made the time references unambiguous.

Background: Travel

The content is largely informational. Discussion could centre on the final paragraph. The Romans built the motorways of their day and it took nearly two thousand years for their achievement to be outdone. And are the amazing advances in the means of travel of the last hundred and fifty years all gain?

Further reading: U. E. Paoli: *Rome: Its People, Life and Customs*, Longman, repr. Bristol Classical Press, pp. 228–31; O. A. W. Dilke: *The Ancient Romans*, David and Charles, chapter 4. The Roman roads in

Britain are particularly straight. If there is one near you, you can discuss it with your pupils.

Source
p. 70, para. 4: Octavian's preference for sea travel: Suetonius: *Augustus* 82.

Illustrations

p. 66: this canal, in point of fact the Canal du Jonction in France, is not uncharacteristic of the canals which line the Pontine Marshes south of Rome.
p. 67: in Horace's day, the Appian Way had to climb over the summit of the White Rocks. The poet complains about the three-mile ascent in carriages to Anxur in his poem about his journey to Brundisium. Later the emperor Trajan cut away the rocks at their base so that the Appian Way could run by the sea shore. The depth of the cutting is marked at intervals of 10 Roman feet, starting from the top.
p. 68: the Appian Way near Rome. This, the first of the great Roman roads, was planned by the blind Appius Claudius in 312 BC. It is still used by traffic, though quite close to the section illustrated it is now rudely bisected by the modern peripheral road around the city.
p. 69 (above): this donkey-drawn vehicle is a tomb painting from Southern Italy. (National Archaeological Museum, Paestum)
    (below): this relief of a *raeda* comes from Klagenfurt. It is from a sarcophagus and dates from the imperial period.

Chapter 45

In this chapter we concentrate on Horace's life in Rome. The main narrative is based on *Satires* 1.9, his encounter with the persistent bore, and it quotes the opening of this Satire. Students will not find this easy, because of the large number of unfamiliar colloquialisms and wide vocabulary. But it is a delightful piece, easily appreciated, and they will find that it repays hard study.

The linguistic features introduced are the uses of the subjunctive in main clauses – jussive, optative (wishes), deliberative and potential. To introduce these simultaneously might appear confusing, but the commonest of these usages (jussive) has already been met frequently and practised; wishes are usually introduced by **utinam** and so are easily recognized; the deliberative subjunctive is always found in the form of a question; the potential subjunctive is uncommon except with a few verbs – **velim, nōlim, mālim, ausim**. And so the different usages are not hard to distinguish.

Vocabulary

āiō: this verb is 'defective'; it has no infinitive, perfect or supine; **āit** is used in past sense as well as present.

Quīntus ā molestō quōdam vexātur

2 **tot carmina**: at this time (after he had beeen admitted to the circle of Maecenas), Horace was working on both the *Epodes* and *Satires* 1. The first book of the *Satires* was published in 35 BC and the *Epodes* in 30 BC. But the poems would have been circulating among his friends before that and some may, for all we know, have been performed at private or even public recitations.
5 **aliquis eī dīceret**: 'someone might say to him'; this is a rather rare type of potential subjunctive. As students have learnt that the imperfect subjunctive may be translated 'might', they may not be bothered by this and it should not delay you.
    utinam: 'would that ...' indicates that the subjunctive is optative; it is glossed 'I wish'.
6–7 **possīs ... sī velīs**: 'you could ... if you wished'.
8 **ausim**: 'I would dare'; this is an archaic subjunctive form of **audeō** (compare **sim, velim** etc. and also **faxim**, from **faciō**). **ausim** is used only in this potential sense.
12ff. *Satires* 1.9.1–21. Metre: dactylic hexameters.
12 **Viā Sacrā**: 'by (= along) the Sacred Way'; this led through the Forum up to the Capitol.
13 **nescioquid ... nūgārum**: 'something or other of nonsense' (**nūgārum** is partitive genitive, compare **aliquid vīnī** = some wine).
16 **cupiō omnia quae vīs**: 'I desire all that you want'; a polite formula.
17 **adsectārētur**: **sector, sectārī** is an intensive form of **sequor** (there are many such intensive forms, all 1st conjugation, and differing little in meaning from the simple form, e.g. **iaciō, iacere – iactō, iactāre; canō, canere – cantō, cantāre**; it might be worth telling your students this).
18 **nōrīs nōs = volō nōverīs nōs**: 'I want you to know me'; **volō** is sometimes followed by the subjunctive with or without **ut**, e.g. **quid vīs faciam?** ('What do you want me to do?', Plautus: *Merc.* 1.2.49). **nōrīs** is a shortened form of **nōverīs**; **nōs** is used for **mē**. The language of this Satire is highly colloquial, e.g. **dulcissime rērum** (line 15), **suāviter, ut nunc est** (line 16).
    doctī sumus: we are learned = we are poets (a common use of **doctus**); but it might mean 'I am a poet' (compare **nōrīs nōs**), which perhaps is better.
18–19 **plūris hōc ... mihi eris**: 'because of this (**hōc**, ablative of cause) you will be worth more (**plūris**, genitive of value) in my eyes (**mihi**, dative of person concerned)'. Students have met all these usages; if they can explain them in this context, they will be doing very

well! Horace replies to the bore's outrageous behaviour with cold politeness; he cannot bring himself to be rude, as the quick tempered Bolanus would have been (see below).

20–21 īre ... cōnsistere ... dīcere: these are 'historic' infinitives, so called because they are particularly common in historical narrative. They occur only when a succession of actions is being described; their subject is in the nominative (here **ego**, line 18) and their meaning is exactly the same as the perfect (aoristic) indicative.

21 puerō: 'to my boy', i.e. the slave who was accompanying him.

22–3 ō tē ... cerebrī fēlīcem: 'O you lucky in your quick temper'. **tē** is accusative of exclamation; **cerebrī** is genitive of sphere of reference (compare **mīlitiae perītus** = skilled in warfare). Bolanus, otherwise unknown, was evidently notorious for his quick temper and would have soon sent the bore packing; Horace wishes he could emulate him.

24 ut ... respondēbam: **ut** + indicative = when; students may need to be reminded of this.

27 persequar ... tibi: 'I will follow (you) from here whither the journey for you is' = 'I will follow you the way you are going'.

27–8 nil opus est tē circumagī: 'there is no need that you should be taken roundabout'. **opus** + accusative and infinitive is rare.

29 cubat: 'he is in bed'; often used of the sick.

    Caesaris hortōs: the gardens of Caesar were a public park, left to the people by Caesar in his will; they lay on the far side of the Tiber near the Janiculum hill, about three quarters of a mile from the Forum.

31 inīquae mentis asellus: 'an ass of unwilling mind' (genitive of description).

34 nīl ēgit: 'he did nothing' = 'he got nowhere'.

34–9 These lines introduce a succession of subjunctives in main clauses; the contexts should enable students to distinguish them without too much difficulty: **utinam ... possim** (lines 34–5), optative: 'I wish I could'; **quid faciāmus**? (line 36), deliberative: 'What are we to do?'; **festīnēmus** (line 36), jussive: 'let us hurry'; **eāmus** (line 39), jussive: 'let us go'; **nōlim** (line 39), potential: 'I would not want'.

47 venī in iūs: 'come to justice', i.e. come to have our case settled.

48 mē servāvit Apollō: Horace claims to be under the protection of Apollo, the god of poetic inspiration.

It is worth quoting part of the Satire in which the bore asks Horace to introduce him to Maecenas (lines 35–60); the passage skilfully develops the insensitive character of the bore and tells us a lot about the relations between Horace and Maecenas:

We had reached the temple of Vesta and by now a quarter of the day was past and it happened he had to appear in court as he was held to bail; if he failed to do so, he would lose his case. 'Please,' he said, 'give me your support in court for a little.' 'Hang me, if I have the strength to stand so long and I know nothing of the civil law; and I am hurrying you know where.' 'I don't know what to do,' he said, 'whether to leave you or my business.' 'Me, please,' I said. 'I won't do it,' he replied and began to lead the way. I follow, for it is hard to fight with one's conqueror. Then he starts up again. 'How do you stand with Maecenas? He's a man of few friends and sound sense. No one has used his good luck more skilfully. You would have a great helper, who would play second fiddle to you, if you were willing to introduce me to him. Hang me, if you didn't push all your competitors out.' 'We don't live the way you think at Maecenas'. No house is purer or more free from nastiness of that kind. It's no disadvantage to me that this man is richer or that more learned than me; each one of us has his own place.' 'What you say is remarkable, indeed scarcely credible.' 'And yet it is true.' 'You make me all the keener to get close to him.' 'Only wish it and, such is your courage, you will take him by storm; he is a man who can be conquered, and that is why he makes the first approaches difficult.' 'I won't let myself down; I'll bribe his slaves with gifts; if I am not admitted today, I'll not give up. I will find out his timetable; I'll meet him at the crossroads; I'll escort him home. Life gives men nothing without great effort.'

(At this moment they meet Horace's friend, who knows the bore well and is thoroughly amused by the situation, pretending not to understand what Horace means when he nods, rolls his eyes and pinches his arm. He goes off, leaving Horace in a rage. But just as Horace despairs, the bore's adversary at law appears and carries him into court: *sīc mē servāvit Apollō*.)

This masterly poem is not satire as we now understand it; he is not attacking bores in general or even a particular bore; it is a little drama in which the leading character is Horace. He laughs at himself and the situation in which he finds himself, as his innate courtesy prevents him from sending the bore packing. You might ask your students to write a piece in which they have a similar experience.

Quīntus urbis strepitum effugere cupit

This passage is suggested by Horace's repeated expressions of longing to escape from Rome to the country, e.g. *ō rūs, quandō tē aspiciam?* (*Satires* 2.6.60). The description of his idle days at Rome is based on *Satires* 1.6.111–31:

I go alone wherever my fancy takes me; I ask how much cabbages and flour are; I wander through the cheating Circus and the Forum as evening falls; I stand by the fortune-tellers; then I take myself home to a simple supper ... Then I go to bed, not anxious because I must get up early for some tiresome business. I lie on until the fourth hour; after that I go for a walk, or, after reading or writing something to please myself in silence, I anoint myself with olive oil ... and when I'm tired and the sun, getting hotter, has warned me to go to take a bath, I avoid the Campus Martius and the games of ball (played there). After a light lunch, just enough to prevent me fasting all day, I idle at home. This is the life of those free from the heavy burden of miserable ambition. I take comfort that I shall live more pleasantly like this than if my father and my grandfather and my uncle had been quaestors.

3 **utinam ... nātus essem**: 'I wish I had been born' (pluperfect, a wish for the past); **utinam ... essem** (lines 3–4): 'I wish I were' (imperfect, a wish for the present). The tenses of the subjunctive used in wishes are the same as those used in 'contrary to fact' conditional clauses.

7 **turba clientium**: 'a crowd of clients'; **turba** suggests a disorganized crowd, a mob. Distinguished men had to suffer the morning *salūtātiō*, at which clients were expected to call on their patrons to pay their respects and then accompany them to the Forum (see background essay). A man's importance could be judged by the size of the retinue which followed him.

19 **urbis mē taedet**: 'it wearies me of the city'; glossed, but you may have to say a word on impersonal verbs.

20–21 **calōrēs aestātis**: the heat of Rome in the summer was intolerable and all who could escaped to the hills, as they still do.

Grammar and exercises

Uses of the subjunctive in main clauses

1 Jussive (exhortations and 3rd person commands). Students were introduced to this usage in chapter 34 and it has occurred periodically in the narratives of subsequent chapters.

Although it is commonest in 1st and 3rd persons, it is also found occasionally in the 2nd person instead of an imperative, e.g. *miser Catulle, dēsinās ineptīre*: 'unhappy Catullus, stop being a fool' (Catullus 8.1). This use is common in comedy but rare elsewhere.

nē + perfect subjunctive is used an an alternative to **nōlī** + infinitive in prohibitions; it seems to be a colloquialism used for emphasis, e.g. *sēcrētō hoc audī; nē Apellae quidem dīxerīs*: 'listen to this in secret; do not tell even Apella' (Cicero: *Ad Fam.* 7.25.2). There is

no need to bother your students with this information.

2 Deliberative questions. These are easily recognized, since the subjunctive (always present) occurs in a question.

3 Optative (wishes). The tenses of the optative subjunctive are the same as those for 'future less vivid' and 'contrary to fact' conditional clauses, i.e. the present subjunctive expresses a wish which may be fulfilled in the future, e.g. (**utinam**) **diū vīvās** = may you live long; the imperfect subjunctive expresses a wish unfulfilled at the present time, e.g. (**utinam**) **valērēs** = I wish you were well (but you are not); the pluperfect expresses a wish unfulfilled in past time, e.g. (**utinam**) **nē domō abiissēs** = I wish you had not gone away from home (but you did).

The regular negative in wishes is **nē**, but **nōn** is occasionally found after **utinam**, e.g. *utinam susceptus nōn essem* = I wish I had never been reared (Cicero: *Ad Atticum* 11.9.3).

4 Potential. This use (negative **nōn**) is commonest with **velim, nōlim, mālim** and **ausim** but occurs with other verbs also, e.g. **fortūnam facilius reperiās quam retineās** = you would find a fortune more easily than you would keep it.

Also **dīcat/dīxerit aliquis** = someone may say.

Students may find these different uses confusing; difficult examples which occur in the narrative will still be glossed. The exercises 45.3 and 45.4 will probably not cause problems.

P.S.

1 (*CIL* 7812) We do not gloss the medical terms in the first two lines of this inscription; intelligent students will be able to guess them. **clinicus** = a physician, someone who attends a patient in bed (Greek: *clinē*). **chīrūrgus** = a surgeon, properly a doctor who works with his hands (Greek: *cheir*) as opposed to one who administers drugs etc. (the old spelling of surgeon was chirugeon).

Students will be interested to see that there were specialists in these various branches of medicine in the ancient world. Since Hippocrates (fifth century BC) had set medicine on a rational basis, it had made great progress, but, as the second inscription shows (*CIL* 9441), surgery was not always successful, any more than it is today.

Background: Patrons and clients

This humiliating system perpetuated the social hierarchy. At its best it could operate to the mutual benefit of patron and client, but in the empire, the period from which most of our evidence comes, the bulk of callers were, according to J. P. V. D. Balsdon, 'on the outer fringe of good society, unsuccessful men who, at the cost of whatever personal humiliation, hoped for gain, favour or advantage considerably greater that the sportula'. He believes that 'it would be a mistake, because of the attention given by Juvenal and by Martial to the rich man's reception of his clients, to think that any very substantial number of Romans passed the first two hours of the day in this degrading manner'. He goes on to remark wisely, 'This is only one of the respects in which the satirist, the epigrammatist and the moralist may leave an altogether false impression of the general social life of their times' (*Life and Leisure in Ancient Rome*, Bodley Head, pp. 22, 24.) Balsdon's commentary on the patron–client system is excellent (pp. 21–4). See also J. Carcopino: *Daily Life in Ancient Rome*, Penguin, pp. 191–3.

Sources

p. 76, para. 1: bribing of slaves: Seneca: *Epistles* 4.10.
Seneca quotation: *De Brev. Vit.* 14.4.
para. 2: infrequent invitations: Juvenal: 5.15–16.
Juvenal on dinner: 5.92–106.
para. 3: Seneca quotation: *Epistles* 19.4.
para. 4: Martial quotation: 8.56.5.

Illustrations

p. 72: this view of the Roman Forum from the Capitoline hill clearly shows the Via Sacra to the left. In the background is the Colosseum, the great amphitheatre of Rome which was opened in AD 80 and could hold probably some 50,000 spectators. To the left are the temple of Antoninus and Faustina (dedicated in AD 141) and (in the foreground) the arch of Septimius Severus (built in AD 203).
p. 73 (above): the Pons Fabricius, which leads to the Tiber island, is the oldest Roman bridge to have survived in the city. It carries an inscription which gives the name of the builder, Lucius Fabricius, and the date, 62 BC.
(below): a sixth-century AD mosaic of a man approaching a suspicious ass with a feed-bag. (Mosaic Museum, Istanbul)
p. 75: this idealized landscape is from the frescoes partially shown on p. 62 and commented on on pp. 28–9 above.

Chapter 46

Cartoon captions

This is a review chapter and neither the captions nor the narrative introduce any new linguistic features. The captions revise the usages of conditional clauses and should cause students no difficulty.

Quīntus rūsticus fit

Maecenas gave Horace the Sabine farm in about 33 BC. The site is generally identified with a villa in the hills above the valley of the Digentia near the modern town of Vicovaro, about 25 miles east of Rome; this villa fits the description of his farm which Horace gives in *Epistles* 1.16.1–16. It was a fair-sized house (*satis ampla*) with a large walled garden. The house contained twelve rooms, including an *ātrium*, two dining-rooms and a bath with a hypocaust. The estate was not small, for it supported five separate families and the farm manager had eight slaves under him as labourers.
34–8 **hoc erat in vōtīs ...**: quoted from *Satires* 2.6.1–5. Metre: dactylic hexameters.
35–6 **hortus ... foret**: the word order is difficult; simplified, it would run: **ubi hortus foret et iugis aquae fōns tēctō vīcīnus et paulum silvae super hīs.**
foret: this subjunctive is formed from **fore**, the alternative future infinitive of **esse**.
37 **bene est**: 'it is well' (a common idiom).
38 **faxīs**: this is an archaic form of the perfect subjunctive of **faciō** (compare **ausim** from **audeō**). The gloss says it is equivalent to **faciās** (present subjunctive), which is true of the sense.

Fōns Bandusiae

For the spring identified with the *fōns Bandusiae*, see illustration; its site is on the hillside above the villa.
15ff. **ō fōns Bandusiae ...**: *Odes* 3.13. Metre: Asclepiads (see Appendix):

ō fōns | Bāndŭsĭaē, | splēndĭdĭŏr | vītrō,

dūlcī | dīgnĕ mĕrō | nōn sĭnĕ flō|rĭbŭs,

crās dō|nābĕrĭs hāe|dō,

cuī frōns | tūrgĭdă cōr|nĭbŭs

The Ode takes the form of a hymn to the *fōns Bandusiae*. All springs were sacred and in mid-October the Fontinalia was celebrated, when offerings of flowers and libations of wine were thrown into the water, and the sacrifice of a kid was made (Varro: *De Lingua Latina* 6.22). The formal characteristics of a hymn are: 1 the invocation – **ō fōns Bandusiae**; 2 the attributes of the deity – **splendidior vitrō**; 3 the functions of the deity (how he/she helps mortals, commonly introduced by **tū ... tē ...** (anaphora). (Compare the Hymn to Mercury, *Odes* 1.10: *Mercurī, fācunde nepōs Atlantis, quī ..., tē canam ... tē ... tē ... tū piās ... animās repōnis ...*)
But this Ode has two digressions: **1** five lines, nearly a third of the poem, are devoted to the kid and its fate. The kid is described sympathetically, and **frūstrā**, both by its meaning and by its weight, isolated between stops in emphatic position at the beginning of the line,

rings out like the knell of doom. Does Horace intend to make us feel revulsion at the fate the playful kid is to suffer?

2 The last stanza begins with a complete change of direction; the spring will be added to the role of famous springs, like Castalia and Arethusa, through the greatness of Horace's poetry. The poem ends with a naturalistic description of the scene, in which the rhythm (the enjambement makes the last lines seem to tumble over each other like the water) and the sounds assist the sense (see Gordon Williams: *Horace Odes Book 3*, Oxford).

So, if we ask what the poem is about, the answer will be complex. It is about the spring and its beauty; it clearly has a dimension of 'nature' poetry. It is also about the kid and the cruelty of animal sacrifice (an unexpected note in ancient poetry). Lastly it is about Horace's own poetry, when he claims that he can confer on the spring the gift of immortality.

It is characteristic of Horace to revitalize old forms, to pack much into a small compass, to change direction of thought, to vary the tone; all this is achieved here in a mere sixteen lines. We will find him performing a similar feat in *Vīxī puellīs* (*Odes* 3.26) in chapter 50.

17 crās dōnāberis: Horace says 'tomorrow you will be offered these sacrifices', which must mean that he is composing the poem just before the festival. The Fontinalia was held in October, but the third stanza gives a picture of midsummer when the burning Dogstar rises (July), and it could be argued that kids, usually born in the spring, would have well-developed horns by October. If there is a discrepancy here, it is not important.

19 et Venerem et proelia: 'both love and battles' = 'battles of love'; hendiadys, compare Virgil: *Georgics* 2.192, *paterīs lībāmus et aurō* ('we pour libations from golden cups'). If the kid reached maturity, it would fight with the other he-goats for the favours of the she-goats.

21 rubrō sanguine: when the goat had been sacrificed, its blood would be ritually poured into the stream, staining its sparkling water.

Grammar and exercises

A review chapter; the exercises give practice in constructions recently learnt.

Exercise 46.2

2 Students may have to reminded that **opus est** is used with the ablative of the thing needed and the dative of the person concerned: 'you need leisure'.

11 composuit ut ... numerētur: 'he composed so beautiful a poem (in the past) that the spring is now counted ...'. In consecutive clauses sequence cannot always be followed; here a past action results in a present consequence.

Background: Houses

We owe much of our evidence about Roman houses to the eruption of Vesuvius on 24 August AD 79. The town closest to the mountain, Herculaneum, was swamped in a flow of volcanic mud; Pompeii was covered with a fall of ash and stones. The excavations of these towns have proved enormously valuable.

Further reading: *Pompeii AD 79*, Royal Academy of Arts; Michael Grant: *Cities of Vesuvius*, Spring Books; U. E. Paoli: *Rome: Its People, Life and Customs*, Longman, repr. Bristol Classical Press, pp. 54–77; *The Oxford History of the Classical World*, pp. 718–37. See also Pliny: *Epistles* 2.17.

Valuable software on Roman houses is available in JPROGS Roman Life (based on Pompeii and Herculaneum). Contact JPROGS, 81 High St, Pitsford, Northants NN6 9AD.

Horace's villa (p. 82, para. 4): there is no conclusive evidence that the villa we describe is in fact Horace's villa. Even so, it is the right kind of villa in the right kind of place.

First question: the 'missing room' in our Plans 1, 2 and 3 is a kitchen. Kitchens had no fixed position in the normal layout of a Roman house. They tended to be poky little holes, fitted in wherever there was some free space in a building. Cooking in these cramped conditions was both difficult and dangerous.

Illustrations

p. 79: this villa in the Sabine hills may be the one which Maecenas gave to Horace.
p. 80: this fountain is a short distance above the villa illustrated on p. 79. It is thus identified with the *fōns Bandusiae*.
p. 82 (above): this peristyle garden is in the House of the Vettii at Pompeii.

(below): this reconstruction is based on Pliny the Younger's detailed description of his Laurentine villa in one of his letters (2.17). (Ashmolean Museum, Oxford)

Chapter 47

For the events leading up to the Actium campaign, see also pp. 16–17 above. When Antony sent Octavia letters of divorce and formally married Cleopatra, Octavian embarked on a war of violent propaganda against him; Antony was represented as the slave of an eastern queen to whom he had given away large parts of the empire (the Donations of Alexandria); it was even rumoured that he intended to move the capital of the empire to Alexandria. Despite this, the consuls of 32 BC and many senators supported Antony. Early in the year

Octavian summoned the senate and surrounded by soldiers made an attack on Antony. Both consuls and over three hundred senators fled from Rome to Antony.

Octavian now prepared for war, first attempting to unite all Italy behind him in a 'just' war which would save Rome from the menace of the East. In the summer his agents organized a sort of plebiscite, an oath of allegiance to him: *iūrāvit in mea verba tōta Italia sponte suā, et mē bellī quō vīcī ad Actium ducem poposcit* ('the whole of Italy swore an oath of loyalty to me and demanded me as leader in the war which I won at Actium', *Res Gestae* 25.2). This was followed by a formal declaration of war against Cleopatra.

Antony led his forces (some thirty legions and five hundred ships) north and took up a defensive position near the promontory of Actium. Octavian, leaving Maecenas in charge of Italy, crossed to Greece in summer 31 BC and encamped just north of Actium, while his fleet, commanded by Agrippa, won control of the sea and began to cut off Antony's supplies. Battle was joined on 2 September. Plutarch's account, which we have followed in our narrative, that Cleopatra fled of her own accord, is probably incorrect; it is more likely that when he was being worsted in the battle, Antony signalled to Cleopatra to retire since her ships carried the war-chest. He followed her and the rest of his fleet was captured or surrendered. His land forces carried on the fight for a week, then they also surrendered.

Actium

3 **in diēs**: 'day by day'.
4–5 **tōta Italia ... poposcit**: compare Augustus' own words from the *Res Gestae* quoted above.
9 **repudiāvit**: see the background essay.
13 **qui ... administrāret**: 'to manage/govern'; the relative with the subjunctive expresses purpose.
14 **Agrippā**: M. Vipsanius Agrippa was an exact contemporary of Octavian; he was serving with him in Apollonia when Julius Caesar was murdered, returned to Italy with Octavian and became his most trusted and successful general; it was he who defeated Sextus Pompeius in two naval battles and he was responsible for the victory at Actium. He married Augustus' (= Octavian's) daughter, Julia, in 21 BC and was marked out to be his successor as emperor but died twenty-seven years before Augustus in 13 BC.
28 **minōris aestimāret quam**: 'valued less than'; students may need reminding of the genitive of value.
35 **clēmentiam ... praebuit**: Augustus made much of his *clēmentia*; in the *Res Gestae* 3 he says: *victor omnibus vēniam petentibus cīvibus pepercī* ('in victory I spared all citizens who asked for pardon'). Nevertheless, it is said that he made the soldiers of Antony who had surrendered fight in the front line at Alexandria.

Vergilius Actium proelium dēscrībit

3ff. **in mediō ...**: *Aeneid* 8.675–90. Metre: dactylic hexameters.
In *Aeneid* 8, Venus, fearing for safety of her son Aeneas in the coming war with Turnus and the Latins, goes to Vulcan and asks him to make magic weapons for him (line 370). These she brings to Aeneas (line 608) – helmet, sword, breastplate, spear and, above all, shield. On this magic shield Vulcan had engraved pictures foretelling Roman history from Romulus onwards. In the centre was represented the battle of Actium, the culminating victory of Roman history, in which Octavian ('Augustus Caesar') was to overcome the threat of the East and open the way for the new age of peace.

The scene is described in the terms of Octavian's propaganda war against Antony. Augustus leads the Italians, the senate and people of Rome, with the Roman native gods and the great gods of Olympus, against a motley collection of eastern barbarians followed by an Egyptian wife.

Linguistically, it is not hard (except for the first three lines) apart from the vocabulary.
4 **vidērēs**: potential subjunctive ('you might see, if you looked'); 'you' is the so-called 'ideal second person', i.e. it means 'anyone', 'one might see'.
6 **Augustus ... Caesar**: when Octavian returned from the East, he was voted the title Augustus and from then on was known as Augustus Caesar.
9 **parte aliā ... Agrippa**: supply **est**.
   ventīs et dīs ... secundīs: ablative absolute, like e.g. **Caesare duce**.

Grammar and exercises

The uses of **cum**
On the uses of **cum** = 'when' see p. 13 above. They are extremely complex and we give students only enough information to enable them to get by in most cases.

3 **cum** = 'since' always takes the subjunctive. Other conjunctions introducing causal clauses (**quod, quia** = because; **quoniam** = since) take the indicative, unless the clause gives an opinion rather than a fact, e.g. **iuvenis condemnātus est quod senem occīderat** = the young man was condemned because (as a matter of fact) he had killed the old man; cf. **iuvenis condemnātus est quod senem occīdisset** = the young man was condemned for killing/on the grounds that he had killed the old man. So in *Satires* 1.6.47–8 (quoted in chapter 43), Horace says that everyone carps at him:

nunc quia sim tibi, Maecēnās, convīctor, at ōlim quod mihi pārēret legiō Rōmānā tribūnō.

now because I am your friend, Maecenas, once because a Roman legion obeyed me.

Here the subjunctives **sim** and **pārēret** are used because the clauses express the grounds on which all say unpleasant things about him; the facts are not in dispute but the clauses are virtually oblique.

4 **cum** = 'although' always takes the subjunctive and usually has **tamen** at the beginning of the main clause, to make the meaning clear. Other conjunctions introducing concessive clauses are:

quamquam = although (always followed by the indicative), e.g. **quamquam adulēscēns est, non est stultus** = although he is young, he is not foolish.

quamvīs = however much (always followed by the subjunctive), e.g. **quis est tam stultus, quamvīs sit adulēscēns** = who is so foolish, however young he may be/although he may be young.

quamquam clauses present the point conceded as a fact, **quamvīs** clauses present the point conceded as a supposition or for the sake of argument.

The uses of dum
1 **dum** = 'while' has long been known to students and they have often met it in past time with the present indicative; this is a type of historic present. We here introduce **dum** + imperfect indicative, used when the action of the **dum** clause and the action of the main clause are contemporaneous.
2 **dum** = 'until', like other temporal conjunctions (**dōnec** = until, **antequam/priusquam** = before, **postquam** = after, **simulac/atque** = as soon as etc.), takes the indicative unless the clause contains some other idea besides time, most commonly purpose (see examples with **dum** in the Students' book).
(3 **dum/dummodo** = 'provided that' is used with the present or imperfect subjunctive, e.g. **ōderint dum metuant** ('let them hate (me), provided that they fear (me)', Cicero: *De Officiis* 1.29.97). We do not deal with this usage in the Students' book.)

The connecting relative
This usage is common in narrative and is easily grasped.

P.S.
Students are likely to meet these alternative forms as soon as they start to read unadapted Latin.
1 has already occurred several times in verse extracts.
2 The syncopated forms of perfects in **-īvī** are commoner than the unsyncopated forms and we use them in the narrative in subsequent chapters. Other syncopated forms are more rare and are glossed when they they occur, e.g. **amāsse** = **amāvisse**, **nōrīs** = **nōverīs**.
3 We have already drawn attention to **fore**, but it is worth reminding students of this form; a subjunctive is

formed from it: **forem** for **essem**.
4 The alternative forms of the imperative are archaic (found mostly in legal formulae); your students need to know **estō, scītō, mementō**.
5 3rd declension **i-** stems: Caesar always has ablative singular **-ī**, not **-e**, e.g. **nāvī**; Caesar and Virgil always have accusative plural **-īs**, not **-ēs** (note that the **ī** is long).

Background: Divorce

Comparisons with the modern world are the obvious area for discussion here. Is divorce easier in some cultures today than in others? If there are significant differences, what do your pupils think of this? How much of a consolation is ease of divorce for a woman if she has to leave her children behind?

The following passage (Aulus Gellius: 43) may provide a profitable source of discussion. In or around 231 BC, Spurius Carvilius Ruga divorced his wife for barrenness when she was guilty of no offence:

> Servius Sulpicius ... declares that legal measures to define wives' property first became necessary when Spurius Carvilius ..., a nobleman, divorced his wife, because there were no children from her body ... Indeed, Carvilius is said to have greatly loved the wife that he repudiated, and to have held her very dear for her sweet character. But he put the sanctity of his oath before his love and inclination, because he had been required by the censors to declare that he would have his wife 'for the sake of begetting citizen children'.

Further reading: J. Carcopino: *Daily Life in Ancient Rome*, Penguin, pp. 108–15; P. Jones and K. Sidwell (eds), *The World of Rome*, chapter 7.

Sources
p. 87, para. 1: the life and death of Terentia: Jerome: *Adversus Jovinianum*: 1.48; Pliny: *Natural History* 8.158.
p. 88, para. 1: Caesar's wife must be above suspicion: Plutarch: *Caesar* 10.6.
frivolous reasons for divorce: Valerius Maximus: 6.3.10–12.

Illustrations

p. 84: in this painting of c. 1635 by the great French painter Nicholas Poussin (1595–1665), Aeneas' loving mother Venus presents to him the magical suit of armour forged for him by the fire god Vulcan. To the left the god of the river Tiber looks on. (Art Gallery of Ontario, Toronto)
p. 85: beneath these white cliffs, some 200 feet high, the battle of Actium was fought. Cape Leucate takes its

name from them (*leukos* is the Greek word for white). There are a few fragmentary remains of the temple of Apollo on top of the cape. The temple was restored by Augustus in gratitude for his victory.

p. 86 (above): this relief of the first century BC from Praeneste may well date from the time of Cleopatra. Note the crocodile on the bows. The legionary soldiers stand on deck while invisible slaves work the oars below. (Museo Pio-Clementino, Vatican, Rome)

(below): this relief of a sea-battle, which shows Roman soldiers fighting alongside mythological or divine figures with corpses on the shore, dates from the third century AD. (Archaeological Museum, Venice)

p. 88: in this relief from the sarcophagus of one of the partners in the wedding illustrated, the solemn moment at which the bride and groom, who holds the wedding contract, join hands is commemorated. Between them stands Cupid holding his torch (both literally a wedding torch and symbolically representing the fire of love) and the *prōnuba* is in the background.

Chapter 48

Cartoon caption

This introduces **nē** + subjunctive after a verb of fearing; as students have learnt that **nē** = lest, this will probably cause no difficulty.

Bellum Alexandrīnum

We follow Plutarch's highly romantic account of the deaths of Antony and Cleopatra, which was used by Shakespeare.

2 **lentissimē ... secūtus est**: Octavian in fact returned to Italy before pursuing Antony to Egypt, where he arrived in summer 30 BC.

11–12 **eī nuntiātum est**: 'it was announced to him'; the impersonal use of the verb in the passive may require comment. In this case we have a similar use in English; the next chapter deals with the impersonal use of the passive of intransitive verbs.

13 **ut sē occīderet**: **sē** refers to Antony, the reflexive referring to the subject of the leading verb (**imperāvit**).

20 **quō cognitō**: 'when he learnt this' ('which thing having been learnt'; connecting relative).

31 **quod dēdecus**: 'this disgrace'; connecting relative.

Mors Cleopātrae

We have not asked any comprehension questions on this passage. You might like to read your students Shakespeare's magnificent version, *Antony and Cleopatra*, Act 5, scene 2.

19 **mulier et formā ... superbō**: 'a woman of

outstanding beauty and proud spirit' (ablatives of description).

The extract from Horace's Cleopatra Ode (*Odes* 1.37.21–32) may be considered an optional extra. Metre: Alcaics (see Appendix):

> fātālĕ mōnstrūm; | quaē gĕnĕrōs|ĭŭs
>
> pĕrīrĕ quaērēns | nec mŭlĭēb|rītĕr
>
> ēxpāvĭt ēnsēm nĕc lătēntēs
>
> clāssē cĭtā rĕpărāv|ĭt ōrās

6–7 **fortis ... tractāre**: 'brave to handle'; **tractāre** is an epexegetic (explanatory) infinitive.

12 **nōn humilis**: not humble = extremely proud, a rhetorical figure of speech called litotes.

Before tackling these difficult lines, you may wish to read your students the translation of the whole Ode which we give below.

> Today is the day to drink and dance on. Dance, then,
> Merrily, friends, till the earth shakes. Now let us
> Rival the priests of Mars
> With feasts to deck the couches of the gods.
>
> Not long ago it would have been high treason
> To fetch the Caecuban from family store-room,
> When the wild Queen was still
> Plotting destruction for the Capitol
>
> And ruin to the Empire with her squalid
> Pack of deseased half-men – mad, wishful grandeur,
> Tipsy with sweet good luck!
> But all her fleet burnt, scarcely one ship saved –
>
> That tamed her rage; and Caesar, when his galleys
> Chased her from Italy, soon brought her, dreaming
> And drugged with native wine,
> Back to the hard realities of fear.
>
> And swiftly as the hawk follows the feeble
> Dove, or in snowy Thessaly the hunter
> The hare, so he sailed forth
> To bind this fatal prodigy in chains.
>
> Yet she preferred a finer style of dying;
> She did not, like a woman, shirk the dagger
> Or seek by speed at sea
> To change her Egypt for obscurer shores,
>
> But, gazing on her desolated palace
> With a calm smile, unflinchingly laid hands on
> The angry asps until
> Her veins had drunk the deadly poison deep,
>
> And, death-determined, fiercer then than ever,
> Perished. Was she to grace a haughty triumph,
> Dethroned, paraded by
> The rude Liburnians? Not Cleopatra.

(James Michie)

The Ode starts as a song of jubilant exultation – **nunc est bibendum** – at the destruction of the drugged Egyptian queen and her train of eunuchs, who suffered a just fate at the hands of a righteous Caesar. She is a **fātāle mōnstrum** (a monster bent on our destruction); but immediately after this striking phrase, the tone changes to admiration for her courage and pride. As so often, Horace surprises the reader by his swift change of direction. If the first twenty lines give the 'politically correct' view of Augustan propaganda, the last twelve seem to give the poet's own estimation of a woman who could hardly fail to inspire admiration.

Grammar and exercises

Clauses of fearing

This construction is easily recognized and presents no difficulty in Latin, though English usage can be confusing. English introduces such clauses by either 'lest' or 'that' or uses no introductory conjunction (see examples in the Students' book); Latin always uses an introductory conjunction. This is nearly always **nē** or, if negative, **nē nōn**, but occasionally **ut** is used instead of **nē nōn**, e.g. **vereor ut veniat** = I am afraid he may not come. We do not bother students with this rare alternative.

timeō, metuō, vereor are all found with the infinitive, meaning 'I am afraid to'. Students should not have any difficulty in distinguishing this use from 'I am afraid that something may happen.'

P.S.

1 The trumphal arch from which this inscription comes stood in the Forum.

The *tribūnicia potestās* = the powers which had been held by tribunes under the republic, in particular the power to introduce legislation and the power of veto. These powers enabled Augustus to control affairs in Rome without holding the consulate. It was assumed by Augustus for the first time in 23 BC (see p. 40 below), and was held continuously by his successors. Claudius became emperor in AD 41, so the arch was dedicated in AD 52, the eleventh year in which he held *tribūnicia potestās* and the fifth year in which he held the consulship.

2 The second inscription is *CIL* 2701.

Background: Cleopatra

To what extent is Cleopatra the victim of the victor Octavian's projected image of her? A woman who is a powerful political figure as well as a symbol of fertility, she was, Maria Wyke argues in *Omnibus* 21, pp. 27–9, hopelessly misrepresented in the official Augustan version. 'Surrounded by the paraphernalia of an Eastern despot,' she writes (p. 28), 'and associated with abuse of political power, with drunkenness, immorality, bestiality, effeminacy and a perverse desire to dominate men, this Roman version of Cleopatra belongs to a long Western tradition in which the East is described as feminine, despotic, and immoral and therefore, according to the logic of sexism, in sore need of control by the supposedly masculine, democratic, and moral West. If, in Horace's *Epode* 9, the soldier in Antony's army is "in bondage to a woman" and capable of service to "wrinkled eunuchs", Octavian is thereby rendered the champion of male liberty, seeking to free a Roman "slave" from a woman's chains.' There is much to discuss here.

It remains indisputable, however, that in *Odes* 1.37 (*Nunc est bibendum*) Horace begins with ecstatic gloating over Cleopatra's demise but then, as we have seen, moves through sympathy to a final unstinting tribute to her noble death in the high Roman fashion.

Plutarch's *Life of Mark Antony* and Shakespeare's *Antony and Cleopatra* offer the most striking pictures of Cleopatra.

Sources

p. 93, para. 1: Shakespeare: *Antony and Cleopatra* Act 2, scene 3, lines 195–205. The final two lines: i.e. surpassing the picture of Venus in which artistic imagination has outdone nature.

Illustrations

p. 89: in this 1978 production of Shakespeare's *Antony and Cleopatra* by Peter Wood for the Royal Shakespeare Company, Glenda Jackson played Cleopatra and Paola Dionisotti played Charmian.
p. 91: this basket of figs is a wall painting from the dining-room of the villa at Oplontis near Pompeii. It was only in 1964 that systematic excavations began here. The villa may have belonged to Poppaea Sabina (died AD 65), the wife of Nero. The property was unoccupied when it was buried beneath ash and pumice from Vesuvius in AD 79.
p. 92: the inscription AEGVPTO CAPTA ('after the capture of Egypt') on this coin is appropriately illustrated by a crocodile. (British Museum, London)
p. 93: this handsome bust of Cleopatra is from the Antikensammlung in Berlin.

Chapter 49

The deaths of Antony and Cleopatra marked the final end of the civil wars. Octavian, or Augustus he was shortly to be called, was ready to embark on the work of reconstruction. He annexed Egypt, not as a province but as his personal possession, to be administered by a Prefect appointed by himself (the first was the poet Cornelius Gallus). He appropriated the treasure of the Ptolemies. He cancelled the Donations of Alexandria and spent some time reestablishing the old provinces; he did not extend the territory ruled by Rome but secured the frontiers by installing loyal client kings on their borders. After making satisfactory arrangements, which were to last for many years, he returned to Rome in summer 29 BC and celebrated triumphs for his victories in Illyricum, Actium and Alexandria.

Peace was finally established throughout the Roman empire and the senate voted that the gates of the temple of Janus should be closed. The army, now swollen to nearly seventy legions, was reduced to twenty-six and the veterans settled, partly on land paid for by the spoils of Egypt. In 28/27 BC he made a constitutional settlement, which he describes in *Res Gestae* (34) as transferring 'the republic from my power into the control of the senate and people of Rome'. On 13 January 27 BC he laid down all powers and resigned all provinces to the disposal of the senate and people. Pressed by the senators, he consented to assume a special commission consisting of proconsular authority over Gaul, Spain and Syria. The basis of his power was now the consulship, which he held repeatedly, and his *imperium* in these provinces, where a large proportion of the legions were stationed. The senate acclaimed the restitution of liberty and conferred on him the name Augustus, a word with religious associations (in Cicero usually conjoined with *sānctus*). From then on he was known as Caesar Augustus. The title by which he preferred to be called and which he applied to himself was *prīnceps*; this was adapted from that given to the senior senator, *prīnceps senātus*, and means no more then 'leading citizen'; it implied no particular powers and had a civilian ring to it.

He then left Rome for a tour of the western provinces and was absent for nearly three years. When he returned to Rome in 24 BC, a crisis supervened; there was a conspiracy led by discontented nobles (the Conspiracy of Murena) and he himself fell seriously ill. He decided to revise the constitutional arrangements. He resigned the consulship, and to maintain his authority in the civilian sphere he assumed the *tribūnicia potestās*, which he held continuously. To maintain his control over the armies and provinces, he was granted *maius imperium prōcōnsulāre*, which enabled him to override the proconsuls in the provinces for which he was not directly responsible. Thus, while in theory the republic continued to function with annual elections, senatorial debates and the other machinery of republican government, in fact Augustus controlled the whole state both through the exceptional powers granted him and by his ever-growing *auctōritās*.

Caesar Augustus

2–3 **bella redintegrāta essent**: since the defeat of Crassus at Carrhae (53 BC), the eastern frontiers of the empire had been insecure. Antony had fought more or less continuous campaigns against Parthia and Armenia between 40 and 34 BC, suffering a major defeat in Armenia in 36 but reversing this in 34. Parthia remained a permanent threat. Augustus decided not to invade Parthia but installed a reliable client king in Armenia, which was to serve as a buffer state. In Asia Minor he kept the three existing provinces (Asia, Bithynia and Cilicia) and left control of the rest to client kings. In Syria he installed a reliable governor (Cicero's son) and strengthened his army. These arrangements secured peace for the time being but Augustus spent the years 22–19 BC in the East when he reached a permanent settlement with Parthia by diplomacy, recovering the standards lost at Carrhae and leaving the Euphrates as the boundary between the two empires.

11 **quasi deum colere**: in 42 BC the senate had voted to deify Julius Caesar; Octavian thus became *dīvī fīlius* and Virgil could write in *Eclogue* 1.6 *deus nōbīs haec ōtia fēcit*. From 29 BC his name was added to those of the gods in hymns. Before 23 BC Horace could write: *praesēns dīvus habēbitur/Augustus adiectīs Britannīs /imperiō gravibusque Persīs* (*Odes* 3.5.2–4). In the towns of Italy cults sprang up dedicated to the worship of Augustus. But despite the effusions of the poets, Augustus himself, while accepting emperor worship in the provinces where the deification of rulers had long been customary, discouraged it in Italy; he allowed only freedmen to become *Augustālēs* (priests of the cult of Augustus). Nevertheless, on his death the senate voted for his deification and he became Divus Augustus.

13 **odiō esse**: **odiō** is predicative dative; see chapter 53.

14 **rēgēs ... expulimus**: the last king of Rome, Tarquinius Superbus, was driven out in 510 BC according to tradition.

18–21 **in cōnsulātū ... trānstulī**: *Res Gestae* 34.

28 **numquam ... sē imperātōrem appellābat**: Augustus was *imperātor* in the traditional sense; nearly all the legions were under his command and all wars were fought under his auspices. In inscriptions his titles begin: *imp. Caesarī, dīvī fīlius, Augustō*. But he wished to disguise the military basis of his power and preferred the vague title of *prīnceps* (see above, introductory note to this chapter).

33 **sī quis nōbilium**: 'if any(one) of the nobles'.

37ff. **bella multīs cum gentibus ...**: We do not go into the various campaigns by which Augustus gradually extended the boundaries of the Roman empire. Although he added more territory to the empire than any of his predecessors, his policy was essentially conservative, dictated not by desire for military glory but to secure the safety of the frontiers of the empire.

He settled the eastern boundary by diplomacy (see introductory note to this chapter). To secure the boundaries of the empire to the north, he undertook the colossal task of advancing them to the Danube; this was accomplished bit by bit through his lieutenants until four new provinces were created – Raetia, Noricum, Pannonia and Moesia, apart from the Alps, which formed two small provinces. The map (p. 110) shows the dates of these conquests.

His only other ambition was to advance the frontier of the north from the Rhine to the Elbe in order to make a shorter line of defence to the Danube; in a series of campaigns between 12 BC and AD 9 Roman armies advanced to the Elbe, but all these gains were lost when the German chief Arminius raised a successful rebellion and destroyed the Roman general Varus and three legions, ambushed in the Teutonberg forest. Augustus then gave up the project of conquering Germany and bequeathed to his successors *cōnsilium coercendī intrā terminōs imperiī* ('the policy of not extending the boundaries of the empire', Tacitus: *Annals* 1.11).

43 poëtae semper canēbant: e.g. Horace: *Odes* 3.5.1–4:

> caelō tonantem crēdidimus Iovem
> rēgnāre: praesēns dīvus habēbitur
> Augustus adiectīs Britannīs
> imperiō gravibusque Persīs.

We believed that Jupiter reigned when he thundered in the heavens: Augustus will be held a god on earth when the Britons and the threatening Persians (i.e. Parthians) are added to the empire.

51 ō Vāre ...: cf. *Quīntīlī Vāre, legiōnes redde* (Suetonius: *Divus Augustus* 23).

Vergilius Augustum laudat

1 ēloquentiam studiaque līberālia: Suetonius (*Divus Augustus* 84) says: *ēloquentiam studiaque līberālia ab aetāte prīmā et cupidē et labōriōsissimē exercuit* ('from his earliest youth he practised eloquence and liberal studies eagerly and most laboriously'). He also tells us that Augustus wrote numerous works in prose and verse, including an autobiography and a tragedy (which he destroyed).

3 poëtās semper fovēbat: besides Virgil and Horace, he counted Livy among his friends, and encouraged Propertius. When Ovid published poetry which ran counter to the moral reforms he was seeking to implement (*Ars Amatoria*), he was sent into exile.

4–5 crēdēbat enim Vergilium sē adiuvāre posse: Augustus recognized that the works of Virgil, Horace and others could be a great help in winning over the educated classes to the new regime. Maecenas, who encouraged poets in his circle to write patriotically, has

been called Augustus' 'minister of propaganda'. This is a crude over-simplification. There can be no doubt that the admiration which Virgil felt for Augustus was genuine and that the hopes which he placed in him were heartfelt. Nor can we doubt that Augustus appreciated Virgil's genius and accepted him as a real friend. Nevertheless, the modern reader may feel that from time to time both Virgil and Horace go over the top in the praise which they heap upon the Princeps.

11–15 fās versum atque nefās ...: the lines quoted are from Virgil (*Georgics* 1.505–11). The following three lines (512–14) conclude the book on a note of despair in a simile which shows the world hurtling to destruction like a chariot out of control:

> ut cum carceribus sēsē effūdēre quadrīgae,
> addunt in spatia, et frūstrā retinācula tendēns
> fertur equīs aurīga neque audit currus habēnās.

as when the chariots have poured out from the starting gates, they gather speed on the course, and the charioteer pulling on the reins in vain is carried away by the horses and the chariot does not obey the reins.

Only Augustus can save the Roman world from destruction; Virgil appeals to the gods of Rome to allow him to succeed (lines 500–501):

> hunc saltem ēversō iuvenem succurrere saeclō
> nē prohibēte.

Do not prevent this youth from saving our age turned upside down.

11 fās versum atque nefās: 'right and wrong are turned upside down'; Virgil attributes the crisis in Roman affairs to moral collapse, a theme he develops at the end of *Georgics* 2; human greed and lust for power are responsible.

12–13 nōn ūllus arātrō/dignus honōs: 'there is no honour to the plough worthy (of it)', i.e. the plough is not given the honour it deserves.

17 Aenēidos: **Aenēis** usually has this Greek form of the genitive.

20–26 nāscētur pulchrā ...: *Aeneid* 1.286–96. In the first book of the *Aeneid* when Aeneas has been driven by a storm from Sicily and wrecked in Libya, Venus, his mother, goes to Jupiter and asks when her son will be allowed to reach Italy and found the new Troy which has been promised. Jupiter tells her not to fear; he will unroll the secrets of fate. He gives a prophecy of the future of Aeneas and his people, culminating in the birth of Augustus, the descendant of Aeneas himself. Augustus will bring to an end the madness which has nearly destroyed Rome and usher in an age of peace.

24 Furor impius: throughout the *Aeneid* the principle of *furor*, the cause of war and strife, is opposed to that of *pietās*, the source of peace and goodness, loyalty to gods, family and state. Aeneas represents the principle of *pietās*; almost the first words he speaks in the *Aeneid* are *sum pius Aenēās* (*Aeneid* 1.378) and he is repeatedly described as *pius*. Augustus, as the bringer of peace, could claim the same title.

Grammar and exercises

Impersonal verbs

mihi placet and **mihi licet** have already occurred (glossed) several times in the narratives. All those listed are 2nd conjugation except for **mē iuvat** which is 1st. They should be learnt with the person, so that students will know whether the person concerned is in the accusative or dative (object or indirect object), and the meanings are best learned in a personal form ('I ought' etc.; not 'it behoves me', which makes little sense to a student today). There are a good many other impersonal verbs which will be learnt as they occur in vocabularies.

Intransitive verbs in the passive

Intransitive verbs are occasionally used impersonally in the passive, e.g. **ventum est** = it was come. There is no such usage in English, and we introduce it by **nūntiātum est** = it was announced, where English and Latin usage appear to coincide; **nūntiō** is not in fact an intransitive verb but it is often used impersonally in the passive. Students may find this usage difficult; it is not common except in the passive of dative verbs.

In exercise 49.3.1 'we reached' = **perventum est**; the person is provided from the context ('we set out').

Background: Augustus

See also the note introducing this chapter. The three questions suggest the essential areas for discussion here. A good book on Augustus is A. H. M. Jones: *Augustus*, Chatto and Windus.

Sources

p. 97, para. 2: *Georgics* 1.501–14.
p. 98, para. 1: Ovid: *Fasti* 1.709–22. The Ara Pacis was set up in the Campus Martius on the banks of the Tiber in honour of Augustus' return from Spain and Gaul in 13 BC. It was dedicated on 30 January 9 BC. The monument was reconstructed under the inspiration of Mussolini near its original location in 1937–8.
para. 2: Tacitus: *Annals* 1.4.

Illustrations

p. 94 (left): this noble statue from Prima Porta in Rome shows Augustus as a general wearing his general's cloak (*palūdāmentum*). (Vatican Museums, Rome)

(right): Augustus is represented as a pious citizen, performing a sacrifice or attending a religious ceremony, with part of the toga drawn up to veil his head. (Museo delle Terme, Rome)
p. 96: the breastplate of the Prima Porta Augustus (see note above on p. 94 (left)). The imagery here has strong links with Horace's *Carmen Saeculare*. At the lower left and right are Apollo, god of music (he holds a lyre), and Diana, goddess of hunting (she rides a stag), and at the top Diana as moon goddess leads the way for Apollo as sun-god while he drives his chariot through the sky. Jupiter presides over the scene. At the centre the recovery from the Parthians of the standards lost at Carrhae is portrayed. Bottom centre shows the personification of Italy holding a horn of plenty (*cornūcōpia*).
p. 98: this large sardonyx cameo, the Gemma Augustea (AD 10–11), shows the deified Augustus seated next to the goddess Rome. (Kunsthistorisches Museum, Vienna)

Chapter 50

Cartoon caption

The cartoon shows Livia, Augustus' wife, spinning wool. Students will need help over the first example of a gerund, **perficiendō**.

Vocabulary

causā: the ablative of the noun **causa** = by reason of, for the sake of; the noun which depends on it always comes before **causā**, e.g. **pācis causā** = for the sake of peace. It is commonly used with the gerund to express purpose, as in **meditandī causā** (line 14 of the passage below): for the sake of meditating = to meditate.

Augustus Quīntum in amicitiam suam accipit

3 **scrībam suum**: Suetonius (*Vita Horatii*) tells us this and quotes from the letter Augustus wrote to Maecenas:

> Augustus epistolārum quoque eī (= Horātiō) officium obtulit, ut hōc ad Maecēnātem scrīptō significat: 'ante ipse sufficiēbam scrībendīs epistolīs amīcōrum: nunc occupātissimus et īnfirmus Horātium nostrum ā tē cupiō abdūcere. veniet ergō ab istā parasīticā mēnsā ad hanc rēgiam et nōs in epistolīs scrībendīs adiuvābit.'

Augustus also offered him the duty of (writing) his letters, as he makes clear in this letter to Maecenas: 'Formerly I myself was capable of writing letters to my friends, but now I'm extremely busy and in poor health and I want to take our friend Horace from you. And so he shall come from that parasite's table (of yours) to this royal table and help me in writing my letters.'

(The words *parasītica* and *rēgia* are used ironically; Horace was not the parasite of Maecenas, nor would Augustus have seriously called himself *rēx*.)

Augustus was a voluminous letter writer and needed a private secretary; the post he was offering Horace was not the office of state later called *ab epistolīs*, which included the management of the whole imperial correspondence (Suetonius held this post under Hadrian, which gave him access to the imperial archives and enabled him to quote, for instance, Augustus' letters to Horace).

5 sufficiēbam scrībendō: 'I was sufficient for writing'; **sufficiō** is commonly used with the dative. Here the noun in the dative is a gerund (a verbal noun). The use of the gerund is not difficult and it would probably pay to explain it at this point. (The use of the gerund in this chapter is intelligible but not always good Latin idiom, since gerundive attraction is usual rather than a gerund + direct object, e.g. here **sufficiēbam scrībendīs epistolīs** (as in Augustus' original letter) and in line 13 **carminibus compōnendīs**, rather than **carmina compōnendō**. Gerundive attraction is explained in chapter 51.)

14 nōlim: 'I would not want'; potential subjunctive – students may need to be reminded of this.

19–21 ille ... habēre: when Horace rejected the emperor's offer on the grounds of ill health, Augustus accepted his refusal without anger; Suetonius (*Vita Horatii*) says:

ac nē recūsantī quidem aut succēnsuit aut amīcitiam suam ingerere dēsiit. exstant epistolae, ē quibus argūmentī grātiā pauca subiēcī: 'sūme tibi aliquid iūris apud mē, tamquam convīctor mihi fueris; rēctē enim et nōn temere fēceris, quoniam id ūsus mihi tēcum esse voluī sī per valitūdinem tuam fierī posset.'

Even when he refused, Augustus was not angry with him and did not cease to press his friendship upon him. There are letters extant, from which I add a few lines as proof of this: 'Assume for yourself some rights (liberties) with me, as if you were my close friend; you will do this rightly and without presumption, since that is the relationship I wanted to have with you, if your health had made this possible.'

22–3 uxōrī eius Līviae: Augustus had divorced his second wife, Scribonia, and married Livia in 38 BC. It was a love match. Livia was beautiful, dignified and intelligent, and Augustus remained devoted to her until his death. She had two children by her first marriage (Tiberius and Drusus), but none by Augustus (Tiberius succeeded Augustus as emperor). She was his trusted counsellor and he often followed her advice; Suetonius (*Claudius* 4) quotes a letter in which he consults her about what to do about her backward grandson Claudius:

I have talked to Tiberius, as you told me, Livia, about what is to be done about your grandson Claudius at the games of Mars. We both agreed that we must decide once and for all what policy to follow about him. For if he is, if I may say so, really normal, why should we hesitate to advance him by the same stages as his brother?

23 recitandī causā: 'to give a recitation (of his poetry)'. We know that Augustus listened to Virgil reciting his poetry; in 29 BC Virgil read the recently completed *Georgics* to him at Naples. We may safely assume that Horace recited to him also. Augustus knew his poetry and had a very high opinion of it; see Suetonius (*Vita Horatii*):

scrīpta quidem eius usque adeō probāvit mānsūraque opīnātus est ut saeculāre carmen compōnendum eī iniūnxerit.

he approved of his writings so highly and thought that they would last that he gave him the task of composing the Secular Song.

On the *Carmen Saeculare*, see chapter 52.

23 quam modestē vīverent: Augustus set an example of modest living and introduced sumptuary laws to try to prevent excessive extravagance.

27 lānam ... faciēbat: one of the traditional duties of the *māterfamiliās* was to spin the wool and weave the cloth from which her husband's toga was made; compare this epitaph on a good wife (*CIL* 1.1007):

casta fuit, domum servāvit, lānam fēcit.

We are told that Augustus even wore the garments made by Livia.

Quīntus caelebs manet

Odes 1–3 include seventeen poems in which love themes are treated. In none of these does he appear to be wholly serious. He says of his own poetry, in refusing to write of Agrippa's military exploits (*Odes* 1.6.17–20):

nōs convīvia, nōs proelia virginum
sectīs in iuvenēs unguibus ācrium
cantāmus vacuī, sīve quid ūrimur,
non praeter solitum levēs.

I sing of dinner parties, I sing of battles waged by
girls fiercely attacking boys with sharpened finger
nails, heart-whole, or, if I do burn at all with
passion, light (in tone) as usual.

He is saying that the themes of his lyric poetry are
traditional – sympotic and erotic. His 'erotic' poems are
usually about others; he watches the battles of love with
amused detachment, as in *Odes* 1.5 (*quis multā gracilis
tē puer in rōsā*). When he does write about his own
loves, he often laughs at himself, as in *Vīxī puellīs*.

1 mātrimōniō liber: 'free from marriage'.

7–8 in iocum rem vertit: 'he turns the theme into a
joke'.

10–21 *Odes* 3.26. Metre: Alcaics (see Appendix):

vīxī pŭēllīs | nūpĕr ĭdō|nĕŭs

ēt mīlĭtāvī | nōn sĭnĕ glō|rĭā;

nūnc ārmă dēfūnctūmquĕ bēllō

bārbĭtŏn hīc părĭēs | hăbēbĭt

10 vīxī: 'I have lived', 'my life (as a lover) is over'.
Compare Dido's last words (*Aeneid* 4.653): *vīxī et quem
dederat cursum Fortūna perēgī* ('I have lived and
completed the course which Fortune had given me').

The Ode opens with what is ostensibly a solemn
pronouncement, though the word **idōneus** may arouse
suspicions of irony; it means 'suitable', especially for
some action. Perhaps it suggests that Horace was a fit,
able-bodied, lover, but **puellīs idōneus** is certainly an
unexpected conjunction.

11 mīlitāvī: for love as a battle, compare Ovid: *Amores*
1.9, who develops the conceit in forty-six lines: *mīlitat
omnis amāns et habet sua castra Cupīdō*. The mock-
heroic tone is carried on, but by now the irony cannot
be missed.

13 barbiton: *barbitos*, a lyre, is a Greek word and has
the Greek form of the accusative.

12–15 nunc ... custōdit: the occasion of the poem now
becomes clear. Horace is retiring from his service in the
wars of love and is dedicating his weapons to Venus,
just as a soldier on retiring from the army dedicated his
weapons to Mars. The idea may have been suggested by
Greek epigrams such as that in which a courtesan, Lais,
on retiring from her profession, dedicates her mirror to
Venus (*Anth. Pal.* 1.6., attributed to Plato).

15 There is a violent break in the middle of this line.
The repeated **hīc** and the plural imperative suddenly

introduce action; we find that Horace has a train of
attendants carrying his weapons, which are arranged in
a crescendo of absurdity: torches, for lighting the night,
crowbars for breaking down the doors which shut him
out, bows, presumably for shooting recalcitrant
doorkeepers (but the bow was also the weapon of
Cupid, so there may also be the idea of metaphorically
shooting an arrow at the heart of his beloved).

The theme of the excluded lover, perishing on the
doorstep of his beloved, appealing to or threatening the
doorkeeper, or even the door itself, was traditional and
appears, for instance, in Horace: *Odes* 1.25, Ovid:
Amores 1.6. Horace is here parodying a traditional
theme.

18–21 As the weapons are dedicated, the poet makes a
prayer to Venus, starting with the traditional invocation,
listing cult centres. But the prayer does not end 'Accept
these gifts now that my days of love are over', but 'Help
me just once more, by raising your whip and sending
Chloe, who has refused me (**arrogantem**) running back
to me.' Horace has not, after all, retired from the lists of
love.

Cyprum ... Memphim: in hymns deities are often
summoned from their cult centres, in any of which they
might be residing. Aphrodite (= Venus) was born from
the sea off Cyprus; she had a temple at Memphis in
middle Egypt (see Herodotus: 2.112).

19 Sīthōniā: 'Thracian', which represents the frozen
north. Chloe was perhaps Thracian by birth (compare
Odes 3.9.9: *mē nunc Thraessa Chloē regit*) and there is
perhaps an implication that Chloe's heart is as frozen as
her birthplace, far removed from the heat of Venus'
homes.

The poem is a dramatic monologue on a tiny scale.
From the hints which Horace drops, it might be
reconstructed as follows: Horace has gone with his train
of attendants to serenade Chloe but this time she refuses
to open the door (she is young – Chloe means 'green' –
and Horace is getting old). In high dudgeon he rushes
off to the nearest temple of Venus, where he solemnly
declares that his life as a lover is over; he hangs up his
lyre and orders his attendants to dedicate the other
weapons he has used in the battles of love. But at the
last moment he changes his mind.

In twelve lines Horace has developed a theme from
epigram with extreme sophistication. The tone changes
three times – the opening is solemn and rather
pompous; the central section is urgent (note the
enjambement) and ludicrous; the concluding prayer
begins with a leisurely invocation with two whole lines
devoted to Venus' cult centres but ends in a wistful
appeal, which is a complete surprise. The poem is
permeated by irony; if you choose to believe that it is
autobiographical, Horace is laughing at himself.

Grammar and exercises

Gerunds

The use of the gerund is not difficult, since we have a verbal noun in English (e.g. writ-ing), which can be used in the same way. In English the same form is used for the present participle, but this causes no problems in understanding and translating Latin.

The gerund declines like **bellum**; it occurs in all cases except for the nominative, where an infinitive is used, e.g. *difficile est longum subitō dēpōnere amōrem* ('To give up a long love suddenly is difficult', Catullus: 76.13). (The infinitive is properly speaking a verbal noun; here **dēpōnere** is the subject of **est**.)

The gerund rarely occurs with a direct object; the gerundive attraction construction is used instead (see chapter 51). **carmina scrībendō** is grammatically correct but the best authors would prefer **carminibus scrībendīs**.

P.S.

1 A vestal virgin (*CIL* 4931)
It is interesting to find so pious an adherent of the old religion at a time when Christianity was spreading and only about fifty years before the acceptance of Christianity under Constantine.

2–3 apud dīvīna altāria: 'at the divine altars'.

3 diēbus noctibusque: 'day and night': one would expect the accusative of duration of time, but the ablative is often used like this in inscriptions, e.g. *Callistē vīxit annīs xvi* (chapter 43, P.S. 2). Even Caesar uses the ablative like this once: *nostrī quīnque hōrīs proelium sustinuērunt* (*B.G.* 1.47).

6 prīdiē Kalendīs Octōbris: the day before 1 October = 30 September.

7 dominīs nostrīs: by this time (AD 257) there were two emperors reigning in tandem; they are referred to as *dominī nostrī*, 'our lords', the title by which a slave addressed his master. Augustus eschewed this title but Nero insisted on it.

2 A British lady in Rome
Martial (AD 40–104) was an exact contemporary of Agricola, the governor of Britain who first encouraged the Britons to adopt Roman customs and live in cities; up to his time they had been thought of (quite wrongly) as woad-painted barbarians. It is interesting to find a British lady at so early a time who had evidently married a Roman and taken a Roman name (Claudia Rufina); she was so thoroughly 'civilized' that Roman mothers could think she was born a Roman and, perhaps even more significant, Athenians that she was one of them; she must have been trilingual in Celtic, Latin and Greek. Archaeologists have found tablets from the second century AD which show British children learning Virgil at school.

Background: Vīxī puellīs

These two translations will give students an opportunity to think about the possible priorities in the translation of Latin poetry. Is literal accuracy the main objective? If West's translation is perceived as the more 'accurate' – at any rate it recreates Horace's three verses – does that mean that it is inferior as poetry to Michie's, which rhymes and scans? How far does West's free verse do the original justice? Your pupils might consider producing their own versions.

Illustrations

p. 99: this relief of a Roman secretary, craning with pen over his book, is from the Rheinisches Landesmuseum, Trier.
p. 100: this basalt bust of Livia is from the Louvre Museum, Paris.
p. 102: the so-called Ludovisi throne (because found in the Villa Ludovisi) is a lustrous masterpiece of the fifth century BC. It shows Venus rising from the sea to the embrace of a towel held by two women representing the seasons, who stand on the pebbled beach. The distinction between the three different types of drapery is just one fine feature of this superb sculpture. (Museo delle Terme, Rome)

Chapter 51

Cartoon caption

We do not attempt to introduce the gerundive in this caption but quote the first two lines from the poem of Propertius which comes in the narrative.

sōle rubente: 'as the sun grows red', i.e. at dawn. Students may be able to infer the meaning of **rubente** from **māne** in the previous line.

Maecēnās poētās fovet

Maecenas formed a circle of poets around him who were encouraged to support the new regime. Sextus Propertius (born c. 50 BC) was primarily a love poet; four books of *Elegies* survive of which the first is entirely devoted to his mistress, Cynthia. In the other books new themes appear besides love; there are poems in praise of Maecenas, Augustus and Virgil, and in the last book poems on the battle of Actium and on the origin of Roman cults. Perhaps his output was a disappointment to Maecenas, since he remained something of a maverick and never supported the regime in the way that Virgil and Horace did.

4 recitātiōnēs: in Greece it was the custom for authors

to give public recitations of their works (it was thus that Herodotus published his *Histories*). Ancient poetry was always written to be read aloud and its sound was of paramount importance. The public recitation became extremely popular in the time of Augustus; authors would hire lecture halls for this purpose and their friends and the general public would flock to hear them. By the younger Pliny's time (born AD 61) there were so many recitations that attendance had become a tiresome duty (see *Letter* 1.13: 'This year has brought a great crop of poets; in the whole of April there's been scarcely a day when someone didn't give a recitation').

9–16 mīrābar quidnam ...: Propertius 3.10.1–8. Metre: elegiac couplets (see Appendix):

> mīrā|bar quīd|nām vīs|īssent | mānĕ Că|mēnae
>
> āntĕ mĕ|ūm stān|tēs∧sōlĕ rŭ|bēntĕ tŏ|rŭm.

9 Camēnae: the Camenae were Roman goddesses, originally water spirits, who from early times were identified with the Greek Muses.

11 nātālis = nātālis diēī: 'of the birthday'.
nostrae for **meae**, as often.

13–16 trānseat ... stent ... pōnat ... aspiciam ... supprimat: the subjunctives all express wishes.

16 Niobae: Niobe, daughter of Tantalus, had six sons and six daughters; she boasted that her family was better than that of Leto, who only had two children, Apollo and Artemis (= Diana). Leto then killed all her children and Niobe herself was turned to stone; the 'rock that was Niobe', could still be seen on Mount Sipylus in Asia Minor; the streams which poured continually down this rock were her tears.

17 Albius Tibullus: Tibullus (48–19 BC) belonged to a rival circle of poets patronized by Messalla Corvinus. Four books of *Elegies* survive under his name, of which two are certainly his. He wrote mostly of love and the joys of country life, only once touching on a political theme. Horace was clearly fond of him but found him too given to melancholy (*Odes* 1.33.1–3):

> Albī, nē doleās plūs nimiō memor
> immītis Glycerae neu miserābilēs
> dēcantēs elegōs

Albius, don't grieve too much remembering cruel Glycera and don't keep singing elegies full of self-pity.

23–4 ad doctrīnam Epicūrī inclīnābātur: Horace was eclectic in his philosophy; he says (*Epistles* 1.1.14–15):

> nūllius addictus iurāre in verba magistrī,
> quō mē cumque rapit tempestās, dēferor hospes.

I am not bound to swear allegiance to any master's words but wherever the storm (of life) carries me, I put in (to port) and make myself at home (*hospes* = as a guest).

Some of the Roman Odes (Book 3, 1–6) suggest a stern Stoic ethic, but as a whole the Epicurean ethic predominates.

28–38 Albī, nostrōrum sermōnum ...: *Epistles* 1.4 (with omission). Metre: dactylic hexameters.
29 quid ... dīcam: 'what am I to say?' (deliberative subjunctive).
30 quod ... vincat: 'something which may surpass'; the subjunctive might express purpose or it might be generic, 'of the sort which ...'.
33 nōn ... sine pectore: 'you were not (i.e. you never were) a body without a heart', i.e. 'you have always been a man of intellect and feeling'.
34 dederunt: the second **e** is scanned short, an alternative form found several times in verse.
35 suprēmum: the adjective is predicative: 'believe that each day that has dawned for you is your last'. So also **grāta** in line 36.
38 dē grege: **grex** is used both of a flock of animals and of a group or school of people. Since Epicurus said that the greatest good for man was pleasure, his opponents accused him, wrongly, of self-indulgence and excess. Horace in fact preached moderation in all things, the golden mean (*aurea mediocritās*: see *Odes* 2.10.5). He is, of course, laughing at himself; he was in fact growing fat – see Suetonius: *Vita: habitū corporis fuit brevis atque obēsus* ('in physique he was short and fat'). He describes himself at the age of forty-four as (*Epistles* 1.20.24–5):

> corporis exiguī, praecānum, sōlibus aptum,
> īrāscī celerem, tamen ut plācābilis essem.

short of stature, grey-haired before my time, given to sun-bathing, quick to anger but easily placated.

Mors Vergilii

1 et Quīntus et Vergilius iam seniōrēs: Virgil died in 19 BC at the age of fifty-one. Horace was then forty-six. In the Roman army those aged seventeen to forty-six were called iūniōrēs, those older than that seniōrēs. The Romans had no term for 'middle aged'; you were either young or elderly.
4 Augustō ... ab Oriente redeuntī: Augustus was in the East from 22 to 19 BC (during his stay there he had made a treaty with the Parthians and recovered the standards lost at Carrhae).
7 Neāpolī: Virgil had lived at Naples for the last ten years of his life. On his tomb was an inscription attributed to Virgil himself:

> Mantua mē genuit, Calabrī rapuēre, tenet nunc
> Parthenopē; cecinī pāscua, rūra, ducēs.

Mantua gave me birth; Calabria carried me off; Parthenope (= Naples) is now my home; I sang of shepherds (the *Eclogues*), the country (the *Georgics*) and leaders (the *Aeneid*).

The *Aeneid* was unfinished when he died, and before setting out for Greece he had asked his literary executors, Varius and Tucca, to burn it if he died. Augustus countermanded this request and ordered them to publish it in its unfinished state.

11–14 nāvis, quae ...: *Odes* 1.3.5–8. Metre: Asclepiads (see Appendix):

nāvīs, | quae tĭbĭ crē|dĭtŭm

dēbēs | Vērgĭlĭŭm, | fīnĭbŭs Āt|tĭcīs

The first Ode of Book 1 is to Maecenas, the second to Augustus, the third to Virgil. In the first eight lines of this Ode he wishes *bon voyage* to Virgil, who is about to sail to Greece; this is followed by a diatribe on the dangers of travelling by sea and the rashness and wickedness of the human race in attempting such exploits. The *bon voyage* poem is a traditional form which can be traced back to a poem by Sappho wishing her brother a safe return from Egypt (Sappho: 5). Equally the diatribe on the wrongness of progress is a commonplace and is handled by Horace in a mock-heroic spirit.

Virgil's proposed voyage cannot in fact be that of 19 BC, since the first three books of the *Odes* were published in 23 BC, but an earlier one of which we know nothing.

Grammar and exercises

Gerundives

There is no part of the English verb corresponding to the Latin gerundive, and so it will undoubtedly cause your students difficulty to start with. (The girls' names Amanda and Miranda are Latin gerundives in form; if you told your students this, it might help them to remember the meaning of the gerundive.) It has two main uses: **1** in gerundive attraction; **2** gerundives expressing obligation, which are dealt with in the next chapter.

Gerundive attraction is an idiom so completely alien to English that the literal translation is virtually unintelligible. It is therefore better to study examples and translate into natural English; gerundive phrases tackled in this way soon become easy enough to understand.

We do not consider it necessary to practise this construction from English into Latin and, for a change, we give as the last exercise of this chapter a piece of continuous English for translation into Latin.

P.S.

These two epigrams by Martial illustrate a form of poetry, the elegiac epigram, in which both Greek and Latin poets had excelled.

1 A nightmare doctor
3 subitae: students know **subito** = 'suddenly' and can deduce the meaning of the adjective.

requīris: if students stumble over this word, ask from what verb it is compounded (**quaerō**).

2 A noisy schoolmaster
Martial is, or imagines he is, a neighbour (**vīcīnī**, line 5) to a noisy schoolmaster, who starts his classes before cockcrow. The epigram shows that girls as well as boys attended his school, that beating was a regular feature of his method and that he seems to have taught in a private house. Students are likely to need more help than we have given in their text.

1 quid tibi nōbīscum est? 'What have you to do with us?'

6 pervigilāre: the prefix **per-** is intensive, 'to lie awake all night' (compare **dūrus** = hard, **perdūrus** = extremely hard).

7–8 vīs ... taceās?: i.e. **vīs accipere (tantum) ut taceās quantum accipis ut clāmēs** ('will you accept as much to keep quiet as you do to keep shouting?'). Martial offers to bribe the schoolmaster to shut up.

Background: The Roman empire

The benefits of Roman civilization were immense and enduring. Your pupils could be encouraged to make a list of benefits derived by provincials from their membership in the Roman empire. However, a list of drawbacks should be drawn up too. (There is a humorous treatment of this in the Monty Python film *Life of Brian*!)

It will be possible to return to this subject if you tackle Calgacus' speech from Tacitus' *Agricola* later in this book (p. 186). But how realistic were any hopes of an alternative to Rome? (Mel Gibson's Oscar-winning film *Braveheart* (1995) offers a relevant comparison here.)

The speech of Agrippa quoted at the end of the essay (p. 109) offers a fertile ground for discussion. Xerxes (para. 2): when Xerxes, king of Persia, invaded Greece in 480 BC, he built a bridge across the Hellespont (linking Asia and Europe) and cut a canal through the promontory of Mount Athos. Defeated later that year, largely by the Athenian navy, at the battle of Salamis, he withdrew to Persia leaving his land forces to be conquered by the Greeks at Plataea in the following year.

Another area which could be explored is whether your students think that former members of the British

47

empire benefited at all from that phase of their history. If so, how?

The Hellenistic era (p. 107, para. 1): we date this from 323 BC (the death of Alexander the Great) to 30 BC.

St Paul (p. 107, para. 2): when St Paul was accused of treason, Festus, procurator (governor) of Judaea, sent him to Rome. As a Roman citizen, he had made use of his right to appeal for judgement there. Reaching the imperial capital after shipwreck and other adventures, he stayed there for two years. We do not know whether he was acquitted.

The *pūblicānī* (p. 107, para. 3): the hatred that they inspired (cf. the 'publicans and sinners' of the Gospels) was shown when, in a revolt instigated by Mithradates, the provincials of Asia massacred tens of thousands of them in 88 BC. Governors who tried to shield the provincials from these jackals were liable to suffer for it. (See H. H. Scullard: *From the Gracchi to Nero*, Methuen, pp. 191, 63 and 103.)

Romanization (p. 109, para. 1): the spread of Roman ways of acting, building and thinking which spead to diverse cultures.

Sources

p. 108, para. 2: Verres and the statue of the lyre-player: Cicero: *In Verrem* 2.1.20.
Catullus reference: 10.12.
para. 3: the reluctance of upper-class Roman juries to condemn one of their own number: Pliny: 2.11.
para. 4: Pliny references: 10.31, 32, 41, 42, 61, 62, 96, 97.
Edward Gibbon (1737–94): *The Decline and Fall of the Roman Empire*, chapter 3.
p. 109, para. 1: Tacitus reference: *Agricola* 21.
Josephus reference: *The Jewish War* 2.356–8, 397.

Illustrations

p. 105: this fine mosaic of the nine Muses originally came from the island of Cos. (Palace of the Grand Masters, Rhodes)
p. 106: a bronze bar with a pig marked on it. When the bronze was melted it ran off into a channel called a sow, the lateral branches of which were called pigs. (British Museum, London)
p. 107 (above): the so-called tomb of Virgil is a *columbārium* (literally a dovecote, in which the compartments could be used for storing urns containing the ashes of the dead) in Naples. It was restored in 1927.

(below): in this relief a Roman tax collector counts a pile of coins while the local farmers, bearded and wearing hooded duffle-coats, wait to pay. (Rheinisches Landesmuseum, Trier)

p. 108: the bust of Verres is in the Museum of Hadrian's villa at Tivoli near Rome.

Chapter 52

Pāx et prīnceps

1 **portae templī Iānī**: Augustus (*Res Gestae* 13) says that the gates of the temple of Janus were closed three times while he was princeps: *Iānum Quirīnum ... ter mē prīncipe senātus claudendum esse cēnsuit*. They had been shut first in 29 BC to mark the end of the civil wars; then in 25 BC after Augustus had completed the pacification of Spain. The date of the third occasion is unknown and we have guessed that their third closure should be associated with the celebration of the Secular Games.

3–4 **lūdīs saeculāribus**: these had been celebrated every hundred years to mark the beginning of a new age perhaps since the early republic, but the dates of only two previous celebrations are known – 249 BC and 149 BC. By juggling the dates Augustus fixed on the year 17 BC for the next celebration, which was to mark the beginning of a new era of peace.

The festival began on 31 May and lasted for three days and nights with an elaborate programme of sacrifice, prayer and games. Horace was commissioned by Augustus to write a hymn in honour of Apollo and Diana, to be sung on the last night by a choir of boys and girls (Suetonius: *Vita Horatii*):

> (Augustus) scrīpta quidem eius usque adeō probāvit mānsūraque opīnātus est, ut saeculāre carmen compōnendum eī iniūnxerit.

> Augustus thought so highly of his poetry and believed that it would last, that he commissioned him to compose the *Carmen Saeculare*.

Carmen Saeculāre
Metre: Sapphics (see Appendix):

> Phōēbĕ sĭlvā|rūmquĕ pŏtēns | Dīānă,
>
> lūcĭdūm cāē|lī dĕcŭs, ō | cŏlēndī
>
> sēmpĕr ēt cūl|tī, dătĕ quāē | prĕcāmŭr
>
> tēmpŏrĕ sāc|rō

We give the first eight lines and lines 57 to 60 (the whole hymn is seventy-six lines long). The choir prays for the greatness of Rome ('May the sun never see anything greater than the city of Rome'), for fecundity of Rome's mothers and of the crops and herds, for a virtuous youth and a peaceful age (lines 45–8):

dī, probōs mōrēs docilī iuventae,
dī, senectūtī placidae quiētem,
Rōmulae gentī date remque prōlemque
    et decus omne.

Gods, grant good morals to a youth quick to learn,
gods, grant quiet and calm to the aged, and to the
race of Romulus grant wealth and offspring, and all
glory.

12 Sibyllīnī ... versūs: the Sibylline verses were a
collection of prophecies which, according to tradition,
had been brought to King Tarquinius Priscus by an
unknown old woman. They were kept by a special
priestly college, the *Quīndecimvirī sacrīs faciundīs*, and
were only consulted at moments of crisis by order of the
senate. Augustus was chairman of the *Quīndecimvirī*,
who conveniently decided that the correct date for the
celebration was 17 BC. The verses in which the form of
the festival was prescribed have been preserved by
chance together with fragments of the senate's decree by
which it was regulated (see E. Fraenkel: *Horace*,
Oxford, pp. 366–9).
16 Fidēs ... Honōs Pudorque: **Fidēs** here means
'trustworthiness'; a true Roman kept his word. **Honōs**
usually means the honour or esteem in which a person is
held, but here must approximate to our 'sense of
honour'. **Pudor** means sense of shame, conscience.
These are the qualities the Romans had lost during the
long years of the civil wars; now they dare reappear on
earth. Like Virgil and Augustus, who had just initiated a
programme of moral reform, Horace attributes the
disasters of the last century to moral failings.
21–2 quibus frētī: **frētus** = 'relying on' takes the
ablative case.
23 saeculum aureum: compare Virgil: *Augustus
Caesar ... aurea condet/saecula* (Aeneid 6.792–3). The
ancients from Hesiod onwards (*Works and Days*
109–201) placed the Golden Age in the remote past, at
the beginning of the world; it was followed by a
continual deterioration – Silver Age, Bronze Age, Iron
Age; the last was the age in which we live. But time
revolves in a circle and when the cycle is completed
there will be a new Golden Age. The Augustan poets
frequently assert that this moment has come at last
(Virgil: *Eclogues* 4.5):

magnus ab integrō saeclorum nascitur ordō

the great succession of the centuries is born anew.

Grammar and exercises

Gerundives of obligation
These are probably more quickly understood than
gerundive attraction, though they do present certain
problems:

1 The person by whom the action must be performed is
expressed by the dative (dative of the agent) instead of
ā/ab + ablative.
2 The phrases are passive in form, but where a person
is expressed English prefers the active, e.g. **hoc tibi
faciendum est** = 'this is to be done by you'; but we
would say 'you must do this'.
3 The gerundive of intransitive verbs is used
impersonally in the passive.
4 Sometimes Latin omits to express the person, e.g.
exercise 52.1.6 **statim proficīscendum est**; English
will supply it from the context: 'you must set out at
once'.
5 The English verb 'must', expressing obligation, can
only be used in the present; to vary the tense, English
says: 'I have to, I had to, I shall have to'.
All this sounds very complex when explained like this,
but if students study the patterns of these gerundive
phrases, they will soon understand them. In this case,
formal analysis may actually hinder understanding.

Exercise 52.4
Another short piece for continuous composition, an
optional exercise which brighter students might enjoy
doing.
1 he liked: **eum iūvit**; remind students of this
impersonal use.
3 he arranged for: **curāvit** + gerundive (see exercise
52.2.2 above).
7 you could scarcely say: **vix dīcere possīs** (potential
subjunctive; give help, if necessary).

P.S.
In this and the next chapter we give memorable lines
from Virgil and Horace which students might like to
learn by heart.
1 In the last of the ten *Eclogues* Virgil tells in pastoral
allegory of the unhappy love of the poet Cornelius
Gallus, who was deserted by his mistress, the actress
Lycoris. Gallus is dying of cruel love. He says that he
will wander abroad but he knows there is no cure:
omnia vincit Amor; et nōs cēdāmus Amōrī.
2 At the end of the second book of the *Georgics*, Virgil
bursts into impassioned praise of the joys of country
life; this is preceded by praise of the intellectual life, of
which the exemplars are Epicurus and his follower
Lucretius; these two freed men from fear of death and
punishment after death by showing that the whole
universe is material and that the soul does not survive
the dissolution of the body:

fēlīx quī potuit rērum cognōscere causās
atque metūs omnēs et inexōrābile fātum
subiēcit pedibus strepitumque Acherontis avārī.
fortūnātus et ille deōs quī nōvit agrestīs
Pānaque Silvānumque senem Nymphāsque sorōrēs.

Happy was he who could find out the causes of things and who subdued beneath his feet all fears, inexorable fate, and the roaring of greedy Avernus. Blessed too is he who knows the country gods, Pan and old Silvanus and the sister Nymphs.

4 This line ends Virgil's introduction to the *Aeneid*, in which he foreshadows the sufferings of Aeneas, who is now being persecuted by Juno, but whose destiny it is to found the new Troy from which Rome shall spring.

5 The Greeks have sailed away from Troy, leaving on the shore the great wooden horse, filled with Greek warriors; when some of the Trojans wish to drag the horse into the city, Laocoon warns them not to.

6 Driven south by a terrible storm as they approach Italy, and wrecked on the shores of an unknown land, the Trojans are in despair. Aeneas tries to raise their spirits by reminding them of the trials they have survived; perhaps, some time they will take pleasure in remembering even their present suffering.

7 Aeneas has sailed from Carthage, and Dido, determined on death, has mounted the pyre and speaks her last words: 'I have lived and completed the course which Fortune had given me, and now my great spirit will go beneath the earth. I have founded a great city, I have seen my walls built, I avenged my husband and punished my wicked brother, happy, only too happy, if only the Trojan ships had never touched our shores.'

8 In the sixth book of the *Aeneid*, Aeneas has to go down to the underworld to see his father Anchises and learn about his destiny. He consults the Sibyl of Cumae about his proposed venture. She warns him of the dangers: 'Trojan son of Anchises, the descent to Avernus is easy. Day and night the gateway to the realm of black Dis lies open. But to retrace your steps, to get out to the air above, that is the task, that is the toil.'

9 When, guided by the Sibyl, he reaches the river Styx, the dividing boundary between the upper and the lower worlds, he finds regiments of souls waiting to cross: 'A whole crowd was rushing this way to the banks, streaming out, mothers and men, the bodies of great-souled heroes whose life was over, boys and unmarried girls, and youths placed on their funeral pyres before the eyes of their parents, as many as the leaves that fall in the woods at the first cold of autumn, as many as the birds which gather, when the cold of the year sends them flying across the sea to sunny lands. They stood praying to be the first to cross the stream and held out their hands in longing for the further shore.' You could have a lively discussion with your students on what Virgil means by the last two lines of this wonderful passage.

Background: Some glimpses of Augustus

These glimpses into more private aspects of Augustus' personality should prove stimulating. The gap between his savagery and his clemency is psychologically not very surprising. It was there in his adoptive father Julius Caesar too. In any case, after he had defeated Antony, he set out to re-make himself: the brutal young man metamorphosed into the pious Augustus.

Suetonius (p. 114, para. 1) was born in AD 69. He was for a short time a lawyer, steered clear of political life and became chief secretary to the emperor Hadrian who ruled from AD 117 to 138. According to the historian Spartianus, he was dismissed for behaving indiscreetly with the empress Sabina. Dean Liddell wrote of him: 'His language is very brief and precise, sometimes obscure, without any affectation or ornament. He certainly tells a prodigious number of scandalous anecdotes about the Caesars, but there was plenty to tell about them; and if he did not choose to suppress those anecdotes which he believed to be true, that is no imputation on his veracity. As a great collection of facts of all kinds, his work on the Caesars is invaluable.'

He ordered every tenth man to be killed (p. 114, para. 6): to kill every tenth man is to 'decimate', a current English word.

Archimedes of Syracuse (p. 115, para. 2): Archimedes (?287–212 BC) was a celebrated mathematician, physicist and inventor from Syracuse in Sicily.

Sources
The references are to the *Life of Augustus* 94.9; 8.1; 13.1–2; 51.1; 24.2; 28.3; 72.1–2; 73; 76.1–2; 77; 84.2; 99.1.

Illustrations

p. 111: the Ara Pacis was set up in the Campus Martius on the banks of the Tiber in honour of Augustus' return from Spain and Gaul in 13 BC. It was dedicated on 30 January 9 BC. There was a precinct wall around the altar; the two long sides showed the procession of the senate, the people of Rome, the magistrates and the family of Augustus. The two short sides had four panels with mythological themes, stressing the piety and fertility of Italy. Beneath the Augustan and mythological scenes was a spreading floral pattern. The monument was reconstructed under the inspiration of Mussolini near its original location in 1937–8.
p. 112: this statue of Apollo is from a bronze original, probably of the fourth century BC. The god steps forward to see the effect of the arrow he has just shot. The graceful elegance and strength of his body and his keen gaze have won much admiration. The statue is

called the Apollo Belvedere because it is placed in the Belvedere, a courtyard built for the display of sculpture in the Vatican.

p. 113: this allegorical figure with her cornucopia (horn of plenty) is by Domenico Passignano (1560–1638). It is called *Allegoria della Felicità Pubblica* and is from the Salone Pubblica of the Villa Medicea in Artimino.

p. 114: this fine bronze bust of Augustus, dating from the first century BC, was found in Meroe, Sudan. (British Museum, London)

Chapter 53

Cartoon captions

The captions introduce predicative datives (1 **odiō**, 3 **summae cūrae**, 4 **magnō auxiliō**). You will need to comment on the first example; the other two may then be immediately intelligible to your students.

Caption 2 introduces **cum** + pluperfect indicative, where **cum** = whenever (see chapter 47). The same usage appears in line 10 of the narrative: **cum vēnerat brūma** = whenever winter came.

Quīntus rūsticus

4–6 **ō rūs ...**: Horace: *Satires* 2.6.60–62. Metre: dactylic hexameters.

8 **plūrimī enim febre corripiēbantur**: the summer months, especially August and September, were notoriously unhealthy in Rome and all who could left for the hills, as they still do today; at this time, says Horace, there are most funerals and 'every father and poor mother goes pale in anxiety for their children' (line 7 of the Epistle quoted below).

14 **quī dīceret sē ... reditūrum esse**: 'to say that he would return'. The relative with the subjunctive expresses purpose.

16 **tantum**: 'only'; students may need reminding of this meaning.

19 **Sextīlem**: August, 'the sixth month', since the Roman new year used to begin on 1 March. The name of the month was later changed to Augustus, just as *Quīntīlis* (July) was changed to Iulius.

22–30 **quīnque diēs ...**: *Epistles* 1.7.1–13 (with omissions). Metre: dactylic hexameters.

23 **mendāx**: 'a liar'; the word is predicative, as in English 'I am proved a liar.'

27 **quodsī**: this usually means 'but if', but here **sī** has a temporal rather than a conditional force, i.e. 'but when'.

30 **cum Zephyrīs**: 'together with the Zephyrs (the warm west winds of spring)'.

36–8 **vīle potābis ...**: *Odes* 1.20.1–3. Metre: Sapphics.

In this Ode Horace invites Maecenas (**cāre Maecēnās eques**, line 5) to dinner but warns him not to expect the grand wines he is used to; he will be served with wine Horace has made himself from grapes from his own vineyard.

37 **Graecā ... testā**: 'in a Greek jar'; Quinn (*Horace: Odes Book 3*, p. 163) suggests that Horace's modest wine was stored in a jar which had held Greek wine to improve its flavour.

40 **tantopere**: 'so greatly'; compare **magnopere** = greatly.

Mūs rūsticus et mūs urbānus

3 **rūsticō mūrī persuādētur**: 'a country mouse is persuaded'; students may need reminding of the impersonal use of dative verbs in the passive voice.

5ff. **ōlim ...**: *Satires* 2.6.79–117 (with omissions). Metre: dactylic hexameters. In this Satire, which begins with the lines quoted on p. 79, *hoc erat in vōtīs ...*, Horace contrasts the pointless bustle of life at Rome with the life of quiet content which he leads on his Sabine farm. He recalls the supper parties he enjoys in the country (**ō noctēs cēnaeque deum**, line 65), so different from dinner parties in Rome, where the guests talk of other people's villas and houses and whether Lepos is a good dancer; at Horace's parties guests discuss whether men achieve happiness by riches or virtue, and what is the nature of good and what is its highest form. 'Then my neighbour Cervius tells old wive's tales to suit the subject. For if someone, ignorant of the cares it brings, praises the wealth of Arellius, he begins: **ōlim/rūsticus urbānum mūrem mūs paupere fertur ...**

The fable, a moral tale in which animals are endowed with human emotions and reactions, had an ancient history in Greek literature, which can be traced back to Hesiod and Archilochus. The earliest collection of fables is attributed to Aesop, who is said to have lived in the sixth century BC. Latin writers adopted the form from Greek.

5 **ōlim**: 'once upon a time'.

6 **fertur**: 'is said'; **ferunt** = men say; **fertur, feruntur** = is/are said to.

11 **patientem**: 'suffering' = 'roughing it'.

13 **mihi crēde comes**: the town mouse continues by expounding the Epicurean philosophy: 'Earthly creatures are allotted mortal souls and there is no escape from death for great or small; and so, good friend, **dum licet, in rēbus iūcundīs vīve beātus**.'

19 **ambō**: 'both'; it declines like **duo** (here nominative masculine plural).

23 **cubāns**: the country mouse reclines on his couch as a guest at a dinner party would.

30 **tenuī ... ervō**: 'with a little vetch'; the country mouse prefers the lowliest source of food in the safety

of his hole to all the rich dishes the town mouse had provided.

Grammar and exercises

The predicative dative

This is another construction in which Latin and English idiom differ, but once seen and understood the predicative dative is unlikely to be forgotten.

The Latin idiom is in fact more logical than English, which appears to use a complement in such sentences as 'He was a help to me.' But the relationship of 'a help' to the subject 'he' is not that of a complement: it expresses purpose or consequence – 'He is for a help to me.' So Latin puts such predicates in the dative together with a dative of the person concerned.

There is a fair number of nouns used in this way (Cicero has over seventy); we give the commonest. The nouns in the dative are never qualified except by simple adjectives of quantity – **magnō**, **tantō**, **summō** etc. They most commonly occur with **esse**, but we find in Caesar, e.g. *equitātuī, quem auxiliō Caesarī Aeduī mīserant* ('the cavalry which the Aeduī had sent as a help to Caesar', *B.G.* 1.18.10 – a good example of the predicative dative expressing purpose).

The relative with the subjunctive

Definite relative clauses with the indicative are well known to your students and they have met several examples of the relative with the subjunctive expressing purpose (glossed, so far). Once this usage has been explained, it causes no difficulty.

The relative with the subjunctive is used to express other shades of meaning as well as purpose:

1 Generic relative, where the relative pronoun does not refer to a definite person but to a class or sort of person, e.g.

Quīntus nōn is est quī tālia faciat.
Quintus is not the sort of person to do such things.

2 Consecutive relative, e.g.
iuvenis dignus est quī praemium accipiat.
The young man is worthy to/deserves to receive the prize.

sunt quī Augustum metuant.
There are some people who fear Augustus.

3 Causal relative (often accompanied by **quippe**), e.g.
peccāvisse mihi videor, (quippe) quī ā tē discesserim.
I think I (I seem to myself to) have made a mistake in leaving you.

We do not introduce students to these usages yet.

Exercise 53.3

Sentences 1–4 refer to various measures which Augustus took to restore order in the Roman world.

1 He reduced the army to twenty-eight legions and stationed them on the boundaries of the empire; the normal distribution was perhaps: three legions in Spain, eight on the Rhine, one in Macedonia, one in Illyricum, seven on the Danube, four in Syria, three in Egypt, one in Africa.

2 Fleets were based permanently at Misenum (Bay of Naples), Ravenna (Adriatic), Forum Iulii (Provence) and Alexandria.

3 In AD 6 he instituted seven cohorts of *vigilēs* in Rome, whose primary duty was to act as a fire brigade. A police force was provided by three *cohortēs urbānae*, instituted in AD 13.

4 The only troops in Italy were the Praetorian Guard (nine cohorts); three of these were stationed in Rome, six in various Italian towns. They not only formed the emperor's bodyguard but maintained order throughout Italy.

Exercise 53.5

The last composition exercise consists of a letter for translation into Latin, again optional. You should remind students of the form of Roman letters.

3 until autumn comes: **dum veniat autumnus**. The subjunctive is usual in **dum** clauses referring to future time, but you might accept future perfect indicative.

4 of fever: **febre**; ablative of cause.

P.S.

1 Horace writes to a friend who is *urbis amātor*; he says: *vīvere nātūrae sī convenienter oportet ... nōvistīne locum potiōrem rūre beātō?* ('If we should live in harmony with nature, do you know any place better than the blessed countryside?')

'You may drive out Nature with a pitchfork, yet she will always come back and imperceptibly break her way through the perverse disdain (of the rich man, who tries to oust nature with artificial luxuries).'

2 Horace tells a friend who has been touring abroad that foreign travel is a pointless way of pursuing happiness: 'Those who run across the sea change their sky but not their state of mind; we busy ourselves by an energetic laziness: we seek to live well by sailing in ships and riding in coaches. What you seek is here.'

3 This is perhaps Horace's most uncompromising statement of the Epicurean ethic: we don't know what will happen tomorrow; it is no use forming long-term hopes; make the most of today's pleasures. 'While we are speaking, jealous time has fled (will have fled); pluck (the flowers of) today, putting no trust in tomorrow.' Compare what the town mouse says to the country mouse, p. 121.

4 From a lament for the death of Quinctilius Varus (*Odes* 1.24), the beloved friend of both Horace and Virgil. It begins:

> quis dēsīderiō sit pudor aut modus
> tam cārī capitis?

> What shame should we feel or what limit should we make to our grief at the loss of so dear a friend?

'He died bewept by many good men, by none more than by you, Virgil.'

5 and **6** Horace advises his friend Dellius to remain calm (level-headed) when things are difficult and to avoids excessive joy when things go well; for death awaits us all, whether we live in sadness or make the most of what life offers. The Ode ends:

> omnēs eōdem cōgimur, omnium
> versātur urnā sērius ōcius
>   sors exitūra et nōs in aeternum
>   exsilium impositūra cumbae.

> We are all herded the same way, the lot of each of us is shaken in the urn and will come out sooner or later and put us on the boat bound for eternal exile (from earth).

Compare James Michie's admirable translation:

> Sheep driven deathward. Sooner or later Fate's
> Urn is shaken, the lot comes leaping out for each of us
>   And books a one-way berth in Charon's
>   Boat on the journey to endless exile.

7 This Ode is in praise of the man who is righteous and sticks to his purpose (*iūstum et tenācem prōpositī virum*); nothing will shake him: 'If the world cracked and collapsed upon him, the ruins will strike him unafraid.'

Background: The town mouse and the country mouse

There should be much profitable discussion of this passage in Rudd's admirable translation.

  Second question: humour: do not miss the bathos of the epic journey of the mice into the town. The bathetic words are printed in bold:

> ambō prōpositum peragunt iter, urbis aventēs
> moenia nocturnī **subrēpere**. iamque tenēbat
> nox medium caelī spatium, cum pōnit uterque
> in locuplēte domō **vestīgia**.

Both complete the proposed journey in their eagerness to creep beneath the walls of the city. And now night was holding its mid position in the sky when each of them set his footprints in a wealthy house.

As for the humour of the piece generally, while Horace surely endorsed the basic idea that the country is preferable to the town, he wishes to satirize the element of cliché in such a view. As we have seen – and not only in *Beātus ille* (chapter 41) – the Romans tended to be more prone to praise the country life than to lead it. There is surely affection as well as mockery in the satire of the town mouse's laid-back Epicureanism.

  Teachers may wish to follow this story up with some fables from Aesop, some poems of La Fontaine and Chaucer's 'Nun's Priest's Tale'.

Illustrations

p. 118: this vault mosaic from Santa Costanza in Rome dates from the fourth century AD and shows *putti* (young cupids) gathering and treading the vintage.
p. 119: these small bronzes of mice are from the British Museum.

Chapter 54

Cartoon

D.M. = **dīs mānibus**, '(sacred) to the spirits of the departed'; this was the usual formula engraved on tombstones, followed by the name of the dead in either the dative or the genitive.
multīs ille bonīs flēbilis occidit: 'he died wept by many good men'; taken from the lament on Quinctilius Varus (*Odes* 1.24.9).

Vocabulary

coepī has no present in common use (though some forms from the old present **coepiō** occur in Plautus); it is past in meaning = 'I began'.
meminī and **ōdī** are perfect in form but present in meaning.

Indomita mors

4–7 eheu, fugācēs ...: *Odes* 2.14.1–4. We know nothing of Postumus, the friend to whom Horace writes this Ode.
10 vīvōrum meminerat: **meminī** and **oblīvīscor** take either the accusative or the genitive; the genitive is usual where the object is personal.
19 multōs abhinc annōs: 'many years ago'; see Part II, chapter 25, in which we imagine Horace attempting to write this poem while in Orbilius' school.
22–3 ūniversōs manēre: 'awaited all men'; **maneō** can be used transitively.
24ff. diffūgēre nivēs ...: *Odes* 4.7 (the fourth book of

the *Odes* was in fact published in 13 BC, five years before Horace's death). We give the entire Ode. Metre: dactylic hexameters, alternating with half-hexameters:

dīffū|gērĕ nĭv|ēs, rĕdĕ|ūnt iām| grāmĭnă| cāmpīs

ārbŏrĭ|būsquĕ cŏ|māe;

26 dēcrēscentia: the rivers were flooded by melting snow; now they are shrinking and again flow between their banks.

28 Grātia cum ... geminīs sorōribus: 'Grace with her two sisters' = the three Graces. With the coming of spring beauty returns to the earth. The best illustration of these lines is Botticelli's *Primavera*.

28–9 audet ... nūda: the Graces can dance naked because the weather is warmer.

30 immortālia nē spērēs: this clause depends on **monet annus**. The melancholy and unexpected change in tone picks up **mūtat terra vicēs**; if spring is here, winter cannot be far away. These words carry the message developed in the rest of the poem; they are pointed by a heavy jarring rhythm, unusual in dactylic hexameters (word stress and verse stress coincide, an effect Augustan poets studiously avoid: see Appendix); and the repeated **ē** sounds of **nē spērēs** are strikingly discordant.

32 prōterit: the verb means properly 'tramples underfoot'.

36–7 damna tamen ... dēcidimus: these lines are the structural hinge of the poem; **damna ... lūnae** looks back to the recurring cycle of the seasons; **nōs ... dēcidimus** looks forward to the one-way road which all men must take down to death.

   nōs: 'but we ...'; **nōs** stands in in emphatic position, with no connecting particle; adversative asyndeton.

   dēcidimus means both 'we have gone down' and 'we have died'.

38 pater Aenēās ... Ancus: all must die, even Aeneas, founder of the Roman race and the kings; Tullus Hostilius and Ancus Martius were, according to tradition, the third and fourth kings of Rome.

39 pulvis et umbra sumus: the body turns to dust, the spirit to an insubstantial shadow.

40–43 quis scit ... animō: since life is so uncertain, Horace says, make the most of today (compare what the town mouse says to the country mouse (see chapter 53):

   dum licet, in rēbus iūcundīs vīve beātus;
   vīve memor, quam sīs aevī brevis.

Accordingly, he tells Torquatus to enjoy his worldly goods while he can and not save them up for his greedy heir. He draws the same moral in *Odes* 2.14 (*Eheu fugācēs*), where after twenty-four splendid and lugubrious lines on the inevitability of death, he ends by telling his host to bring out the best wine, which will

otherwise be drunk by his heir.

   For the modern reader, **cūncta manūs ... dederis animō** can hardly fail to strike a jarring note, coming in the middle of so splendid and melancholy a poem. But they are very much in character. Horace frequently surprises by such sudden changes of tone and finds it hard to remain completely serious throughout.

44 Mīnōs: one of the three judges of the underworld.

46 Torquātus: the addressee of the poem is only known otherwise from *Epistles* 1.5, in which Horace invites him to dinner; from this Epistle it emerges that he was an advocate, hence **fācundia**.

48–51 īnfernīs ... Pērithoō: after the ringing rhetoric of the previous stanza (**nōn ... nōn tē ... nōn tē ...**) the Ode ends on a quieter note of melancholy resignation; if the heroes of myth, the friends of the gods, cannot escape the chains of death, how much less can we expect to.

The poet and classical scholar A. E. Housman surprised his class with a rare outburst of emotion after he had dissected this Ode 'with the usual display of brilliance, wit, and sarcasm. Then for the first time in two years he looked up at us, and in quite a different voice said: "I should like to spend the last few minutes considering this Ode simply as poetry." ... He read the Ode aloud with deep emotion first in Latin and then in an English translation of his own. "That," he said hurriedly, almost like a man betraying a secret, "I regard as the most beautiful poem in ancient literature"' (from a letter to *The Times* from Dora Pym, a former student of Housman, quoted by Grant Richards, *Housman 1897–1936*, p. 289).

   We append his translation (the only Ode of Horace he translated):

   The snows are fled away, leaves on the shaws
       And grasses in the mead renew their birth,
   The river to the river-bed withdraws,
       And altered is the fashion of the earth.

   The Nymphs and Graces three put off their fear
       And unapparelled in the woodland play.
   The swift hour and the brief prime of the year
       Say to the soul, Thou wast not born for aye.

   Thaw follows frost; hard on the heel of spring
       Treads summer, sure to die, for hard on hers
   Comes autumn, with his apples scattering;
       The back to wintertide, when nothing stirs.

   But, oh, whate'er the sky-led seasons mar,
       Moon upon moon rebuilds it with her beams:
   Come we where Tullus and where Ancus are,
       And good Aeneas, we are dust and dreams.

Torquatus, if the gods in heaven shall add
    The morrow to the day, what tongue has told?
Feast then thy heart, for what thy heart has had
    The fingers of no heir shall ever hold.

When thou descendest once the shades among,
    The stern assize and equal judgement o'er,
Not thy long lineage nor thy golden tongue,
    No, nor they righteousness, shall friend thee more.

Night holds Hippolytus the pure of stain,
    Diana steads him nothing, he must stay;
And Theseus leaves Perithous in the chain
    The love of comrades cannot take away.

54–5 mortuus est Maecēnās: Maecenas died a few months before Horace, who died on 27 November 8 BC.
60 Horātiī Flaccī ut meī estō memor: 'Be mindful of Horatius Flaccus as of me', i.e. 'Remember Horatius Flaccus like myself.'

Grammar and exercises

P.S. Augustī testāmentum
1 'Those who murdered my father (Julius Caesar)': he means primarily Brutus and Cassius.
vīcī bis aciē: he refers to the two battles of Philippi. It is hardly true to say that he drove Brutus and Cassius into exile; they left Italy and took up the provinces they had been assigned by the senate.
cum bellum īnferrent reīpūblicae: Brutus and Cassius were defending the republic against tyrants. Augustus cannot fairly claim that he was fighting for the republic at this time.
2 The civil wars: Philippi, Actium, Bellum Alexandrinum; the foreign wars were those he waged pacifying Spain and in extending the frontiers of the empire to the Danube.
veniam: it is true that he practised a policy of *clēmentia* after the amnesty (39 BC) and attempted to unite all Italy behind him. It is also true that he treated the peoples who were incorporated into the empire without rancour and did all he could to see that they were well governed.
3 The gates of the temple of Janus were closed first in January 29 BC, to mark the end of the civil wars; secondly in 25 BC when Augustus had completed the pacification of Spain; thirdly at an unknown date, perhaps in association with the *Lūdī Saeculārēs* (17 BC), which were intended to inaugurate a Golden Age of peace.
4 For the extension of the Roman empire up to the Danube with the addition of four new provinces, see p. 41 above. Egypt was added to the empire not as a regular province but as the personal possession of the emperor, governed by a praefectus appointed by himself. On the title Augustus, see p. 40 above.

5 On the constitutional settlement of 28–27 BC see p. 40 above.
6 Augustus' claim to have ruled through his *auctōritās* rather than any particular powers conferred on him is very dubious. Under the first settlement of 27 BC he had an exceptionally large *prōvincia*, which gave him direct control of most of the legions and he held repeated consulships, which gave him control in the civilian sphere. But he found that even this was not enough to secure his position, and by the settlement of 23 BC he received an even larger *prōvincia*, which gave him direct control of almost all the legions, and *maius imperium* in the provinces not directly under his control, which enabled him to override decisions of governors appointed by the senate. Although he ceased to hold repeated consulships, he controlled the civilian sphere by the vague powers of the *tribūnicia potestās*, which he held continuously. At the same time he steadily increased his admininistrative powers by appointing prefects to take over the functions of the regular magistrates.

Tacitus saw Augustus' principate very differently. He claims to write his history *sine īrā et studiō* (= partisan feeling), but in fact he was prejudiced by the events of his own boyhood and youth, when the principate had degenerated into a tyranny under Nero, followed by another terrible civil war, and he had more recently served under the tyrant Domitian. As he saw it, the seeds of these disasters had been sown by Augustus who had monopolized all real power. To him all Augustus' talk of restoring the republic was pure sham, an attempt to hide his tyranny under an empty name.

    The picture which he paints of Augustus' principate is not altogether convincing, since he reads back into Augustus' time characteristics of the rule of later emperors. Thus gifts or bribes to the soldiers were regularly given by his successors at the beginning of their reign to secure the loyalty of the legions. The corn dole (*annōna*) was reduced by Augustus but used unscrupulously by some of his successors to keep the people quiet.
1 dulcēdine ōtiī pellexit ('he seduced by the attractions of *ōtium*') is a highly emotive way of describing Augustus' restoration of peace to a war-torn world; **ōtium** has both a good and a bad sense; it can mean either 'tranquillity, peace' or 'idleness'; in conjunction with **dulcēdine pellexit** it suggests the latter meaning. But it is true that Augustus did continually increase his administrative powers in the interests of efficiency.
3 nūllō adversante: after the conspiracy of Murena (23 BC), there was virtually no overt opposition; it is also true that most of the die-hard nobles had perished either in the civil wars or in the proscriptions of 43 BC;

and the senate did tend to become steadily more subservient to Augustus – a feature of the times which particularly disgusts Tacitus.

Your students might well like to discuss whether men are likely to be happier under a regime of benevolent despotism (Augustus) or chaotic liberalism (the old republic). Do the lessons of history suggest that democracy is the form of government most likely to give happiness to the largest number?

P.P.S. The death of Lucilius

The introduction of the centurion Lucilius in chapter 35 was an anachronism, which we put right here. The passage in its adapted form is not particularly hard but may be considered an optional extra, which students might read on their own.

The revolt of the legions stationed in Pannonia took place shortly after the accession of Tiberius (AD 14); according to Tacitus the soldiers hoped that a change of emperor offered a chance to get higher pay and better terms of service. It was followed shortly by a mutiny by the legions stationed on the Rhine.

2–3 **circumstantium umerīs**: 'on the shoulders of bystanders'.

4 **quis frātrem mihi?**: it turned out that Vibulenus had no brother. He was simply stirring things up.

5 **gladiātōrēs**: Blaesus probably kept a troop of gladiators to provide entertainment for the soldiers.

6 **in exitium mīlitum**: 'for the destruction of his soldiers'.

7 **nē hostēs quidem ...**: 'not even enemies begrudge burial (to their enemies)'; **invident** is here constructed with the ablative of the thing begrudged.

Background: Death

The question at the end, inviting comparisons between Roman funerals and those of today, is the obvious field for exploration here. What do your pupils think of the idea of professional mourners? Does a Roman funeral strike them as absurd in its excess of grief? What do they feel about the jeering clowns (p. 125, para. 3)? Another point that could discussed is the sensational gap between the funerals of the grand and great and the poor. How far does this still apply (final para.)?

Further reading: there is an excellent chapter on funeral rites in U. E. Paoli: *Rome: Its People, Life and Customs*, Longman, repr. Bristol Classical Press, pp. 128–32.

Sources

p. 125, para. 3: the Vespasian reference is to Suetonius: *Vespasian* 19. In his Vespasian disguise, the clown, Florus, kept going up to the emperor's accountants and asking, 'How much is this great funeral going to cost?'

They replied, 'Ten million sesterces,' and the pseudo-Vespasian cried out, 'Ten million sesterces! Give it to me this minute and then throw me into the Tiber right away.'

p. 125, para. 4: Polybius: 6.53.1ff.

Illustrations

p. 123: the three Graces are a detail from the famous *Primavera* by Sandro Botticelli (1444–1510). (Uffizi Gallery, Florence)

p. 124: this glass urn, containing the ashes of a cremated body, dates from the first or second century AD. (Old Speech Room Gallery, Harrow School)

p. 125: this funeral scene from a sarcophagus of the first century BC or AD shows musicians, pall-bearers and mourners. Artistic licence has allowed the sculptor of the relief to raise the pall which would have covered the corpse, who is seen reclining rather than lying on his back as a dead person would. (Museo Aquilano, Aquila, Abruzzi)

p. 126: this statue of a Roman nobleman carrying the busts of his ancestors is from the first century BC. (Capitoline Museum, Rome)

Appendix 1 Rome's imperial mission

This appendix both provides longer passages of continuous Latin for the brighter student to read and deals with a topic in Roman history which has been neglected in the main narrative, by giving three views on Rome's imperial mission, first that of Augustus himself, then that of Virgil and finally that of Tacitus. The Latin in these passages has not been changed from the original but some omissions have been made.

The three lines from *Aeneid* 6 that begin the section sum up the attitude of Augustus and Virgil to Rome's imperial mission; Roman rule will bring peace to the world and wars will be fought only to extend this peace.

2 **pācīque impōnere mōrem**: this is a difficult phrase: 'to impose custom on peace' must mean 'to make peace customary, habitual'. Some editors prefer to read **pācis**, following Servius, the ancient editor of Virgil; this would mean 'to impose (on the conquered) the habit of peace'. But there is no manuscript authority for this and the harder reading should be accepted.

You might ask students whether they think that 'imposing peace' on other peoples is ever a practical or justifiable policy (the examples of Ireland and Yugoslavia provide food for thought).

1 Augustus

The map (p. 110), with the dates of the various conquests, clarifies Augustus' words, which give a purely factual account. But notice that he uses the word **pacāvī** three times; like Virgil, Augustus looked on his extensions of the empire as wars fought in the cause of peace.

1 **mare pācāvī ā praedōnibus**: piracy in the Mediterranean had been a growing problem ever since Rome had eliminated the Hellenistic kingdoms in the second century BC. By the mid-first century there was a crisis, when huge pirate fleets swept the Mediterranean and interrupted Rome's food supplies. Pompey was given a special commission to deal with this menace in 67 BC and cleared the seas of pirates for the time being. But the trouble was always liable to recur, since Rome had no permanent navy until Augustus established four fleets stationed at different bases in the Mediterranean (see note on exercise 53.2.3).

    omnium prōvinciārum ...: this is not strictly true; he did not advance the frontiers in the East, where he kept the Euphrates as the boundary between the Roman and Parthian empires, and his attempt to extend the northern frontier to the Elbe failed.

3 **Galliās et Hispāniās**: Augustus conducted campaigns which finally pacified Gaul and Spain from 27 to 19 BC. He claims to have made the Ocean the boundary from Cadiz to the mouth of the Elbe; Germany from the Rhine to the Elbe had been reduced to a tributary province by AD 9 when it was lost through the revolt of Arminius. We might suppose that Augustus wrote this before AD 9; the claim is certainly untrue after that date when he abandoned the attempt.

5 **Alpēs** ...: the Alpine region from the Adriatic to the Tuscan sea was 'pacified' in a series of campaigns between 35 and 6 BC. This was certainly a boon to the people of northern Italy who had been subject to the continual depradations of Alpine tribes.

6–7 **nūllī ... per iniūriam**: Augustus claims not to have waged an unjust war against any people; this is a question of how you look at it (most of the Salassi, an Alpine tribe, were sold into slavery). But at least the Alpine campaigns brought security to the people of Italy.

7 **Aegyptum**: Augustus annexed Egypt after the death of Cleopatra as his personal possession, i.e. it did not become a province but was governed by *praefectī* whom he appointed himself.

8ff. **Pannoniōrum gentēs** ...: the extension of the empire to the Danube, bringing Moesia, Pannonia and Illyricum under Roman control, largely the work of his stepson Tiberius, was Augustus' greatest military achievement. It was probably necessary to secure the safety and tranquillity of the rest of the empire and it is certainly true that within these boundaries the provinces flourished exceedingly.

illustration: a wall from the temple of Rome and Augustus at Ancyra (modern Ankara, Turkey). Here is the best preserved copy of the *Res Gestae*, the so-called Monumentum Ancyranum.

2 Virgil

There are three passages in the *Aeneid* in which Virgil directly links the story of Aeneas with his own times: first, Jupiter's prophecy to Venus in Book 1; second, the pageant of Roman heroes to come which Anchises shows Aeneas in the underworld, in Book 6; third, the future of Rome portrayed on the magic shield Vulcan makes for Aeneas in Book 8. In all three the culmination of Roman history coincides with the victories of Augustus which will bring peace to the Roman world.

    Virgil does not play down the military aspect of Rome's imperial mission; the Romans are to be 'lords of creation' (**rērum dominōs**) and Augustus will extend the bounds of empire to the Ocean; they are to 'war down the proud', who do not willingly submit. But this is to serve a higher purpose, to bring peace to the world; Augustus' military exploits are wars to end war and to usher in the *pāx Rōmāna*.

Aeneid 1.276–96
When Venus saw Juno stir up the storm which drove Aeneas and the Trojans away from Italy and wrecked them on the shores of Libya, she appealed to Jupiter and asked how long he would allow her son to be driven over the seas and when he would fulfil his promise that the Trojans should settle in Italy and found the race from which the Romans would spring. He tells her that the fates remained unchanged. And to calm her fears he reveals the secrets of the fates. He tells how Aeneas will fight a war in Latium and after victory found a city there; his son Iulus will move the city to Alba Longa, and after three hundred years Romulus, the son of Mars, will be born and found Rome.

3 **mētās rērum**: 'bounds of things' = 'bounds of power'.

    nec tempora pōnō: 'nor do I lay down times', i.e. Rome's future is for ever – Rome is the eternal city.

4 **quīn**: 'and what is more'. **quīn** is sometimes used at the beginning of a sentence to make a strong addition to what has been said already.

6 **rērum dominōs**: 'lords of things', i.e. 'lords of the world' (the imperial aspect of Rome's destiny); **gentemque togātam**: 'and the togaed race' (Rome's achievements in the sphere of peace). (Suetonius says (*Div. Aug.* 40) that on one occasion Augustus quoted this ironically when he saw a mob of ill-dressed citizens agitating at a public meeting in the forum: *ēn rērum dominōs gentemque togātam*. He gave orders that no

one should stand in the forum unless properly dressed in the toga.)

7 Caesar: scholars debate whether Julius Caesar or Augustus Caesar is referred to. In our view Augustus is meant, not only because of the general context but also because in the following line (omitted), Jupiter says 'One day you will receive him safe, loaded with the spoils of the East,' which can only refer to Augustus' triumphal return to Rome after the campaigns at Actium and Alexandria and perhaps also to the recovery of the Roman standards lost at Carrhae.

8 quī terminet: the subjunctive is consecutive.

10ff. cāna Fidēs ...: Austin in his commentary remarks: 'In this ornate and richly-constructed passage Virgil expresses the full meaning of the *pax Augusta* to come: law and order shall be established on ancient, honoured institutional concepts; civil war shall be ended, and the madness which inspired it shall be imprisoned and impotent.'

Aeneid 6.788–853

In his review of Aeneas' posterity Anchises follows chronological order up to Romulus; he jumps to Augustus, in the passage quoted, but then reverts to the first kings of Rome and heroes of the republic. In juxtaposing Augustus to Romulus he implies that Augustus is the second founder of Rome.

6–7 rēgnāta ... Sāturnō: 'ruled by Saturn'; **Sāturnō** is dative of the agent. According to legend, Saturn was the first king of Latium; honoured as a god after his death, he was later identified with the Greek god Chronos, father of Zeus, and so was said to be the father of Jupiter. Saturn's rule in Latium was a Golden Age of peace and innocence.

7 Garamantas et Indōs: the Garamantes, a tribe in North Africa, were conquered by the Romans in 19 BC; Augustus had received an embassy from the Indians while he was in the East from 20 to 19 BC. Virgil died in 19 BC and so this passage must be one of the last he wrote. It would have been unrevised, which may explain the obscurity of **iacet extrā sīdera tellūs ...**

11–13 excūdent aliī ...: the supremacy of the Greeks in the arts, rhetoric and sciences was freely admitted by the Romans, who prided themselves on their practical skills, above all on the arts of government.

3 Tacitus

Tacitus had a more cynical view of the achievements of Augustus and a more realistic view of what the *pāx Rōmāna* meant to the conquered.

Ancient historians from Herodotus on had all invented speeches for their leading characters at key moments in their narratives; there was no pretence that these were 'historical'. The speech which Tacitus attributes to Calgacus is a rhetorical exercise using the traditional criticisms of Roman imperialism which were often made in the schools of rhetoric. It is nevertheless a remarkable exercise in empathy in which he imagines what it meant to a proud people to lose their freedom.

No doubt Calgacus exaggerates the evils of the empire; there were certainly excesses and abuses. Although Augustus and most of his successors tried to ensure good government of the provinces, the grievances Calgacus lists were real enough and things could go badly wrong; for instance, excesses of the infamous procurator Catus Decianus were partly responsible for Boudicca's revolt. Agricola himself was an enlightened governor, who began the policy of 'civilizing' the Britons by encouraging them to adopt Roman ways; and in campaigning in Caledonia to complete the conquest of Britain he was doing what Augustus had done on a larger scale, attempting to ensure the peace and security of the whole island.

A consideration of Rome's imperial mission raises vital moral issues which are still alive today. Can we ever be justified in imposing 'civilization' on more 'primitive' peoples? Should we ever wage wars to establish peace?

2 tandemque doctī: 'taught at last that' + acc. and inf.

5 super trīgintā mīlia: 'above (more than) 30,000'.

10–11 hodiernum diem cōnsēnsumque vestrum: the two noun phrases form one idea – 'the unity you have achieved this day'.

16–17 quōrum superbiam frūstrā ... effugiās: 'whose pride you would vainly (try to) escape'; the subjunctive is potential.

21 opēs atque inopiam: 'wealth and want'; i.e. they want to conquer everyone, whether rich or poor; this looks back to the previous sentence: they satisfy their greed by conquering the rich, their ambition by conquering the poor.

25 dīlectūs: Britons might be conscripted for tasks such as road-building and it was not long before we find them serving as auxiliaries in the Roman army.

26 coniugēs sorōrēsque: the Roman conquerors were often accused of rape and one of the causes of Boudicca's revolt in AD 61 was the rape of her daughters.

27 nōmine amīcōrum atque hospitum: 'in the name of friends and hosts' = 'by those who called themselves friends and hosts' (a typical example of Tacitus' conciseness of expression leading to obscurity of meaning).

28 tribūtum: the taxes levied on provincials included land tax (*tribūtum solī*), property tax (*tribūtum capitis*) and customs dues (*portoria*); besides these there were corn requisitions to provide grain for the legions and the governor and his staff.

annus = **annōna**, the first meaning of which is annual produce.

29 **silvīs ac palūdibus ēmūniendīs**: **ēmūnīre** = 'to fortify', 'make secure', but here it appears to mean 'to make roads through'; Agricola's advance into Scotland was accompanied by a massive road-building programme, using native labour. Calgacus mentions all the common grievances of the subject peoples: conscription, tribute, corn requisition and forced labour.

30 **mancipia**: **mancipium** means first 'taking by the hand', which as a legal term means 'taking formal possession of a purchase'; it then means a possession, and lastly 'a slave'.

31 **vēneunt**: **vēnīre** = 'to be sold' (active in form but passive in meaning).

ultrō (beyond) = 'and what is more'.

32 **sublāta**: perfect passive participle of **tollō** = I remove, eliminate.

Appendix 2 Continuous indirect speech

The simplified rules for continuous indirect speech given here are sufficient for your students at this stage, and there is not much in them that is new; the one feature which may need stressing is that where an indirect command is introduced into the middle of indirect speech, it is expressed by the subjunctive without any introductory **ut**.

Appendix 3 Uses of the indicative and subjunctive

This summary introduces nothing new except:

2(e)(ii) Causal clauses with the subjunctive, giving the alleged cause (students may look on this as a kind suboblique usage; the cause is what some person or persons alleged, not necessarily a fact).

2(f)(ii) Temporal clauses with the subjunctive where there is an idea of purpose as well as time; this has been touched on in connection with **dum** (chapter 47).

2(g) Concessive clauses with the subjunctive after **quamvīs**. In this usage the concession is advanced for the sake of argument and is not necessarily true.

2(h) Relative with the subjunctive; we add a simple example of the consecutive relative, after **dignus**.

We do not claim that all Latin syntax has been covered in Part III, but enough has been done to enable students to read unadapted texts with a commentary which draws attention to rarer usages.

Translations

Chapter 34

Cartoon captions

1   Quintus and Pompeius visited Delphi to see Apollo's shrine.
2   Quintus said, 'Come on, Pompeius, let's hurry lest we arrive late.'
3   They climbed the Sacred Way to come to the temple.
4   Many suppliants were waiting in front of the temple to receive the oracles of the god.

Quintus visits Delphi

When Quintus heard of the death of Cicero, he was deeply moved. He wanted to hurry to Macedonia to serve with Brutus and avenge the death of his friend's father. But before he left Athens, he decided to visit Delphi to see Apollo's famous shrine, to which men came from all parts of the world to seek the oracles of the god.

And so he went to find a friend called Pompeius and said, 'Pompeius, will you come with me to visit Delphi?' 'Certainly,' he said, 'I will come with you. For I've long wanted to visit Delphi. Let's start the journey as quickly as possible.' Quintus said, 'Let's go to Theomnestus at once and say goodbye to him. We will start our journey tomorrow.' They found Theomnestus in his study reading a book. He praised their plan and advised them to look at everything carefully.

And so the next day they left Athens. At first they walked on flat, straight roads, but on the fourth day the journey became more difficult; they were climbing the hills and soon entered the mountains; they met no one except shepherds, who were driving their flocks down from the mountains and a few travellers who were returning from Delphi.

Suddenly they saw Delphi before them, situated on the side of a mountain between two huge cliffs, which shone in the light of the setting sun. For a while they stood silent, deeply moved by the majesty of the place. To the left they looked down on a plain lying far below, on the right mountains rose sheer to the sky; in the middle the shrine of Apollo clung to the sides of the mountain.

At length Quintus said, 'Let's hurry, lest night fall on us before we arrive.' The sun had set when they arrived at Delphi; they dined in a little inn and went to sleep at once.

The next day Pompeius woke Quintus and said, 'Come on, Quintus, let's climb the hill to see Apollo's temple.' They slowly climbed the Sacred Way. The doors of the temple were open. In front sat some people waiting for the Pythia. Soon the Pythia herself was led in by a priest, dressed in a white robe and holding a branch of laurel in her hand. She went down into the inner shrine. Then murmurs were heard echoing from the shrine; the Pythia, inspired by the god, was uttering the divine oracle. The murmurs ceased. The Pythia ascended from the shrine and with eyes lowered to the ground went silently out of the temple. The priest handed the oracle written on a tablet to the suppliant. He received the oracle with the greatest reverence, read it through and gave thanks to god.

Quintus, watching this (so) ancient ceremony, was deeply moved. He turned towards the statue of Apollo, which stood in the furthest part of the temple; he lifted his hands towards heaven and prayed to the god to be propitious to him. At that very moment he knew this: he was going to be a poet and a prophet of Apollo. He left the temple silently and went down the hill with Pompeius. Near the road was the Castalian spring, sacred to Apollo and the Muses; Quintus stopped and drank the water.

Quintus and Pompeius prepare to go to Brutus

When Quintus had returned to Athens, he hesitated no longer. He hurried to the Academy to tell Theomnestus what he had in mind. He met Theomnestus going into the theatre and told him his intention. He did not try to turn him from his purpose. 'You are doing rightly, Quintus,' he said. 'You must do your duty. Alas! How many young men have now gone off to the war!'

Quintus hurried from the Academy to the city to look for Pompeius; for he had decided to go to Brutus with Quintus. Quintus found him packing up his things. 'Are you nearly ready, Pompeius?' he said. 'Let's stay in Athens today. Early tomorrow let's go to the Academy to say goodbye to our friends. Then let's hurry to the Piraeus to find a ship which will carry us to Brutus.'

And so the next day Quintus and Pompeius first

hurried to the Academy to say goodbye to their friends; then they walked to the Piraeus to look for a ship which was going to go to Asia; for Brutus was now campaigning there with his army. When they arrived at the harbour, they met a captain drinking in a pub, who was going to sail to Asia that very day. He accepted them gladly and did not ask for a fare, because he wanted to help the cause of Brutus.

Exercise 34.1

vocem, dormiam, defendam, festinem, faciam, studeam, adsim

Exercise 34.2

1 we say
2 we said
3 we shall say
4 let us say
5 let him/her come
6 he/she is coming
7 he/she will come
8 he/she came
9 they are helping
10 they helped
11 they will help
12 let them help
13 let us have
14 we have
15 we had
16 we shall have

Exercise 34.3

1 Let us fight bravely.
2 Let us not flee.
3 Let them return to the camp at once.
4 Let us love our country; let us obey the senate.
5 Let the boys work hard.

Exercise 34.4

1 We are hurrying to help you.
2 Quintus is making a journey to Delphi to see the shrine of Apollo.
3 Men come from all parts of Greece to Delphi to seek the oracles of the god.
4 Many young men will sail to Athens to study in the Academy.
5 Come together, young men, to the theatre, to listen to Theomnestus.
6 The boys are hurrying to school so that they may not arrive late.
7 The girls will return home quickly lest they upset their parents.
8 The mother calls back her daughter lest she fall

into danger.

Exercise 34.5

1 We were hurrying to help you.
2 Quintus made a journey to Delphi to visit the shrine of Apollo.
3 Men used to come from all parts of Greece to seek the oracles of the god.
4 Many young men used to sail to Athens to study in the Academy.
5 The young men had come together to the theatre to listen to Theomnestus.
6 The children were hurrying to school that they might not arrive late.
7 The girls returned home quickly lest they annoy their parents.
8 The father wrote a letter to his son to warn him of the danger.
9 Marcus had gone away to Macedonia to serve with Brutus.
10 Brutus had raised an army to defend the liberty of the Roman people.

Exercise 34.6

1 take!
2 I took
3 we may take
4 he/she was taken
5 he/she might take
6 he/she may lead
7 we were led
8 I might lead
9 you led
10 he/she will lead
11 you may call
12 I had been called
13 we are being called
14 he/she might call
15 we shall be called

Exercise 34.7

1 *vīderent.* Quintus and Pompeius made a journey to see Delphi.
2 *īnspicerēmus.* We were climbing the hill to look at the temple of Apollo.
3 *spectēmus.* We shall stay here a long time so that we may see everything.
4 *redīrent.* At last they departed from Delphi to return to Athens.
5 *mīlitāret.* When they had returned to Athens, Marcus had gone away to serve with Brutus.
6 *dēfendam.* He had left a letter for Quintus, in which he had written: 'I have hurried to Macedonia to defend liberty with Brutus.'

Exercise 34.8

1 Quīntus ad Acadēmīam festīnāvit ut amīcōs suōs vidēret.
2 iter Delphōs faciam ut templum Apollinis vīsam.
3 multī hominēs prope iānuam templī exspectābant ut ōrāculum audīrent.
4 Quīntus Pompēium prīmā lūce excitāvit nē ad templum sērō advenīrent.
5 Delphōs vēnimus ut vēra cognōscāmus.
6 trēs diēs Delphīs mānsērunt ut ōrāculum audiant.
7 puellae dīligenter labōrābant ut magister sē laudāret.
8 puerī dīligenter labōrant nē magister sē pūniat.

P.S.

where?	everywhere
where from?	from all sides
who?	each one
which of two?	each of two, both

Chapter 35

Cartoon captions

1 The master said, 'Sit down, children, and be quiet.' (The master tells the children to sit down and be quiet.)
2 The master said, 'Quintus, bring me your tablet.' (The master asks Quintus to bring him his tablet.)
3 The master said, 'Decimus, don't annoy Gaius.' (The master told Decimus not to annoy Gaius.)
4 Quintus said, 'Master, won't you dismiss me?' (Quintus persuaded the master to dismiss him.)

Quintus becomes a soldier

At midday the sailors cast off the ship. There was a following wind, and towards nightfall they arrived at Delos, the little island where the god Apollo was born. Quintus wanted to visit the monuments and asked the captain not to cast off the ship until he had returned. When he had landed, he hurried with Pompeius to look at the sacred place where Apollo had been born. When they had looked at everything, the sun had set; and so they decided to spend the night on land. The next day, as soon as they had returned to the ship, the captain told the sailors to cast off the ship.

The rest of the journey was completed without incident. On the third day they saw the shore of Asia and at midday arrived at the port of Ephesus. Quintus and Pompeius hurried to the city and, when they were sitting in the forum, they met a soldier who was serving with Brutus. They persuaded him to lead them to the army. They started the journey without delay and towards evening they arrived at the camp. When they had entered the camp, the soldier led them to a centurion and said, 'These young men have come from Athens to serve with Brutus.'

He (the centurion) told them to come with him to the headquarters of the legion. When the centurion had led them into the headquarters, they saw a military tribune (tribune of the soldiers) called Rufus, who happened to be known to them. He greeted them cheerfully. 'And so,' he said, 'you too have come to service with us? I will take you to the legionary commander.' The commander received them courteously. 'Rufus', he said, 'will look after you; tomorrow I will take you to the general.'

The next day before dawn Rufus woke them up and told them to hurry to the commander. He took them to Brutus, who asked them many questions. Finally he said, 'You seem sensible and energetic young men. I will accept you into my army.' He turned to the legionary commander. 'Send these young men', he said, 'to the commander of the tenth legion. Tell him to look after them and teach them military discipline.' He said this and dismissed them.

The commander of the tenth legion looked at them gloomily. 'So,' he said,' you've come from Athens? You were studying philosophy in the Academy? Now you want to become soldiers? Immortal gods! Soon we shall have not an army but a school of philosophers. Rufus, take these young men to Lucilius; tell him to teach them some discipline.'

Lucilius introduces Quintus to military discipline

Rufus took Quintus and Pompeius to Lucilius. He was a centurion, a brave man long skilled in military discipline. He used to punish idle soldiers savagely; he was called by them 'Give me another'; for whenever he had broken his vine staff on the back of a soldier, he called for another and then again for another. Quintus and Pompeius were quickly introduced to military discipline by him. They learnt to throw javelins, to strike with the sword, to construct works. They made long marches carrying their arms and packs. Lucilius never let them rest; he was always telling them not to idle. They had never been so tired.

On the twentieth day Lucilius, whose habit it was to find fault, praised them: 'Young men,' he said, 'you are not completely useless. You've learnt a bit of military discipline. And so let's go to the commander. I will recommend you to him.'

When Lucilius had led them to the commander, he looked at them gloomily: 'And so,' he said, 'you've now learnt military discipline? In twenty days you've become soldiers? We shall see. Meanwhile Brutus has ordered me to accept you into my legion. Lucilius will tell you what you must do. Go now and perform your duties diligently.' Then, looking at them more kindly, 'Without doubt,' he said, 'you will show yourselves brave and diligent and will soon become soldiers worthy of the tenth legion.' When he had said this, he dismissed them.

Exercise 35.1

1 The mother ordered her daughter not to play in the road.
2 The daughter asked her mother to take her to the forum.
3 The mother told her daughter to stay in the house and help her.
4 The girl persuades her father to take her to the forum.
5 The girl said to her mother, 'I shall not stay in the house; for I have persuaded father to take me to the forum.'
6 The mother said to her husband, 'What are you doing, my husband? I asked you not to take our daughter to the forum.'
7 Her husband replied, 'The girl has persuaded me to take her with me.'
8 The mother said to her husband, 'The girl has behaved very badly. I advise you not to spoil her like that.'
9 But the father did not forbid his daughter to come with him.

Exercise 35.2

1 *Quīntus Pompēiō imperāvit ut ad urbem festīnāret.* Quintus ordered Pompeius to hurry to the city.
2 *centuriō iuvenibus imperāvit ut sēcum venīrent ad prīncipia legiōnis.* The centurion ordered the young men to come with him to the headquarters of the legion.
3 *Rūfus Quīntum excitāvit imperāvitque ut surgeret./Rūfus Quīntō excitātō imperāvit ut surgeret.* Rufus roused Quintus and told him to get up.
4 *Rūfus eōs ad Lūcīlium dūxit et eī imperāvit ut iuvenēs aliquid disciplīnae mīlitāris docēret.* Rufus led them to Lucilius and ordered him to teach the young men some military discipline.
5 *Lūcīlius Pompēiō saepe imperābat nē cessāret.* Lucilius often told Pompeius not to be idle.

Exercise 35.3

1 Quīntus mīlitī persuāsit ut sē ad Brūtī castra dūceret.
2 mīles Quīntum rogat nē festīnet, quod fessus est.

3 ubi ad castra advēnērunt, centuriō quīdam 'venīte mēcum' inquit 'ut lēgātum legiōnis videātis.'
4 centuriō 'hī iuvenēs' inquit 'vēnērunt ut cum Brūtō mīlitent.'
5 lēgātus Rūfō imperāvit ut eōs cūrāret.
6 Rūfus Quīntō persuāsit nē ē castrīs discēderet.

Exercise 35.4

1 they might have ruled
2 we rule
3 let us rule
4 we shall rule
5 we might rule
6 sleep!
7 I slept
8 you will sleep
9 let us sleep
10 to sleep
11 let us see
12 we shall be seen
13 you might see
14 they were seen
15 he/she might have seen

Exercise 35.5

1 When he had returned to the ship, Quintus at once fell asleep.
2 When we had arrived at port, we hurried to the city.
3 When we were waiting in the forum, we saw many soldiers.
4 When a soldier had led us to Brutus' camp, we met a tribune of the soldiers known to us.
5 When the tribune saw us, he greeted us cheerfully.

Exercise 35.6

1 mittāmur
2 mitterētur
3 missī essent
4 amēminī
5 amārer
6 amātus essēs
7 custōdiantur
8 custōdītus esset
9 custōdīrētur
10 captī essēmus

Exercise 35.7

1 Brutus killed Caesar lest the Roman people should be ruled by a tyrant.
2 When he had been attacked by Antony, he fled from Rome.
3 He sailed to Athens lest he should be caught by

Antony.

4 He stayed in Athens a long time to draw the young men to his cause.

5 He persuaded Marcus Cicero to serve with him.

6 When very many young men had been brought over to the cause of the republic, he hurried to Macedonia.

7 When Marcus' father had been killed by Antony's soldiers, Quintus also wanted to serve with Brutus.

8 He persuaded Pompeius to sail with him to Asia.

9 When they had arrived at Ephesus, they hurried to the forum.

10 When they were sitting in the forum, they met a soldier who took them to Brutus' camp.

Exercise 35.8

1 cum Flaccus ab agrō rediisset, Scintillam salūtāvit quae in hortō sedēbat.

2 cum cēna parāta esset, eum in casam vocāvit.

3 cum cēnārent, Scintilla 'ānxia sum,' inquit; 'Quīntus epistolam nōbīs nōn mīsit.'

4 cum Flaccus haec audīvisset, 'nōlī ānxia esse,' inquit. 'sine dubiō ad nōs mox scrībet.'

5 sed Flaccus quoque ānxius erat. cum cēnam cōnfēcisset, exiit ut amīcōs suōs vidēret.

6 cum in tabernā sedēret, nūntius Rōmā advēnit.

7 nūntius 'Brūtus' inquit 'multīs iuvenibus persuāsit ut Athēnīs discēderent et in exercitū suō mīlitārent.'

8 cum verba nūntiī audīta essent, Flaccus domum festīnāvit ut Scintillae omnia dīceret.

9 Scintilla epistolam ad Quīntum scrīpsit eumque ōrāvit nē in bellum ā Brūtō dūcerētur.

10 sed Quīntus in Brūtī exercitū iam mīlitābat cum hanc epistolam accēpit.

P.S.

I run to, I run round, (I) run together, I run down, (I) run in different directions, I run into/against, I run between, I run in the way of/I meet, I run through, I run in front, I run forward, I run back, I run to help, I run across

Chapter 36

Cartoon captions

1 Scintilla was sitting in the cottage when the postman came in and handed her a letter.

2 Scintilla did not delay but read through the letter at once.

3 Flaccus had already set out to the field, but when he heard his wife's shouts he returned quickly.

4 Flaccus tried to console his wife. They talked about Quintus' letter for a long time.

Scintilla despairs

All the people of Venusia were extremely anxious. Every day worse news was being reported from Rome; the republic was drifting into civil war, just as Flaccus had foretold.

Scintilla was sitting in the cottage when the postman came in and gave her a letter. She broke the seal at once and quickly read through the letter; overcome by terror, she shrieked aloud. Flaccus had already set out for the field but when he heard his wife's shouts, he ran back to the cottage. Entering, he said, 'What's the matter (what have you suffered), dearest?' She said, 'Oh (my) husband, Quintus has left Athens; he has followed Brutus to Asia.' Flaccus said, 'What are you saying, dearest? Surely our son doesn't want to be a soldier?' She replied, 'He is defending the liberty of the Roman people, (as) he says. Oh black day! Immortal gods, keep our son safe. O Flaccus, fetch Decimus; he will help us.'

Flaccus said, 'Quintus is not a boy now but a brave and good man; he must perform his duty. We can't stop him from defending the liberty of the Roman people against tyrants. But, if you like (if it pleases you), I will fetch Decimus so that we can put the matter to him.'

Flaccus hurried to Decimus' house. He met him about to set out for Brundisium but persuaded him to return with him to Venusia. Entering the house, they found Scintilla in floods of tears. Decimus went up to her and said, 'Don't cry, Scintilla. Without doubt Quintus will soon return to Athens and study in the Academy again. The war won't go on (won't be waged) for long. But Quintus is foolish, if he has joined (himself to) Brutus; for Antony is a very skilful soldier (very skilled in warfare) and has better troops. When he has conquered Caesar's assassins, without doubt he will restore the republic. The republic now needs a strong man who will give back peace to the citizens. I myself am about to set out for Brundisium to join the army of Antony.'

When Flaccus heard this, he could not restrain himself. 'What are you saying, you traitor?' he said. 'Do you intend to serve in the army of that tyrant? Do you care nothing for liberty? Be off! Never enter this house again.'

Decimus turned and went out silently. Flaccus went up to Scintilla and tried to comfort her. But she did not cease crying. 'How many troubles shall we suffer!' she said. 'Citizens will fight with fellow citizens, fathers with sons. How many mothers will mourn their sons! Wicked Mars will rage throughout the whole world.' After saying this she fell to the ground in a faint.

Playlet: Quintus and Pompeius are introduced to military discipline

Characters: Quintus, Pompeius, Lucilius

Enter Quintus and Pompeius at the double; they are carrying very heavy packs and shields and swords. Lucilius follows.

Lucilius: Hurry up, young men; you are not studying philosophy in the Academy now. Run!

Pompeius: I can't run any further.

Lucilius: Halt!

Quintus (*panting*): We've already run five miles, Lucilius. We are worn out. Let's sit under a tree and rest a little.

They put their arms down on the ground and sit under a tree.

Lucilius: You've rested enough now, young men. Get up. It's no time to delay. Look! the enemy are advancing against us. Don't you see them? They are hiding in that wood.

Pompeius: What are you saying, Lucilius? I see no enemy.

Lucilius: The enemy are hidden. Take care that you don't fall into an ambush. What should you do?

Quintus: We should send scouts ahead and advance cautiously with swords drawn.

Lucilius: Good, Quintus! Send your scouts ahead, in case you are caught off your guard and go forward cautiously.

Quintus advances cautiously brandishing his sword. Pompeius follows muttering quietly.

Pompeius: What a silly game this is! Lucilius is mad; he's trying to finish us off by hard labour.

When they reach the wood, Quintus shouts at the top of his voice and strikes the undergrowth with his sword.

Quintus: Look, Lucilius! I've killed an enemy. The rest have fled.

Pompeius: Look, Lucilius! I'm wounded; I'm dying.

Lucilius: Halt, boys. Come back to me. Run, Pompeius! I don't want to break another vine staff on your back.

Quintus and Pompeius run to Lucilius.

Lucilius: You've played enough, boys. You are not completely useless. I've seen worse recruits, but not often. Let's go back to camp, so that I can recommend you to the commander. Now march off with the right foot. Oh Quintus, you've started with the left foot. Oh dear, you'll never make a soldier.

Exercise 36.1

1 We will try to help our father.
2 We followed him to the field.
3 On the way I talked for a long time with friends.
4 Having entered the field I called my father.
5 I stayed/delayed in the field a long time.
6 In the evening I set off for home.

Exercise 36.2

1 we are following
2 we shall follow
3 let us follow
4 to follow
5 we followed
6 you were following
7 they might follow
8 following
9 send
10 I sent
11 to be sent
12 sending
13 they may be sent
14 let us send
15 they sent
16 they had been sent
17 they were afraid
18 to fear
19 having feared
20 fearing
21 they may fear
22 you will fear
23 we feared
24 they were fearing

Exercise 36.3

1 We are trying to return home.
2 You seem sensible, friends.
3 We want to talk with you, girls.
4 Setting out/having set out at first light, we entered the city at midday.
5 I have decided to follow Brutus to Asia.
6 Fearing the danger the women stayed in the house.
7 Many citizens died in the civil war.
8 Going out of the house Flaccus set out for the field.
9 On the way he met a friend with whom he talked for a long time.
10 Entering the field, he worked hard.
11 The mother ordered her daughter who was delaying in the house to hurry to the spring.

12 Setting out at once, the girl found many women chatting near the spring.

13 She drew water quickly and was returning home when she slipped.

14 Fearing her mother's anger she went back to the spring and filled her urn again.

Exercise 36.4

1 (*active*) monē, monēte; (*passive*) monēre, monēminī
2 (*active*) verte, vertite; (*passive*) vertere, vertiminī

Exercise 36.5

1 Come here, young men, and try to help me.
2 Stay in the city for three days, son; then set out for home.
3 Follow me to the field, boys; go into the field and help the farmers.
4 Stay, friend, and talk with us.
5 Don't fear the enemy, soldiers, but advance bravely.
6 Be warned by me, friends; don't slip into danger.

Exercise 36.6

1 Brūtum in Asiam sequēmur.
2 statim profectī, Ephesum nāvigāvimus.
3 cum advēnissēmus, Brūtī exercitum invenīre cōnātī sumus.
4 castra ingressī, centuriōnī cuīdam occurrimus.
5 'mē sequiminī' inquit 'ad prīncipia legiōnis.'
6 nōn morātī sumus sed eum continuō secūtī sumus.
7 lēgātō occurrimus ē prīncipiīs ēgredientī.
8 'manēte in prīncipiīs, iuvenēs,' inquit; 'mox reveniam.'
9 mox regressus nōbiscum diū colloquēbātur.
10 tandem 'iuvenēs prūdentēs vidēminī,' inquit. 'vōs ad Brūtum dūcam. mē sequiminī.'

P.S.

that is	compare!
for (the sake of) example	and the following
and the rest	he/she flourished
before midday	each year
after midday	pounds
in the year of our Lord	may he/she rest in peace
to the greater glory of God	(in) number
at the end	things written by hand
from the beginning	note well!
after the writing	

Chapter 37

Cartoon captions

1 As the sun rose Quintus and Pompeius got up and put on their arms.
2 After putting on their arms they ran to the headquarters.
3 Brutus called together the soldiers and made a speech.
4 After finishing his speech Brutus dismissed the soldiers.

Philippi

For some time Brutus stayed in Asia with his army while the soldiers exercised and prepared for war. Quintus was present at several battles which they fought in Asia. He showed himself brave and energetic. In one battle he saved the legionary commander, who had fallen into the greatest danger.

A few days later, after finishing his labours, he was resting in his tent when an orderly came in and told him to come to the general's headquarters. When he had entered the headquarters with an anxious mind, Brutus rose and greeted him kindly. 'Greetings, Horace,' he said; 'I have heard very good reports of you; you have not only fought bravely but saved your commander himself from danger. And so I have decided to make you a military tribune.' After saying this, he dismissed Quintus.

The next day Brutus called together all his forces and made a speech. He ascended the platform and greeted his soldiers. 'Fellow soldiers,' he said, 'Antony and Octavian, the heirs of the tyrant, have assembled a huge army and are preparing to attack us. They have already started the journey to Greece. It is necessary for us to march to Greece to meet them. And so get ready for a long and laborious march. But let us remember this: when we have won the victory, liberty will be restored to the Roman people and civil wars will be finished.'

The soldiers applauded Brutus and joyfully got ready for the march. A few days later Brutus set out for Greece with all his forces. On the march Cassius met them with twelve legions. So Brutus and Cassius united their two armies and marched from Asia to Greece.

They met Antony and Octavian near Philippi. When battle was joined, on the right wing Brutus defeated Octavian. On the left Cassius was defeated by Antony and after suffering such a disaster he despaired and killed himself. The battle had been indecisive; very many were killed on the field of battle, amongst whom the commander of the tenth legion himself died fighting very gallantly.

Brutus is defeated

Three days later Quintus was called to the general's headquarters. Brutus seemed sadder than before but greeted Quintus kindly. 'Quintus,' he said, 'as (appointed) military tribune you have done very well and showed the greatest courage in that deadly battle. And so, since the commander of the tenth legion is dead, I appoint you yourself as commander. Soon we shall join battle again. I pray the gods that we may be more successful and after defeating the enemy restore liberty to the Roman people.'

Leaving the headquarters, Quintus did not return straight to Pompeius but for a long time reflected alone about the words of Brutus. He was elated by the confidence Brutus put in him but worried by the magnitude of so great a duty.

Not much later Brutus was forced to join battle. At first his troops attacked the enemy with the greatest vigour and defeated them; Quintus led the tenth legion gallantly. But soon Antony drove them back and after breaking through Brutus' left wing surrounded the whole army. They (Brutus' men), terrified, turned their backs and throwing away their arms fled to their camp.

Exercise 37.1

1 **collēctum** agrees with **exercitum**, the object of **dūcēbat**:
   Antony collected a very large army and led it to Greece.

2 **collēctus** agrees with **exercitus**, the subject of **contendēbat**:
   The great army collected by Antony was marching to Greece.

3 **collēctō** agrees with **exercitū**, which is neither subject nor object of **contendit**; the phrase is in the ablative (ablative absolute):
   After collecting a very large army, Antony marched to Greece.

Exercise 37.2

1 After finishing his labours, Quintus was talking with his friends.
2 While Quintus was talking with his friends, a centurion approached, who summoned him to Brutus.
3 Brutus called together the soldiers and made a speech.
4 'When the enemy are conquered,' he said, 'we shall restore liberty to the Roman people.'
5 The soldiers, dismissed, prepared for the journey.
6 While Scintilla was sitting in the house, the postman entered.

7 Scintilla after reading the letter called Flaccus.
8 Hearing her shouts Flaccus returned to the house anxiously.
9 Flaccus tried to comfort Scintilla who was weeping.
10 As Scintilla despaired, Flaccus went out to summon Decimus.

Exercise 37.3

1 *Caesare occīsō.* When Caesar had been killed, Flaccus ordered Quintus to sail to Athens.
2 *longō itinere cōnfectō.* When his long journey was finished, Quintus at last arrived in Athens.
3 *monumentīs spectātīs.* After looking at the monuments, Quintus hurried to the Academy.
4 *Marcum in ātriō vīsum.* Quintus saw Marcus in the hall and greeted him.
5 *Marcō in tabernā bibente.* While Marcus was drinking in a pub, Quintus was studying hard.
6 *Quīntō Theomnēstum audiente.* While Quintus was listening to Theomnestus, Marcus was drinking in a pub.
7 *epistolam ā patre scrīptam.* Marcus handed Quintus the letter written by his father.
8 *epistolam perlēctam.* After reading through the letter Quintus returned it to Marcus.

Exercise 37.4

1 (having been) heard
2 he/she was being heard
3 they might hear
4 to be heard
5 we shall be heard
6 let us hear
7 talking
8 he/she will talk
9 talk!
10 he talked
11 he/she was talking
12 to talk
13 I shall warn
14 we warned
15 he might be warned
16 let us warn
17 be warned/you are warned
18 (having been) warned

Exercise 37.5

1 Horātia mātre salūtātā casam intrāvit.
2 Scintilla cēnā parātā Flaccum vocāvit.
3 Flaccus, fīliā vīsā, gāvīsus est/gaudēbat.
4 cēnā cōnfectā, diū colloquēbantur.
5 tandem Horātia parentibus relictīs domum rediit.

Exercise 37.6

1 Quīntus Pompēiusque Delphīs regressī in Asiam nāvigāvērunt ut Brūtum invenīrent.
2 itinere cōnfectō ad Brūtī castra festīnāvērunt.
3 Brūtus in Asiā aliquamdiū morātus exercitum in Graeciam dūxit.
4 Brūtus proeliō commissō Octāviānum vīcit.
5 sed Cassius ab Antōniō victus sē occīdit.
6 Quīntus Brūtō mortuō cum comitibus fūgit.

Exercise 37.7

1 When Quintus was a boy, very many farmers lived in Venusia.
2 As the wind was favourable/With a following wind we quickly arrived at the harbour.
3 When Pompey and Crassus were consuls/In the consulate of Pompey and Crassus, Caesar was fighting in Gaul.
4 When Brutus was leader/Under the leadership of Brutus, Quintus and Pompeius fought at Philippi.
5 When Caesar was dictator Brutus decided to free the republic.

P.S.

narrator, supporter, writer, reader, traitor
surrender, recommendation, greeting, warning, inquiry/question
song, return, warning, laughter/smile, ascent

Chapter 38

Cartoon captions

1 Quintus threw away his shield and fled from the battle towards the camp.
2 The enemy, pursuing (them), were about to break into the camp.
3 Quintus, following his comrades, ran into the woods.
4 The next day, about to set out for Athens, he looked sadly at his sleeping comrades.

Quintus flees to Athens

When Antony broke through Brutus' left wing, Quintus threw away his shield and fled from the field. Of his comrades few were still resisting the enemy; more were fleeing with Quintus towards the camp, forgetting their courage. They cared for nothing except to reach the camp as soon as possible.

In the camp they were greeted with a terrible report. For Brutus, despairing for the future, had run on his own sword; he was dead. When Quintus heard this, he was deeply moved. But it was not the time to delay. The enemy were about to climb the rampart; Quintus could already hear their shouts. Following his comrades, who were escaping from the other side of the camp, he ran into the woods.

Quintus and his comrades lay down, hidden in the woods, and sadly waited for the day. Quintus could not sleep; he violently blamed himself and his men, because they had betrayed their general and turned their back(s). Now the general was dead, what was he going to do? At least he had saved his life; he was luckier than many of his comrades, who were either dead on the field of battle or had been captured and fallen into the hands of the enemy. Now he wanted nothing except to return home and see his parents again; and so he decided to walk to Athens alone.

As the sun rose, he got up, about to set out for Athens; he looked at his comrades (who were) still sleeping. For a little he hesitated, then set out alone. For twenty days he made a laborious journey; in the day time he slept, hidden in the woods, lest he should be caught by the enemy. At night he went on by deserted ways. Sometimes he met peasants, who usually received him kindly and gave him food.

At last he saw Athens far off. As the sun set he entered the city and hurried to the house of Theomnestus and knocked on the door. Theomnestus opened the door and scarcely recognized Quintus, but after looking at his face more closely, he said, 'Immortal gods, surely I'm not looking at Quintus? What has happened to you (what have you suffered?)? Come in quickly.' Quintus went in and told him everything. 'Quintus,' he said, 'you are starving. First have dinner, then go to bed. Let's consider tomorrow what you should do.'

Quintus slept for a long time. At midday Theomnestus woke him and said, 'Come, Quintus, you can't stay in the city lest Antony's soldiers catch you. What are you going to do?' Quintus wanted nothing but to return home. And so they set out for the port to look for a ship which was going to leave for Italy.

Quintus returns to Italy

When Quintus was about to board the ship, Theomnestus embraced him and handed him a bag of money. 'Take this money,' he said; 'sometime you will be able to repay me. Now farewell and look after yourself. May the gods keep you safe.' Quintus was going to thank him, but after saying this he had turned and was hurrying towards the city.

The sailors, already about to cast off the ship, were waiting for the signal of the captain, who told Quintus to make haste. He had scarcely boarded the ship, when the sailors cast off the ropes and rowed into the open sea.

Soon they raised the sails, and the ship ran quickly. They completed the journey without incident and on the fourth day arrived at Brundisium.

Quintus at once set out to reach home as soon as possible. When he was approaching Venusia, he stopped on the top of a hill and looked down on the colony. With the greatest joy he thanked the gods that he was at last seeing his beloved home.

He was about to go down to the colony when he saw an old man by the road who was laboriously tilling a field. Quintus recognized him. He was Ganymedes, an old friend of his father. He approached and greeted him. The old man gazed at his face for a long time and said at last, 'Immortal gods, can I be seeing Quintus? Why have you come back here? Surely you are not going to enter the colony?' Quintus said, 'I've come back to see my home and parents again. Why do you ask me this? What has happened?'

Exercise 38.1

1 having set out
2 to set out
3 set out!
4 they are setting out
5 about to set out
6 having died/dead
7 dying
8 about to die
9 they were dying
10 to die
11 he/she read
12 he/she is reading
13 about to read
14 (having been) read
15 he/she will read

Exercise 38.2

1 While the enemy followed, Quintus and his comrades fled to the camp.
2 When Brutus was dead, Quintus decided to return to Athens.
3 (When he was) about to set out for Athens he looked at his comrades sleeping.
4 When he arrived at Athens, he asked Theomnestus to help him.
5 Theomnestus persuaded Quintus, who was delaying in Athens, to set out for Italy.
6 After saying this Theomnestus led Quintus to the harbour, where they found a ship about to leave for Italy.
7 When the ship was about to leave, Theomnestus said goodbye to Quintus.
8 As the sun was rising, the ship sailed out of port.
9 Quintus, about to return home at last, rejoiced.

10 When he approached Venusia, he saw many strangers about to enter the colony.
11 As the sun set, he was about to go into the colony.
12 But he did not want to see his home occupied by strangers; he turned round, about to make the long journey to Rome.

Exercise 38.3

1 Flaccus in agrum profectūrus erat, sed clāmōribus Scintillae audītīs in casam recurrit.
2 in casam ingressus, eam invēnit flentem.
3 epistolā Quīntī perlectā, eam cōnsōlārī cōnātus est.
4 sed nōn poterat eī persuādēre ut sē audīret.
5 illa, cum loquī posset, eum rogāvit ut Decimum arcesseret.
6 Flaccus statim profectus est ut Decimum invenīret.
7 aedēs eius ingressus, Decimum invēnit Brundisium profectūrum.
8 Decimus Flaccō sequente ad casam festīnāvit.

P.S.

other, otherwise/differently, someone, sometimes, some number/several, several times, for some time, elsewhere

Chapter 39

Cartoon captions

1 The master said, 'Why have you come late, boys?' (The master asked the boys why they had come late.)
2 The master said, 'What are you doing Decimus? Why aren't you working?' (The master asked Decimus what he was doing and why he was not working.)
3 The master says, 'What are you doing, Sextus? Why aren't you writing your letters?' (The master asks Sextus what he is doing and why he is not writing his letters.)
4 Gaius said, 'Master, when will you dismiss us?' (Gaius asked the master when he would dismiss them.)

Quintus revisits Venusia

The farmer looked sadly at Quintus. 'Don't you know', he said, 'what has happened? Haven't you heard what a disaster our colony has suffered?' Quintus said, 'What do you mean? What has happened? Tell me where my parents are.' He replied, 'You won't find your parents here. For they've gone away. Come, Quintus, sit under a tree and listen to me. I will tell you everything.

'When Octavian returned from Greece to Italy, he dismissed his legions; it was necessary to give his veteran soldiers lands. And so he decided to take away their lands from the states which had not helped his side and divide them amongst the veterans. We knew nothing about these matters until a commission of ten men arrived at Venusia to take the lands from us. Our citizens complained bitterly; we drove the commission out of the colony. But they returned with soldiers whom we could not resist.

'Very many citizens lost their lands; amongst them was your father, Quintus. Some remained here deprived of their land, living a wretched life in poverty, like me, who was not rich but had enough; now I possess nothing but this little field, full of stones and thistles. Others went away to seek a better life elsewhere, like your father. What I tell you is sad but true. The whole of Italy is turned upside down; neither right nor laws prevail. The fields are filthy, since the farmers have been expelled. The veterans refuse to till the fields but squander their wealth in idleness.'

Quintus, moved by anguish, interrupted the old man. 'Tell me,' he said, 'where I shall find my parents. Do you know where they have gone?' The old man (replied), 'You will never find your parents, Quintus. The whole of Italy is full of needy citizens wandering this way and that.'

Hearing this, Quintus was filled with complete desperation. For a long time he sat on the ground, tears falling down his cheeks. At length he said goodbye to the old man, who asked him where he would go. He answered, 'I do not know where I shall go. The only thing I know is this: I shall search for my parents throughout the whole of Italy.'

He got up and went down the hill. But when he reached the gates of the colony, he stopped. He did not want to enter the colony and see his home occupied by strangers. He turned and took the road which led to Rome.

Quintus searches for his parents

Quintus now made the journey, which he had made so quickly with his father ten years ago, very slowly. He stayed a long time in all the villages to look for his parents. Sometimes he met people from Venusia on the road whom he asked anxiously whether they had seen his parents, but none of them could tell him where he would find them.

When he was approaching Capua, he met an old friend; Gaius, with whom he used to go to the school of Flavius, was leading a wagon which was drawn by two oxen; it was full of goods of every sort, above which sat Gaius' wife and two small children.

Quintus ran up and greeted Gaius. He gazed at Quintus and said, 'Quintus, I scarcely recognized you; for I've not seen you since you set out for Rome with your father. How are you? Why are you walking to Capua?' Quintus explained everything to him and asked Gaius whether he had seen his parents. He answered, 'I don't know where your parents are now. When the commission of ten had driven us from our lands, Flaccus and Scintilla set out from Venusia with us. But when we reached Beneventum, we delayed (there) a little, they went on to Capua. And so if you hurry to Capua, perhaps you may find them there.'

Quintus thanked him. 'You are the first person to have given me some hope,' he said. 'I will accompany you to Capua to search for my parents there.'

Exercise 39.1

1 Theomnestus asks Quintus what he has suffered (what has happened to him).
2 Theomnestus asks Quintus what he is going to do now.
3 Theomnestus asks Quintus where he wants to go.
4 We want to know when the ship is going to leave.
5 Ask the captain why the ship has not yet left.
6 I don't know when we shall arrive at port.
7 Quintus asks the old man whether he has seen his parents.
8 The old man asks Quintus whether he is going to enter the colony or journey to Rome.

Exercise 39.2

1 Theomnestus asked Quintus what had happened to him.
2 Theomnestus asked Quintus what he was going to do now.
3 Theomnestus asked Quintus what he wanted to do.
4 We wanted to know when the ship was going to leave.
5 I asked the captain why the ship had not yet left.
6 I did not know when we would arrive at port.
7 Quintus asked the old man whether he had seen his parents.
8 The old man asked Quintus whether he would stay in the colony or journey to Rome.

Exercise 39.3

1 When Quintus arrived at Venusia he did not know what had happened.
2 An old man, whom he met near the road, asked him why he had returned to Venusia.
3 'Don't you know,' he said, 'how many troubles have befallen our colony?'
4 Quintus asked the old man whether his parents

were still staying in Venusia.

5   The old man replied, 'They have left Venusia. I don't know whether they have gone to Rome or are staying in the country.'

6   Leaving Venusia, Quintus entered the road which led to Rome.

7   Setting out for Rome he asked all whom he met whether they had seen his parents.

Exercise 39.4

1   *vīdisset*. While Quintus was journeying to Rome, he met an old friend whom he asked whether he had seen his parents.

2   *sint*. He said, 'I don't know where your parents are.'

3   *discessissent*; *īrent*. Quintus asked him when his parents had left Venusia and where they were going.

4   *maneant*; *profectī sint*. He answered, 'Your parents were walking to Capua, but I don't know whether they are still staying in Capua or have set out for Rome.'

5   *factūrus esset*. He asked Quintus what he was going to do.

Exercise 39.5

1   nescīmus quō colōnus ierit.

2   puerōs rogābō num eum vīderint.

3   'scītisne, puerī, ubi colōnus sit?'

4   'eum rogāvimus utrum domum reditūrus esset an in agrō mānsūrus (esset); sed ille nihil respondit.'

5   mox colōnum vīdimus agrum intrantem. eum rogāvimus cūr nōs nōn exspectāvisset.

6   ille 'nesciēbam' inquit 'quandō mihi occurrere vellētis. domum rediī ut cēnārem, quod fessus eram.'

P.S.

1   axioms 'given'.

2   an examination of a corpse after death

3   'under the judge', i.e. the case is still being tried

4   things said in passing (not relevant to the main theme)

5   acting in the role of parent

6   by right; in fact

7   without a fixed date

8   no one speaking against, i.e. unanimously

9   great work

10   they all leave (the stage)

Chapter 40

Cartoon captions

1   While Quintus was asleep, the god Apollo seemed to stand by him.

2   Apollo said, 'Don't be afraid, Quintus; I will look after you,' and saying this he handed him his lyre.

3   Trusting in Apollo, Quintus dared to enter Rome.

4   Marcus and Quintus used to sit in the garden drinking wine.

Quintus meets an old friend

Quintus stayed ten days in Capua looking for his parents, but he made no progress. At last he sadly left Capua and took the road which led to Rome. On the way he always asked travellers whether they had seen his parents, but no one could tell him what had happened to them. At last he approached Rome but did not dare enter the city; he sat by the road, worn out by cares; soon he fell asleep.

In his sleep the god Apollo seemed to stand by him; he carried his lyre in his hands and looked at Quintus with a kind expression. 'Quintus,' he said, 'listen to me. You will never see your parents again; do not fight against fate. It is time to enter a new course of life. You must serve me and the Muses. Trusting in me, go into Rome bravely. I will look after you.' After saying this he handed Quintus his lyre; when he had done this, he vanished.

When Quintus woke up, he rejoiced at the dream. He got up and entered the city. He did not know what he was going to do in Rome, but trusting in Apollo he no longer feared for the future.

A few days later he was crossing the forum when a young man called him. He turned and saw Marcus Cicero running towards him. He embraced Quintus and said, 'Greetings, Quintus. How are you? And so you've dared to return to Rome. Come with me and tell me all that has happened to you since we were defeated at Philippi.'

Marcus took him home and when they were sitting in the garden drinking wine, he said, 'Tell me how you escaped from the battle and what you did afterwards.' Quintus told him everything; Marcus listened to him intently, then he asked what he was going to do. Quintus answered sadly; 'I don't know what I am going to do. I am wasting away from poverty. I must undertake some work to get myself bread.' Marcus was silent for a little, then he said, 'Quintus, listen to me; I have a plan. I've lately been made quaestor of the treasury. Will you help me? Will you become a clerk of the treasury? The duties are not heavy and you will receive enough money. I will gladly use your help,

Quintus. If you come to the treasury tomorrow at the second hour, I will make you a clerk.'

Quintus was delighted by Marcus' confidence (in him) and thanked him. 'My dearest friend,' he said, 'you have given me new hope. I shall be delighted to help you in the treasury. I shall be there tomorrow at dawn.' He said goodbye to Marcus and hurried home to get ready for his new duties.

The next day at dawn he was present at the treasury. He was received kindly by the chief clerk, because he was a friend of Marcus. He explained to Quintus what he had to do. The duties, as Marcus had said, were not onerous; he had to look after the public records; he gave answers to the magistrates if they asked anything about some public matter. Every day he was at the treasury at dawn; at midday his duties were finished and he used to return home.

Quintus is vexed by a malicious senator

Quintus was working in the treasury when a senator came in and summoned him in a loud voice. Quintus, occupied by business, did not run to him at once. He (the senator), a man of noble birth, was fat and arrogant; he complained because Quintus had not left his business at once and answered him. 'Hurry up, clerk,' he said; 'Don't delay. I can't hang about all day.' Quintus hurried to him; 'Greetings, my senator; forgive me. I was engrossed in business. What do you want?'

He looked at Quintus maliciously and asked who he was and who his father was. Quintus answered, 'My name is Quintus Horatius Flaccus. My father, who lived at Venusia, is dead.' When he heard this, the senator said, 'Now I remember. You are a friend of Marcus Cicero. Wasn't your father a freedman? And you, a freedman's son, became a military tribune in Brutus' army and dared to command a whole legion? No wonder Brutus was defeated, if he was forced to make the sons of freedmen tribunes.'

Quintus, who was used to hearing such insults, made no reply to this but again asked him what he wanted. He said, 'I won't do my business with a freedman's son. Call another clerk.' Quintus called another clerk who did the business with the senator. He himself retired to the record office, angry at being so insulted by such a man.

Playlet

Characters: Quintus, Sextus (the chief clerk), Metellus (an arrogant senator), Rufus (his companion)

Quintus is working in the treasury. He is putting the public record in order.

Quintus: What a lot of tablets lie in a muddle! I don't know where I should put these tablets. I must consult the chief clerk. (*he shouts*) Sextus, will you help me? Where should I put these tablets?

Sextus comes up to him.

Sextus: Look, Quintus, you must put these tablets onto that shelf, where the other tablets are placed which concern the replies of the censors.

Enter Metellus and Rufus.

Metellus: Clerk! Clerk! Come here. I want to consult you.

Quintus, who is putting the tablets in their shelf, delays a little.

Metellus: Hurry up, clerk. Don't dawdle. Hey, young man. I can't wait for you all day.

Quintus hurries to Metellus.

Quintus: Greetings, my senator. Forgive me. I was extremely busy. How can I help you?

Metellus: I am accustomed to come to the treasury often but I've never seen you before. Tell me who you are and who your father is.

Quintus: My name is Quintus Horatius Flaccus, my senator; my father, who lived at Venusia, is dead.

Metellus: Now I remember. Someone told me all about you. You are a friend of Marcus Cicero. Wasn't your father a freedman? Immortal gods, your father was a slave!

Quintus: My father was a good and honourable man. I shall never be ashamed of him.

Metellus: And you, a freedman's son, became a military tribune in Brutus' army!

Quintus: Yes indeed, my senator. I became a military tribune and was put in command of a legion at Philippi.

Metellus: No wonder Brutus was defeated if he put freedmen's sons in command of legions. Rufus, come here. Look, this clerk is the son of a freedman. What do you feel? Isn't it disgraceful to entrust the public records to the son of a freedman?

Rufus: There's no reason for you to despise him like this. Without doubt he is an active and clever young man. What does it matter if his father is a freedman? He is a Roman citizen and performs his duties well.

Metellus: Don't talk nonsense, Rufus. It's a very disgraceful business and contrary to the custom of our ancestors. I refuse to do business with a freedman's son. Call the chief clerk.

Sextus hurries to Metellus. Quintus retires into the treasury, very angry.

Exercise 40.1

1 'Do you want to buy this horse? I bought it for thirty denarii but I am willing to sell it to you for twenty denarii.'
2 'If you value it so highly, why are you willing to sell it to me so cheaply?'
3 'I am willing to sell it cheaply, because I need money now.'
4 'I value the horse much less highly than you. Moreover I already have a better horse.'
5 'Your horse is much worse than mine. How much do you think my horse is worth?'
6 'I don't think your horse is worth much (I value it at a little). I'll give you five denarii.'
7 'What do you say? Five denarii! Don't talk nonsense. I am willing to sell it to you for ten denarii.'
8 'I don't need the horse, but because you're in need of money, here, I'll give you eight denarii. But I don't know when I'm going to use such a horse.'

Exercise 40.2

1 they were rejoicing
2 having rejoiced (rejoicing)
3 rejoice!
4 you rejoiced
5 to rejoice
6 you were accustomed
7 we were accustomed
8 they are accustomed
9 having dared (daring)
10 you dared
11 I was becoming/was being made
12 she became/was made
13 to become, to be made
14 he/she is becoming/is made
15 they had become/had been made

Exercise 40.3

1 Quintus, trusting in Apollo, dared to enter Rome.
2 Quintus, having been made a secretary of the treasury, rejoiced.
3 Every day he was accustomed to hurry to the treasury, where he performed his duties diligently.
4 Quintus, insulted by the senator, was becoming angry.
5 But, being accustomed to bear such insults, he was not troubled for long.
6 For he did not put much value on the words of such an arrogant man.

Exercise 40.4

1 in maximō perīculō sumus. opus est nōbīs auxiliō. hostēs oppugnāre nōn audēmus.
2 numquam solitī estis hostēs timēre.
3 num ignāvī iam factī estis?
4 eā virtūte ūtiminī quam saepe anteā praebuistis.
5 multō fortiōrēs semper fuistis hostibus/quam hostēs.
6 deīs cōnfīsī, mē sequiminī, mīlitēs, fortiterque pugnāte ut patriam dēfendātis.

Exercise 40.5

1	(a) loquēbāmur	(b)	locūtī sumus
2	(a) gaudēbant	(b)	gāvīsī sunt
3	(a) pōnēbātis	(b)	posuistis
4	(a) fīēbant	(b)	factī sunt
5	(a) cōnfīdēbās	(b)	cōnfīsus es

P.S.

here	hither (to here)	hence (from here)
there	thither (to that place)	thence (from that place)
there	thither	thence
where?	whither? (to where?)	whence? (from where?)

Chapter 41

Cartoon captions

1 The boys are bad. (The master tells their parents that the boys are bad.)
2 The boys threw away their tablets. (The master tells their parents that the boys threw away their tablets.)
3 The boys have been sent home. (The master tells their parents that the boys have been sent home.)
4 The master will punish the boys. (The master tells their parents that he will punish the boys.)

Quintus writes poems

Quintus was now getting enough money to live modestly; he was enjoying enough leisure to compose poems. So he spent two years contentedly. He often met Marcus Cicero who learnt that he was writing poems; he asked him to recite the poems to him. When he heard them, he said that Quintus was an excellent poet. He told his friends that he had found a new poet; they wanted to hear the poems. So Quintus' reputation gradually spread abroad. Quintus hoped that he would soon complete a whole book of poems.

We quote one of these poems here, in which he praises the life of a rustic farmer:

'Happy is he, who far from business, like the ancient race of men, tills his ancestral fields with his own oxen, free of all debt. He is not roused by the savage trumpet as a soldier, nor trembles at the angry sea (as a sailor), and he avoids the forum and the proud doors (thresholds) of (over)powerful citizens. He either watches his wandering herds of lowing cattle in a remote valley, or stores the honey he has pressed in clean jars, or clips the weak ewes. He loves to lie now under an ancient ilex tree, now in the clinging grass. Meanwhile the water glides by in the deep streams, the birds complain in the woods, and the springs murmur with flowing water, which invites light sleep.' ...

When Alfius the money-lender, always on the point of becoming a country man, had said this, he called in all his money on the Ides, and sought to lend it out (again) on the Kalends.

Virgil seeks Quintus' friendship

One day, when Quintus had left the treasury, he was sitting in a pub under a tree, when a young man he did not know approached him. 'Greetings, Horace,' he said, 'I've been looking for you for a long time. I am Publius Vergilius Maro. A friend told me that you write poetry. I've long wanted to get to know you.' Quintus got up and greeted him; he answered that he had read Virgil's poems and greatly admired them.

Virgil smiled at him; he said, 'I am glad you approve of my poems. But what are you going to do today? or are you at leisure? Will you come home with me?'

Quintus was delighted that Virgil was seeking his friendship and followed him home. They sat in the garden until late at night talking to each other. Quintus recited to him the poem he had written recently about Alfius.

Virgil laughed and said, 'I too am trying to write a poem about country matters. The things which you treat jokingly, I am expounding seriously; for I sing of the toils of the farmers, the beauty of the countryside, and the innocent and peaceful life of the peasants.' Quintus asked him to recite to him some of this poem, but he said that he would not recite the poem to him. 'I've scarcely finished anything,' he said; 'I shall recite this to no one until it is finished.' At last Quintus got up and said that he must return home. When Virgil said goodbye to Quintus, he said that he had very much enjoyed their talk. 'I hope', he said, 'that you will often come here and recite your poems to me.'

Exercise 41.1

(a)	*active*	*passive*
present	dare	darī
perfect	dedisse	datus esse
future	datūrus esse	

(b)	*active*	*passive*
present	mittere	mittī
perfect	mīsisse	missus esse
future	missūrus esse	

Exercise 41.2

1 Quintus learns that his parents have left Venusia.
2 He hopes (that) he will find them on the road.
3 Gaius says that he has not seen them.
4 He believes that they have set out for Capua.
5 Apollo promises that he will look after Quintus.
6 Quintus at last knows that he will never see his parents again.
7 Marcus says that Octavian has granted him pardon.
8 Quintus rejoices that he has been made a secretary of the treasury.

Exercise 41.3

1 Quintus learnt that his parents had left Venusia.
2 He hoped he would find them on the road.
3 Gaius said that he was journeying to Capua.
4 Quintus replied that he would follow Gaius.
5 Those whom Quintus met on the road said that they had not seen his parents.
6 The friends to whom Quintus had recited his poems said that they were very good.
7 Quintus was delighted that Virgil was seeking his friendship.
8 He hoped that Virgil would approve of his poems.
9 Virgil said that he had been delighted by Quintus' poems.
10 Quintus replied that he greatly admired Virgil's poems.

Exercise 41.4

1 dīxit magistrum īrātum esse.
2 dīxit Quīntum in Italiam rediisse.
3 dīxit Quīntum parentēs quaesīvisse.
4 dīxit colōnōs ab agrīs expulsōs esse.
5 negāvit Quīntum parentēs Venusiae inventūrum esse.

Exercise 41.5

1 Marcus dīxit sē Quīntum adiūtūrum esse.
2 dīxit sē quaestōrem aerāriī factum esse.
3 spērāvit/spērābat Quīntum sē adiūtūrum esse.

4 Quīntus gaudēbat Marcum sibi cōnfīdere.
5 Quīntus sciēbat officia nōn difficilia fore/futūra esse.
6 spērāvit/spērābat sē multa carmina scrīptūrum esse.
7 amīcīs dīxit sē pauca carmina scrīpsisse.
8 amīcī eius dīxērunt carmina optima esse.
9 Quīntus contentus erat; negāvit sē unquam tam laetum fuisse.

Chapter 42

Cartoon caption

It is sweet for me to run mad when I've got my friend back.

Quintus and his friends celebrate the return of Pompeius

A few days later Quintus ran into another old friend in the forum. For he caught sight of Pompeius hurrying to the Palatium. He ran up and greeted him. 'Pompeius,' he said, 'have you returned to your fatherland at last? Come with me and tell me where you have been, what you have done and what you are going to do.' They entered a pub and ordered wine. When they had sat down, Pompeius told what he had done and what he was going to do.

He said that he had fled from the field of Philippi with the rest; for a long time he had hidden in the mountains and woods. At length he had decided to go to Sextus Pompeius and renew the war for the republic. 'He was in Sicily; I got there with great difficulty. For two years I served with him, but he was achieving nothing for the republic, he cared for nothing except getting gold and silver for himself. Finally, when Octavian promised pardon to his enemies, I slipped out of Pompeius' camp and sailed to Italy. Now at last I have returned to Rome and I am hurrying to Octavian to ask for pardon.'

'Good!' said Quintus; 'I'm glad you've come back to your country at last. I am sure Octavian will grant you pardon. For he is very keen to reconcile all his enemies to himself and to bring back Italy to peace and tranquillity (leisure). But tell me, friend, what are you going to do tomorrow? Will you dine with me? We will hold a party to celebrate your return.'

Pompeius answered that he would gladly come to dinner and went off to the Palatium to look for Octavian. Quintus hurried home to get everything ready for the party. He invited many friends to dinner and many very beautiful girls. He told his slaves to prepare the best food and wine; he sent out others to pick flowers and make garlands.

The party was magnificent; all the guests were delighted that Pompeius had returned to Rome safe; he was extremely happy because Octavian had granted him pardon. They all got extremely drunk. At last Quintus called for silence and recited a poem which he had composed to celebrate the return of his friend.

Quintus celebrates Pompeius' return with a poem

O Pompeius, who were often led into the ultimate danger with me when Brutus was commander of our army, who has given you back to the gods of our fathers and the skies of Italy, as a citizen of Rome, Pompeius, the first of my comrades? With you I often broke the lingering day by (drinking) wine undiluted, after crowning my shining hair with Syrian perfume.

With you I felt (the shock of) Philippi and swift flight, abandoning my little shield dishonourably, when Virtue was broken, and those who had threatened (so high) touched the ground with their chins in disgrace. But me Mercury swiftly carried off through the enemy in a thick mist while I trembled: (but) you the wave(s) sucked back into war again and carried you over stormy seas.

So now render to Jupiter the feast you owe him, and lay your side, tired out by long warfare, beneath my laurel tree, and do not spare the jars (of wine) marked out for you ... It is sweet for me to run mad when I've got my friend back.

Exercise 42.1

1 parāminī
2 monērī
3 regī
4 audītus es
5 caperēmur
6 positus/posita est
7 monēminī
8 lātī/lātae sumus
9 factī/factae sunt
10 āctus/ācta esset

Exercise 42.2

1 When Quintus caught sight of Pompeius in the forum, he ran to him.
2 He greeted his friend and asked him when he had returned to Rome.
3 Pompeius said he had returned to Rome to seek pardon from Octavian.
4 Quintus was certain that Octavian would grant him pardon.

5 He asked Pompeius to come to dinner. He answered that the next day he would gladly dine with Quintus.

6 Quintus called together his slaves and told them to prepare everything for dinner.

7 'Hurry up!' he said; 'get everything ready so that we may celebrate Pompeius' return.'

8 Very many friends after entering Quintus' home greeted Pompeius.

9 As the sun set Quintus told his friends not to return home.

10 'Wait a little,' he said, 'to hear the poem I have composed about Pompeius' return.'

Exercise 42.3

1 Pompēius dīxit sē in montibus cēlātum diū mānsisse.

2 dīxit sē iam Rōmam rediisse ut veniam rogāret.

3 Quīntus prō certō habēbat Octāviānum eum benignē acceptūrum esse.

4 Pompēium rogāvit ut ad cēnam venīret; dīxit multōs amīcōs invitātōs esse.

5 Pompēius prōmīsit sē ventūrum esse.

6 cum omnēs convīvae advēnissent, cēnā optimā gaudēbant multumque vīnum bibēbant.

7 cēnā cōnfectā Quīntus carmen recitāvit quod dē Pompēiō composuerat.

8 omnēs convīvae, carmine dēlectātī, Quīntum laudāvērunt.

Chapter 43

Cartoon captions

1 Quintus was sitting in the garden thinking over a poem when in ran Virgil.

2 'Come with me, Quintus,' he said; 'your poems please Maecenas so much that he wants to get to know you.'

3 Maecenas said, 'Greetings, Horace; Virgil has spoken to me of you so often that I want to hear your poems.'

4 Quintus was so shy that he could scarcely say anything.

Quintus is introduced to Maecenas

A few months later Quintus was sitting in the garden thinking over a poem, when in burst Virgil, very excited. 'Quintus,' he said, 'come with me; make haste. Maecenas is waiting for you. I have told him that you compose excellent poems; I've recited several of your poems to him, which please him so much that now he wants to get to know you.'

Maecenas was an outstanding man, an old friend of Octavian; he was rich and noble, who said that he was sprung from Etruscan kings. He had never sought office but, although he was a private knight, Octavian valued him so highly that he always consulted him about matters of the greatest importance. He cultivated the Muses and studied literature. He had helped many poets, some of whom he had received into the number of his friends.

Quintus followed Virgil and soon arrived at Maecenas' house. When they entered the reception room, Maecenas was sitting at a table reading a book. He was of short stature and fat; he was not wearing a toga but a loose tunic.

Virgil went up to him and said, 'Maecenas, I should like to introduce to you my friend Quintus Horatius Flaccus. He is a witty poet, as I have told you, and learned.' Maecenas looked at Quintus with a kindly expression and said, 'Greetings, Horace. Virgil has spoken to me about you so often that I have long wanted to get to know you. Tell me something about your parents and your career (course of life).'

Quintus was so shy that he could scarcely speak. But he spoke a few words haltingly; he did not say that he was the son of a famous father but told the truth. Maecenas answered shortly and soon dismissed Quintus. Quintus was upset because he had so failed himself that he showed himself unworthy of friendship with so great a man. Eight months passed. Maecenas did not recall him. Quintus thought that he had not pleased Maecenas; but Virgil said that Maecenas had liked him and thought highly of (approved of) his poems; but he was so busy that he was neglecting his friends; he had been away from Rome for a long time; without doubt he would recall Quintus.

Maecenas receives Quintus into the number of his friends

Quintus himself describes how he was first received by Maecenas; in this poem he says Maecenas was a noble but did not despise him because his father was a freedman. 'Many', he says, 'despise unknown men. If anyone seeks office, they ask who his father is ...

'Now I return to myself, born from a father who was a freedman, whom all run down as a freedman's son, now because I am your friend, Maecenas, but once because a Roman legion obeyed me as a tribune ... When I came into your presence, I said a few words haltingly, for dumb shyness stopped me from saying more. I do not say that I was born of a famous father ... but speak the truth. You reply shortly, as your way is: I go away; and eight months later (in the ninth month afterwards) you call me back and tell me to be numbered amongst your friends. I consider this a great thing, that I pleased you ... not because I had a famous father but because my life and heart were pure.'

He adds this: 'If I have a good character, the reason for this is my father, who, a poor man with a little farm, did not want to send me to the school of Flavius, where the big boys, sons of big centurions, went ... but dared to take me as a boy to Rome, to be taught the arts which any knight or senator has his own children taught.'

Quintus so loved his father that he always praised and thanked him. Although he was a friend of many great men and even the emperor himself, yet he was never ashamed of his father.

Exercise 43.1

1 Maecenas was so wise that Octavian always trusted him.
2 He was so keen on literature that he helped many poets.
3 He valued Virgil so highly that he accepted him into the number of his closest friends.
4 Virgil had spoken so often to Maecenas about Quintus that he wanted to get to know Quintus.
5 When Virgil had introduced Quintus to Maecenas, he was so shy that he could not speak.
6 Quintus thought that Maecenas despised him.
7 But Virgil said that Maecenas had liked him and had been delighted by his poems.
8 At last Maecenas recalled Quintus and told him to be in the number of his friends.

Exercise 43.2

1 multī tam stultī erant ut Quīntum contemnerent quod lībertī fīlius erat.
2 sed Maecēnās omnēs magnī aestīmābat quī ingeniōsī erant.
3 nōn rogāvit utrum lībertōrum fīliī essent an nōbilī genere nātī.
4 Maecēnās rēbus tam occupātus erat ut Quīntum nōn statim revocāverit.
5 nōnō tamen mense eum revocātum in numerō amīcōrum suōrum esse iussit.
6 dīxit sē Quīntī carminibus dēlectātum esse; prōmīsit sē eum adiūtūrum esse.

P.S.

1 To the departed spirits. To Simplicia Florentina a most innocent soul, who lived ten months. Felicius Simplex centurion of the Sixth Legion her father made (this monument).

2 Sacred to the departed spirits. Calliste lived sixteen years, three months, six and a half hours; she was about to marry on 15 October but died on the 12th. Panathenais her devoted mother made (this) for her dear daughter.

3 Sacred to the departed spirits. To Aurelia Vercella his sweetest wife, who lived more or less seventeen years. 'I was not, I was, I am not, I care not.' Anthimus, her husband (made this monument).

4 To the girl Aurelia Maria, a most innocent maiden, who is going in holiness to the just and elect in peace. Who lived seventeen years, five months, eighteen days, betrothed to Aurelius Damas for twenty-five days. Aurelius Janisireus, a veteran, and Sextilia her parents (made this monument) against their prayers for their most unfortunate daughter, their sweetest and most beloved child. As long as they live, they feel great grief. Holy Martyrs, keep Maria in mind.

Chapter 44

Cartoon captions

1 Maecenas asked Quintus whether he wanted to make a journey with him to Brundisium. 'If you hurry,' he said, 'you will be able to set out with Virgil.'
2 Quintus learnt that Virgil had already set out for Brundisium. If he had come earlier, he would have made the journey with Virgil.
3 Quintus said to Heliodorus, 'Don't let us set out today. If we set out tomorrow, we shall reach Aricia at midday.'
4 They arrived at Aricia in the evening. If they had walked quicker, they would have arrived there at midday.

Quintus makes a journey to Brundisium

One day Maecenas sent for Quintus and said, 'I have to make a journey to Brundisium. Do you want to accompany me? Virgil will be there and other friends. If you set out at once with Virgil, I will meet you at Anxur. For I'm so tied up with business that I cannot start today.'

Quintus hurried to Virgil's house but when he arrived, he learnt that he had already started with other friends. And so he went on to Heliodorus; for he had learnt that he too was going to make the journey. But unless he had hurried, he would have arrived too late; for he found Heliodorus just about to set out. 'Heliodorus,' he said, 'it is nearly midday. If we were to leave at once, we would not get far before night. If we start early tomorrow, we shall reach Aricia at midday.' And so they decided to set out the next day.

And so they left Rome early and walked to Aricia and stayed the night in a modest inn. The next day, when they reached Forum Appi, they found the roads filled with sailors. Heliodorus said, 'Why are there so many sailors running this way and that? What are they doing?' Quintus said, 'No doubt those sailors steer the barges along the canal.' 'What do you mean, Quintus?' said Heliodorus; 'where is that canal? I'm very tired. If we go on on foot, I shall die of exhaustion (toil). Let's hurry to the canal. If we were to board a barge, we would travel much more easily.' And so they decided to board a barge, so that they could sleep, while the mule dragged the barge along the canal.

Horace himself describes the journey like this:

When I left great Rome Aricia received me in a modest inn: my companion was the rhetor Heliodorus, far the most learned of the Greeks; from there we went on to Forum Appi, stuffed full of sailors ... Now night was preparing to draw darkness over the earth and to scatter the constellations in the sky ... While the fare(s) are taken, while the mule is harnessed, a whole hour passes. Nasty mosquitoes and marsh frogs prevent sleep, while a sailor plastered with lots of cheap wine and a passenger sing in competition of their absent girlfriend(s): at last the passenger, worn out, begins to sleep, and the lazy sailor sends the mule to graze, ties its halter to a rock, and snores lying on his back. And now day was at hand, when we realized that the barge is static (proceeding not at all), until one quick-tempered passenger jumps up and whacks the head and loins of mule and sailor with a willow club. Eventually at the fourth hour we are put ashore.

When Quintus was put ashore, he said, 'We've completed this journey slowly, certainly, but easily, Heliodorus. If the canal were longer, I should prefer to go on in the barge rather than on foot. Now we must climb laboriously to Anxur.' They climbed slowly to Anxur, which is situated on top of a hill which shines with white rocks, where they met Maecenas. Then they hurried on to Sinuessa:

The next dawn rose most welcome (to me); for Plotius and Varius and Virgil met us at Sinuessa.

A long and laborious journey still awaited them. Sometimes they experienced very bad roads, sometimes they suffered heavy rain. Heliodorus was nearly worn out by the effort; if Quintus had not helped him, he would have given up the journey. They passed Venusia; Quintus would have entered and seen his old home, if he had not known that the colony was full of strangers and empty of friends. At last they reached Brundisium, the greatest port of all Italy.

Maecenas reconciles Antony with Octavian

The next day Quintus and Virgil accompanied Maecenas to the port and said goodbye to him. He said, 'Goodbye, friends, and thank you for making the journey with me; if I had travelled alone, I should have died of boredom. Now you must go back the same way. Don't dawdle. If you were to set out at once, you would reach Rome in fifteen days.' After saying this, he boarded the ship.

Maecenas had to sail to Athens to meet Antony. For Octavian had sent him to Athens to reconcile Antony, who was becoming hostile, to him. If Maecenas had not managed the business with the greatest skill, he would not have effected a reconciliation. But he finally persuaded Antony to come to Italy and help Octavian against Sextus Pompeius.

But soon Antony returned to the East, sent back to Italy his wife Octavia, Octavian's sister, and summoned Cleopatra queen of Egypt to Syria. When his sister had been so insulted, Octavian was moved with such anger that he decided to make war on Antony.

While Antony dallied in Egypt with Cleopatra and neglected public affairs, Octavian prepared for war; he won over the whole people of Italy (to himself) and little by little increased his authority. Day by day he became more powerful.

Exercise 44.1

1 If you had fought bravely, you would have conquered the enemy.
2 If our father were alive, he would be giving us advice.
3 Unless Quintus had fled from the field (of battle), he would have been captured by the enemy.
4 If Quintus were wise, he would not be serving in Brutus' army.
5 If we set out at once, we would get home before night.
6 If the boys had been good, the master would have told them a story.
7 The master said, 'Boys, if you were to work hard, I would tell you a story.'
8 The mother said to her daughter, 'If you helped me, father would praise you.'
9 The girl said, 'Mother, if I were at leisure, I would gladly be helping you.'
10 If the girl had not been busy, she would gladly have helped her mother.

Exercise 44.2

1 Unless Pompeius had served with Sextus Pompeius, he would have returned to Italy long ago.
2 If Pompeius at last returns, we will all rejoice.

3 If you had asked Octavian for pardon, he would have forgiven you.

4 If Octavian were to pardon me, I would stay in Rome.

5 If you dine with me, we will celebrate your return.

6 If you drink more wine, you will be completely drunk.

7 Unless we were celebrating the return of Pompeius, we would not be drinking so much wine.

8 If Quintus recites another poem, I shall go off home.

9 Unless there were pretty girls here, I would have gone off long ago.

10 You are a barbarian, if you were not delighted by this poem.

Exercise 44.3

1 (*future vivid*) sī mox domum redieris, omnia tibi dīcam.

2 (*future less vivid*) sī statim proficīscāris, duōbus diēbus hūc adveniās.

3 (*contrary to fact*) sī Rōmae nōn morātus essēs, tibi Capuae occurrissem.

4 (*simple fact*) sī mē Capuae exspectāvistī, stultissimus erās.

5 (*contrary to fact*) sī nunc adessēs, sub arbore mēcum sedērēs vīnum bibēns.

Chapter 45

Cartoon caption

I happened to be going along the Sacred Way.

Quintus is persecuted by a bore

Meanwhile Quintus was living in Rome contented with his lot. He performed his duties in the treasury conscientiously. He had now written so many poems that his reputation was spreading more widely. Many praised his talents. A few, inspired by envy, ran him down. Others cultivated his acquaintance because they hoped he would help them. So someone might say to him, 'I wish I could be received into the number of Maecenas' friends! You are an intimate friend of his. And so you could introduce me to him, if you wanted. Come on, won't you take me to him?' Quintus used to answer, 'Forgive me, friend. I would not dare to introduce to Maecenas a man I scarcely know.'

He tells a story about a bore who hoped Quintus would introduce him to Maecenas:

I happened to be going along the Sacred Way, as my custom is, thinking over some nonsense, entirely engrossed in it. Up runs someone known to me only by name and seizes my hand. 'How are you doing, my dear fellow?' he says. 'Very nicely, at present,' I say, 'and I want all that you do.' When he followed me, 'Do you want anything,' I put in. '(I want) you to make my acquaintance,' he said; 'I'm a learned man/poet.' Then I replied, 'For this you will be worth all the more in my eyes.' Miserably wanting to get away, I sometimes walked quicker, sometimes stopped, whispered something or other into my slave's ear, while sweat poured down to the bottom of my ankles. 'O Bolanus, blessed in your quick temper,' I said to myself, while he was talking some nonsense or other, praising the streets or the city. When I made him no answer, 'You are miserably longing,' he said, 'to get away. I've seen this long ago; but you are getting nowhere; I'll cling on to you. I shall follow you from here wherever you are now going.' 'There's no need for you to be taken out of your way,' (I answer); 'I want to visit someone you don't know: he's in bed a long way off, across the Tiber, near the gardens of Caesar. 'I've got nothing to do and I'm not lazy: I'll follow you the whole way.' I put back my ears like a bad-tempered donkey, when too heavy a burden lands on its back.

The bore, as he had promised, followed Quintus the whole way. Quintus tried to send him away but got nowhere. He said to his boy, 'I wish I could get rid of this bore, but he keeps holding on to me. What are we to do? Let's hurry home as soon as possible.' Then he (the bore) tried to persuade Quintus to introduce him to Maecenas. When Quintus said he could not do that, he replied, 'I don't believe you; let's go to him at once. I should not want to lose such an opportunity.'

At that very moment a friend of Quintus ran into them. Quintus greeted him and gave a sign, rolling his eyes, for him to rescue him. But he, who grasped the whole situation, pretended not to understand; he said goodbye to Quintus; the wicked fellow fled and left Quintus in the hands of the bore.

Quintus had been reduced to absolute desperation, when an opponent at law of the bore ran up to him and shouted in a loud voice, 'Where are you going, you villain? Come to justice.' He rushed him off to the law-courts. 'So' said Quintus, 'Apollo saved me.'

Quintus wants to escape the racket of the city

Quintus was living a modest life, contented with his lot. He did not envy the rich and powerful men with whom he was now friends. He never said to himself, 'I wish I had been born of a noble family! I wish I were a senator!' For the nobles were always tied down by business and duties, (while) he himself enjoyed leisure so that he could compose his poems free from care. When they (the nobles) were hurrying through the streets of the city to some business, a crowd of clients and slaves always accompanied them; himself (Quintus) he used to walk alone wherever he wanted to go. Sometimes he went to the shops and asked how much cabbage and flour were; in the evening he wandered round the Circus and the Forum; he used to stand by the fortune-tellers who (fore)told fortunes. From there he he made his way back (took himself) home to a modest dinner. Then he went to bed, not worried because he had to get up early tomorrow. The next day he would lie in bed until the fourth hour; when he had got up, he would either read or write something. 'This is the life', he said, 'of men free from miserable and oppressive ambition.'

Exercise 45.1

1 What am I to say to you?
2 Where are we to go?
3 Are we to resist the enemy or flee?
4 How am I to get rid of that bore?
5 When are we to depart from Rome?

Exercise 45.2

1 Long life and good health! (May you live and be healthy!)
2 I wish I were rich.
3 I wish you had not said this to me.
4 May the gods preserve you.

Exercise 45.3

1 (*deliberative*) What am I to do, friend? How am I to persuade Octavian to pardon me?
2 (*jussive*) Let us go to the palace. I am sure he will pardon you.
3 (*optative*) May Octavian receive us kindly!
4 (*potential*) Octavian, I should like to introduce my friend Pompeius to you.
5 (*optative*) Greetings, Pompeius. I wish you had not helped my enemies so long.
6 (*potential*} But I rejoice that you have at last come to ask for pardon. I gladly forgive you. For I would not want to punish anyone who asks for pardon.
7 (*jussive; optative*) Let us lay down all enmity. From now on may we always enjoy peace and harmony.

Exercise 45.4

1 utrum hīc maneāmus an domum festīnēmus?
2 hīc maneāmus; nōn possumus domum ante noctem pervenīre.
3 nōn ausīm iter noctū facere.
4 utinam nē tam sērō profectī essēmus.
5 utinam domī incolumēs iam essēmus.
6 in magnō perīculō sumus. utinam deī nōs servent.

7 prīmā lūce domum proficīscāmur.

P.S.

1 Publius Decimius, freedman of Publius, Eros Merula, doctor, physician, surgeon, oculist, priest of Augustus. This man gave 50,000 sesterces for his freedom. He gave 2,000 sesterces to the republic for his priesthood. He gave 30,000 sesterces for setting up statues in the temple of Hercules. The day before he died he left an estate of ? sesterces.

2 To the departed spirit(s) of the freedman Euhelpistus. He lived twenty-seven years, four months, eleven days: sudden death stole from him the years of his prime. A most innocent soul, whom the doctors cut and killed. Publius Aelius, freedman of Augustus, Peculiaris (made this monument) for his foster child.

Chapter 46

Cartoon captions

1 Maecenas said, 'Quintus, if you are at leisure, come with me tomorrow to the Sabine hills.'
2 Night had come when at last they arrived at the farm. If they had hurried, they would have arrived before sunset.
3 Maecenas said, 'If we had ridden more quickly, you could see the whole farm now.'
4 The next day Maecenas said goodbye to Quintus. If he had been free, he would have stayed with Quintus on the farm.

Quintus becomes a countryman

A few months later Maecenas summoned Quintus. When Quintus had arrived, he was led into the study. Maecenas was alone. He got up and smiled at him. 'Quintus,' he said, 'I have summoned you because I should like to offer you a gift. You have now become a distinguished poet. You need leisure, so that you can compose your poems far from the smoke and racket of Rome. If you owned a house in the country, you could enjoy tranquillity. And so I've decided to give you a little farm. It's thirty miles away from the city, lying in the Sabine hills. If you come back tomorrow at the first hour, we will go there together to inspect the farm.'

Quintus had always wanted to live in the country but scarcely hoped that he would ever own a farm. The next day Maecenas and Quintus set out at the first hour to inspect the farm. After advancing into the Sabine hills, they at last entered the valley of the Digentia and if they had hurried, they would have arrived at the farm before night. But they rode slowly, enjoying the beauty of the countryside. Night was already falling when they arrived.

Quintus was astonished; for it was not a little farm, as Maecenas had said, but a fair estate. On the side of the hill was placed a villa, large enough; there were eight slaves there who would look after Quintus and till the fields. Near the house was a spring of ever-flowing water. The place was lovely, the view most beautiful. The next day Maecenas led Quintus all round, delighted that he was so pleased.

At last, 'Quintus,' he said, 'if I were at leisure, I would be staying here with you, but I am so loaded with business that tomorrow I must return to Rome. But you may, if you like, stay here.' Quintus was so delighted that he could scarcely speak. 'Dearest friend,' he said, 'I shall never be able to give you adequate (worthy) thanks. You have given me what I most wished for.' Maecenas smiled at him; 'Quintus,' he said, 'you have well deserved all this; you are a faithful and modest friend. Unless I had wanted to keep you in Rome, I would have given you the farm long ago.'

The next day, when Quintus had said goodbye to Maecenas, he inspected everything again; going into the garden, he sat under a tree and composed these verses:

This was one of my wishes: a plot of land, not so very big, where there would be a garden and, near the house, a spring of ever-flowing water and above these a little woodland. The gods have done more generously and better (than this). It is well. I ask for nothing more, son of Maia, except that you should make these gifts my own (for ever).

The spring of Bandusia

Quintus got up; he called the farm manager and said, 'If you are at leisure, I should like to inspect the farm.' The farm manager led him first to the vineyard, then to the olive grove. Finally, when they had watched for some time the slaves reaping the crops, they climbed the hill to the spring. Cool water, brighter than glass, was leaping down from the hollow rocks into a pool, from which a stream flowed into the valley with a gentle murmur. Above the spring was a tall ilex tree which gave welcome shade to both men and beasts. Quintus was greatly delighted by this place. He turned to the farm manager and said, 'How lovely this place is! What is the name of this spring?' 'The spring is called Bandusia,' he said. 'Does it please you?' 'It pleases me very much,' said Quintus. 'I will stay here a while.'

Quintus sits on the bank; he looks at the water leaping down into the pool and the goats lying in the shade of the ilex tree, while the kids play on the grass. Inspired by the beauty of the place, he composes this poem:

O spring of Bandusia, more sparkling than glass, deserving (offerings of) sweet wine together with flowers, tomorrow you will be given a kid, whose forehead, swelling with its first horns, marks it out for battles of love; in vain! for the child of the wanton flock will stain your cool stream with red blood. You the cruel hour of the burning Dogstar cannot touch, you give coolness welcome to the oxen worn out by the plough and to the wandering flock. You too will become one of the famous springs, when I tell of the ilex tree which stands upon the hollow rocks from which your chattering waters leap down.

Exercise 46.1

1 amēmus
2 dīcerent
3 secūtī essent
4 proficīscāmur
5 gaudeant
6 sint
7 vellent
8 ferrēmus
9 nōlim
10 possīs

Exercise 46.2

1 Maecenas said that he would give Quintus a little farm.
2 He said, 'You need leisure, so that you may compose poetry. I should like to help you.'
3 He asked him to return the next day at the first hour.
4 'Let us go', he said, 'to the Sabine hills to look at the farm.'
5 When Quintus had seen the farm, he was so happy that he could scarcely speak.
6 After seeing the farm Quintus tried to thank Maecenas.
7 But Maecenas said that he (Quintus) had well deserved all this; for he was a loyal and modest friend.
8 Unless he had been occupied by much business (many businesses), he would have stayed with Quintus on the farm.
9 The next day, when Maecenas had set out for Rome, Quintus called the farm manager and said, 'Come with me; I should like to inspect the farm.'
10 After inspecting the whole farm, Quintus composed a song sitting by the spring.
11 He composed such a beautiful song that the Bandusian spring is now numbered amongst the famous springs.
12 He valued the farm so highly that he always wanted to stay there and returned to Rome reluctantly.

Chapter 47

Actium

While Quintus rested on his Sabine farm, the republic was again being rushed into civil war. When Octavian and Antony accused each other of the most serious crimes, they conceived more hatred for each other every day. At length Octavian prepared openly for war. The whole of Italy swore allegiance to him and demanded him as leader in the war. Those senators who supported Antony left Rome and fled to Antony.

But Antony divorced Octavia, whom he had sent back to Rome long ago, and proclaimed that Cleopatra was his wife. When the senators learned this, they at once declared war on Cleopatra.

Without delay Antony assembled huge forces and led them to Greece to meet Octavian. But Octavian, leaving Maecenas in Rome to govern Italy, set out for Brundisium with Agrippa, who was the best of his generals. When he had transported his forces across the sea to Greece, he pitched his camp at Actium, not far from Antony's camp.

Agrippa joined battle with Antony's fleet and defeated the enemy so (soundly) that he controlled the sea. Antony, since his soldiers besieged by land and sea were dying of disease and hunger, was finally forced to break out. He left nineteen legions on the shore to defend his camp and led his fleet out of harbour, with Cleopatra following.

For four days there were such tremendous storms that they could not join battle. On the fifth day, when the sea was calm, each fleet advanced to battle. For a long time they fought on equal terms, when suddenly Cleopatra turned her ship and led the Egyptian fleet into flight. When he saw this, Antony ordered his helmsman to follow the queen. He burnt with such love for Cleopatra that he valued his own honour and the safety of his men less than one woman.

While Antony was fleeing with Cleopatra, his fleet and his land forces, although they were deserted by their leader, bravely resisted the enemy; but at last they gave up hope and surrendered to Octavian. He treated the captives humanely. He thought that neither Antony nor Cleopatra could resist him any longer; now he ruled the whole world. And so he showed mercy so that he freed all who had surrendered and received them into his army.

Virgil describes the battle of Actium

This battle, by which the fate of the Roman empire was decided, Virgil describes in the *Aeneid* as follows:

In the middle (of the shield) it was possible to see the bronze-beaked ships, the battle of Actium, and you could see the whole of Leucate seething with warships in formation and the waves gleaming with gold. On this side was Augustus Caesar, leading the Italians into battle, together with the Fathers and the people, the gods of Rome and the great gods, standing on the high poop ... in another part Agrippa, standing out, leading his column with the help of the winds and the gods ... On that side Antony with the help of barbarians and motley arms brings Egypt and the powers of the East and furthest Bactra with him, and there follows him (what wickedness!) an Egyptian wife. All rush together ...

Exercise 47.1

1 Quintus and Maecenas, when they had left Rome at the first hour, rode into the Sabine hills.
2 It was already evening when they reached the villa.
3 Although Quintus was tired, he still wanted to inspect the villa.
4 Maecenas said, 'Since it is night, we can see little.'
5 Quintus said, 'As soon as the sun has risen, I shall inspect everything.'
6 The next day when Maecenas had set out for Rome, Quintus called the farm manager.
7 Although the farm manager was busy, he nevertheless hurried to Quintus.
8 They had looked at everything when Quintus dismissed the farm manager.
9 Since Quintus wanted to rest, he sat near the spring.
10 When he was resting under a tree, he composed a poem.
11 Whenever summer came, Quintus hurried to the hills.
12 Whenever he returned to Rome, he always longed for his farm.

Exercise 47.2

1 While Antony delayed at Actium, Octavian's forces pitched camp not far off.
2 While (all the time that) Antony was being besieged by land and sea, his soldiers were dying of hunger and disease.
3 Agrippa besieged Antony until he (Antony) was forced to break out.
4 Antony waited in camp for the sea to be calm/until the sea should be calm.
5 While Antony was attacking Agrippa's fleet, Cleopatra suddenly fled.
6 While (all the time that) Antony was fleeing with Cleopatra, his forces were fighting bravely.
7 Octavian waited for them all to surrender.
8 While Antony was fleeing to Egypt, Octavian received the captives into his army.

Exercise 47.3

1 Cleopatra led her fleet into flight. When Antony saw this, he followed her.
2 Antony saw Cleopatra fleeing. He loved her so much that he also fled from the battle.
3 When Agrippa saw this, he attacked Antony's fleet even more fiercely.
4 At last Antony's soldiers surrendered. Octavian treated them humanely and received them into his army.
5 When Antony learnt this, he despaired.

Chapter 48

Cartoon caption

Cleopatra, fearing she might fall into the hands of Octavian, killed herself.

The war at Alexandria

After Antony had fled to Egypt with Cleopatra, Octavian followed them very slowly through the East. The next year, while his fleet sailed for Alexandria, he himself led his army through Syria into Egypt. Antony was so desperate that he did not attempt to resist Octavian as he entered Egypt. Battles were joined near Alexandria by land and sea. Antony's fleet deserted to Octavian in the middle of the battle; on land his army was easily defeated.

Then at last Antony was afraid that, if he fell into the hands of the enemy, he would be taken as a captive to Rome. He said to his armour bearer, 'May I die before I suffer such a disgrace. But I fear Cleopatra may be taken by the enemy. Let us hurry to the city.' On returning to Alexandria it was reported to him that Cleopatra had died by her own hand. When he heard this, he ordered his armour bearer to kill him. But he, a loyal youth, drew his sword and killed not Antony but himself. Antony, looking at the young man lying on the ground, said, 'You have done well; you have given me an example. May I be no more cowardly than you.' So saying, he drew his sword and drove it into his belly.

He fell to the ground, gravely wounded but not yet dead. While he lay there, up ran Cleopatra's secretary and reported that the queen was still alive. When Antony learnt this, he told his soldiers to carry him to Cleopatra. She had shut herself up in a high tower, which she refused to leave, fearing that she would be betrayed to Octavian. When the soldiers arrived there carrying Antony, she told her slaves to lower ropes from the window and lift Antony to her. So Antony died in the arms (lap) of Cleopatra.

At that very moment a messenger arrived sent by Octavian, to persuade Cleopatra to leave the tower and give herself up. Octavian promised that he would treat her with the utmost humanity. But she did not believe him and refused to leave the tower. For she was afraid that Octavian wanted to lead her captive through the streets of Rome when he celebrated his triumph; this disgrace she could not bear.

The death of Cleopatra

When Octavian had taken Alexandria, he again tried to persuade Cleopatra to give herself up. When Cleopatra refused to leave the tower, he took her by a trick. For while Cleopatra was talking to a messenger sent by Octavian, he sent two men to climb into the tower; they moved a ladder up to the tower and burst through a window and seized Cleopatra.

When Octavian had captured Cleopatra he guarded her with the greatest care, in case she should kill herself. But she found a way to death. An old man entered the prison and asked the guards to admit him to the queen; he said he wanted to give Cleopatra a gift; he showed them a basket full of figs and told them to taste the figs. They suspected nothing and admitted the old man to the queen. Cleopatra accepted the gift and sent then old man away.

When she was alone, she looked at the basket carefully; under the figs were hidden two little serpents. She sent everyone away except two faithful maidservants; she put on her most beautiful clothes and all her royal regalia. The she lifted the serpents from the basket and applied them to her breasts. She quickly drank down the poison into her body. So died the last queen of Egypt, a woman of excellent beauty and proud heart.

Horace's ode on the death of Cleopatra

... She sought to die more nobly; she did not tremble at the sword like a woman, and did not make for hidden shores with her swift fleet; she dared to look on the ruins of her palace with face serene, she had the courage to handle the cruel serpents, to drink their black poison deep in her body, all the fiercer because she had planned her death, begrudging, surely, the fierce Liburnian galleys that she should be led no more a queen in the proud triumph, no humble woman.

Exercise 48.1

1 Maecenas was afraid that they would not arrive at the farm before night.
2 'Hurry up, Quintus,' he said; 'I am afraid we may arrive late.'

3 Quintus said, 'My horse is tired; I am afraid to ride more quickly.'

4 The boys, fearing that the master would be angry with them, were working hard.

5 They were afraid the master would not let them go.

6 The girls, fearing that the boys may follow them, are hurrying home.

Exercise 48.2

1 Following our leader we soon arrived at the city.

2 Setting out at first light I returned home before night.

3 Cleopatra, fearing that she would be betrayed to Octavian, refused to leave the tower.

4 Cleopatra, gazing at Antony, knew that he would die.

5 The old man, entering the prison, greeted the guards.

Exercise 48.3

1 festīnēmus; timeō nē sērō adveniāmus.

2 puerī, veritī nē magister sibi īrāscerētur, extrā iānuam lūdī exspectābant.

3 puellae intrāre nōn timēbant; sciēbant enim magistrum sibi nōn īrātūrum esse.

4 Cleopātra, verita nē Antōnius vincerētur, cum nāvibus suīs fūgit.

5 Antōnius nōn timēbat pugnāre, sed amōre Cleopātrae superātus eam secūtus est.

P.S.

1 To Tiberius Claudius, son of Drusus Caesar Augustus Germanicus, high priest, holding tribunician power for the eleventh year, consul for the fifth time, emperor, father of his country, the Senate and Roman people (dedicated this arch) because he conquered eleven kings of Britain without any loss and received their submission (received them into surrender) and first brought under the control of the Roman people the barbarian nations living beyond the Ocean.

2 To Gaius Gavius, son of Lucius, Silvanus, senior centurion of the sixth legion Augusta, commander of the second cohort of watchmen, commander of the thirteenth urban cohort, commander of the twelfth praetorian cohort, donated gifts by the Divine Claudius in the British war, chains, bracelets, medals, golden crown; patron of his colony. (This monument was set up) by the decree of the town councillors.

Chapter 49

Caesar Augustus

When Antony and Cleopatra were dead, Octavian decided to delay in the East to settle things there. If he had not done this, without doubt wars would have been renewed. And so he strengthened the provinces of the Roman empire with strong garrisons; he made treaties with neighbouring kings, so that there should not be wars on the borders of the empire. At last, when all was settled, he could return to Rome.

The senate and people received him with the greatest joy and the highest honours. All believed that wars were finished and that never again would citizens fight with citizens. Many said, 'This man, a second Romulus, has founded Rome anew; he alone has saved our empire; we should worship him like a god.'

At that time, if Octavian had wanted to become king, he could easily have attained this; but he knew that the name of king was hateful to the Roman people. 'Many years ago,' he said, 'we drove out the kings; we must not restore them now.' Although he had now won control of everything, yet he said in the senate that he wanted to restore the republic and give the people back their liberty. Many years afterwards, when he was advanced in age and near to death, he published a testament, in which he wrote these words: 'In my sixth and seventh consulship, after I had put an end to civil wars, and had won control of everything through the agreement of all, I transferred the republic from my power into the control of the senate and people of Rome.'

The senators heaped thanks upon him but begged him not to fail the republic and not to lay down power. They loaded him with more honours; amongst other things they voted that he should be called by the name Augustus; this name so pleased him that from that time he called himself Caesar Augustus. At last he yielded to the prayers of the senators and received a sphere of power by which he governed several provinces. But he never called himself 'emperor', but 'leading citizen'.

And so in words he restored the republic, but in fact he so excelled all in authority that he was always increasing his power. Most of the citizens accepted this state of affairs gladly; for all were weary of wars and were afraid that, unless one man ruled Rome, civil wars would start again. If any of the nobles could not bear his power, he either kept quiet, or, if he could not keep quiet, he was allowed to retire into exile.

But although he had put an end to civil wars and given the Roman people peace again, Augustus himself was not allowed to enjoy peace and leisure. For it was necessary to undertake wars with many foreign peoples.

Beyond the borders of the Roman empire lived barbarian tribes which were always threatening the provinces. He realized that the Roman empire would never be safe, unless he extended its boundaries to the Rhine and the Danube rivers. To do this, for many years either he himself or other leaders campaigned and added many peoples to the Roman empire.

The poets were always singing that Augustus would both cross the sea to conquer the races of Britain and would lead his army against the Parthians, lest he should leave the disaster suffered by Crassus unavenged. But Augustus decided not to do these things. He never ceased to seek peace and embarked on no war unless it was necessary to fight. In the East he made a treaty with the Parthians. He suffered no disaster except, when he was old, in Germany, where three legions under the command of Varus fell into an ambush and were totally destroyed. Augustus always grieved for this disaster; they say he often shouted in his sleep: 'Varus, give me back my legions.'

Virgil praises Augustus

Augustus loved to practise eloquence and liberal studies from his first youth. He not only studied literature and wrote poems himself, but he also always encouraged poets, especially Virgil, whom he held in the number of his closest friends; for he believed that Virgil could help him, if he praised the new state of affairs in his poems. And Virgil thought that all good men should praise Augustus, because he had at last given Italy peace; for he (Virgil) had seen the republic torn apart by continual wars, he had seen right and wrong turned upside down, he had seen the Roman empire almost brought to destruction. This is what he had written when civil war was still raging:

... right and wrong are turned upside down: so many wars throughout the world, so many forms of wickedness, no honour worthy of the plough, the fields are unkempt, the farmers evicted, and curved sickles are beaten into unbending swords ... Wicked Mars rages throughout the whole globe.

Virgil now believed that Augustus alone could preserve peace. In the first book of the *Aeneid*, when Jupiter is revealing the secrets of the fates to Venus, he says that one day Augustus will bring the peoples of the world a golden age and restore peace throughout the globe:

Caesar shall be born, a Trojan of glorious origin, to bound his empire with the Ocean, his glory with the stars ... then wars shall cease (be laid aside) and the generations of violence shall grow gentle: the terrible ... gates of War shall be closed; inside wicked Madness sitting on top of his savage arms ... shall growl horridly with his bloodstained mouth.

Exercise 49.1

1 Octavian decided to delay in the East.
2 It was necessary to strengthen the provinces with garrisons.
3 At last he was allowed/he could return to Rome.
4 All the citizens were tired of civil wars.
5 When shall we be allowed to enjoy peace?
6 We ought to obey Octavian, because he has restored peace to the Roman people.
7 Maecenas delighted to look after poets.
8 Quintus was tired of the racket of the city.
9 Maecenas decided to give Quintus a farm.
10 Quintus ought to have returned to Rome, but he decided to stay at the farm.

Exercise 49.2

1 It was announced to Antony that Octavian was advancing into Egypt with all his forces.
2 He decided to join battle near Alexandria.
3 There was a fierce battle by land and sea; but at last Antony's forces fled.
4 All the captives were spared by Octavian.
5 Octavian's forces advanced to Alexandria. When they came into the city, he sent a messenger to Cleopatra.
6 Cleopatra was ordered to leave the tower.
7 The messenger said, 'If you surrender, you will be pardoned.'
8 But she was not persuaded to surrender.

Exercise 49.3

1 prīmā lūce profectī in collēs festīnāvimus; ante merīdiem ad summum montem ventum est.
2 nōbīs placuit ibi duās hōrās manēre.
3 sed nōbīs nōn diū quiēscere licuit.
4 nam pāstor quīdam nōs monuit nē morārēmur nōbīsque persuāsum est ut statim dēscenderēmus.
5 iter longum erat et difficile, et antequam domum advēnimus, montium mē taeduit.

Chapter 50

Cartoon caption

Livia made the wool with her own hand; she never failed in performing the duties of a Roman matron.

Augustus receives Quintus into his friendship

Maecenas and Virgil had introduced Quintus to Augustus; soon he too was received into the number of the friends of the emperor, who was so fond of him that he wanted to make him his secretary. For he sent a letter to Maecenas in which he said this: 'Up till now (before) I was capable of writing letters to my friends: but now, as I'm extremely busy and weak in health, I want to take our Horace from you. And so he will come and help me in writing my letters.'

Maecenas sent for Quintus and told him what Augustus wanted. 'You ought', he said, 'to obey the emperor, but I don't believe this will please you.' Quintus was glad that the emperor had such confidence in him and had offered him so great an honour, but he did not want to change his present course of life. When he had heard Maecenas' words, he said, 'Dear friend, if I were to obey the emperor, I should not have enough leisure to write poetry nor could I revisit my farm to reflect. And so I would not want to do this.'

Maecenas said, 'Don't worry yourself; be brave. Tell him you are not worthy of so great an honour; say you are not strong enough to undertake so great a task. You can be certain that he's a sensible and kind man; he will understand the situation; he won't be angry with you.'

And so Quintus answered the emperor as Maecenas had advised. Augustus accepted his excuse patiently and did not cease to keep him in the number of his friends.

Quintus often went to the palace to recite his poems to Augustus and his wife Livia. He was amazed how modestly they lived. Livia provided an example of the Roman matron. She was a chaste woman, loyal to her husband, of outstanding beauty and sharp intellect; and she never failed in performing the duties of a Roman matron; she ran the household herself; she made the wool with her own hand. She was always loved by Augustus, who died with these last words: 'Livia, live on and don't forget our marriage; farewell.'

Quintus remains a bachelor

Quintus himself had never married; he preferred to live free from marriage to cultivate his art. But he had loved many girls, had been loved by many, and had written many love poems. In these poems he never seems to burn with passion, but laughs gently at either the girl or other lovers or his own self. For he looked on human life (affairs) as a comedy, which should arouse laughter rather than tears. Often if he began to treat a subject seriously, he drove out sadness and turned the matter into a joke. When you start to read a poem, you cannot know where he's going to lead you. When he was getting older, he said goodbye to girls like this:

I have lived till recently a paragon for the girls and have fought gloriously (in the wars of love). Now this wall shall keep my arms and my lyre whose wars are over, this wall which guards the left-hand side of (the temple of) sea-born Venus. Put here, put here the shining torches and crowbars and bows which

threatened doors shut in my face. But queen, goddess, who dwell in blessed Cyprus and Memphis which knows not Scythian snow, lift your whip and touch Chloe, who was proud, just once.

Exercise 50.1

1 Quintus learnt the art of speaking at Rome.
2 Then he came to Athens to study philosophy.
3 By studying hard he learnt many things there.
4 He left Athens to serve with Brutus.
5 He showed himself very brave in resisting the enemy.
6 When Brutus was dead, he returned to Italy to look for his parents.
7 After being made a secretary of the treasury by Marcus, he had enough leisure for writing poems.
8 By pardoning his enemies Octavian won over all the citizens to himself.
9 Pompeius returned to Rome to ask for pardon.
10 Quintus called together all his friends to celebrate Pompeius' return.

Exercise 50.2

1 vēnimus ad mīlitandum cum Brūtō.
2 nam pugnat lībertātem dēfendendī causā.
3 nōnne audīvistis signum prōgrediendī?
4 nōlīte morandō vōs servāre cōnārī.
5 fortiter pugnandō hostibus victīs rempūblicam servābimus.
6 Quīntō imperātum est ut legiōnem in Antōniī cōpiās dūceret. (Quīntus iussus est ... dūcere.)
7 fortiter pugnātum est sed tandem victus est Brūtus.
8 Quīntus, scūtō abiectō, ad castra currendō sē servāvit.
9 ibi nūntiātum est Brūtum mortuum esse.
10 omnēs sē servāvērunt in silvās fugiendō.

P.S.

1 To Flavia Publicia, chief vestal virgin, a most holy and religious woman, who through all the steps of the priesthood serving duly with pious heart at the divine altars of all the gods and at the eternal fires day and night, deservedly came to this position in the course of time (literally: with age), Bareius Zoticus together with his Flavia Verecunda (dedicated this memorial) because of her outstanding kindness to them. Dedicated on 30 September when our lords Valerianus Augustus (for the fourth time) and Gallienus Augustus (for the third time) were consuls.

2 Although Claudia Rufina was born from the woad-painted (blue) Britons, how Latin is her heart (literally: how she has the heart(s) of the Latin

race)! What beauty of figure! Italian mothers can believe that she is Roman, Athenian that she is one of them (their own) ... So may it please the gods that she always rejoice in her only husband and her three children.

Chapter 51

Cartoon caption

I wondered why the Muses had visited me early in the morning, standing before my bed as the sun rose red.

Maecenas encourages poets

Maecenas held Virgil and Horace amongst his closest friends, but he encouraged other poets too and urged them to compose songs. From time to time he called a number of his friends to his house to listen to recitations. Amongst others Sextus Propertius sometimes attended these recitations, a poet of passionate temperament, who wrote very many poems to his girl, called Cynthia. This is how he celebrates Cynthia's birthday: he says that as the sun was rising the Muses visited him to remind him of his girl's birthday:

I wondered why the Muses had visited me early in the morning, standing before my bed as the sun rose red. They brought a sign of my girl's birthday and three times clapped their hands in sounds of happy omen. May this day pass without a cloud, may the winds stand still in the sky, and may the waves lay their threats softly on the shore. May I see none grieving in today's light, and may that very stone which was Niobe cease her tears.

Another poet, Albius Tibullus, was a friend of Horace who often sang of country matters and enjoyed a course of life free from both business and riches.

Horace wrote a letter to him when he had retired to the Pedane district to write poems and study philosophy; he followed the precepts of the Stoics, who said that the wise and good man should care for nothing but virtue. But Horace inclined towards the teaching of Epicurus, who asserted that the highest good for men was pleasure. Albius was often sad and querulous. In this letter Horace was trying to comfort him by reminding him how many good things the gods had given him:

Albius, honest critic of my *Satires*, what should I say you are doing in the Pedane district? Writing something to outdo the little works of Cassius of Parma? Or strolling silently among the health-giving woods, pondering (caring for) whatever is worthy of the wise and good man? You were never a body without a heart. The gods have given you good looks, the gods have given you riches and the ability to enjoy them ... You should believe that every day that has dawned for you is your last. The time (hour) which is not expected will arrive to your delight. You will find (visit) me fat and sleek, in good condition, when you want a laugh, a pig from Epicurus' sty.

The death of Virgil

Time was flying; both Quintus and Virgil were now older. Virgil, who had never enjoyed good health, was now often ill. But he made a journey to Greece to visit the monuments. But when he had arrived in Athens, he met Augustus who was returning from the East, who persuaded him to come back with him to Rome. On the journey he was attacked by illness and died at Brundisium. Augustus brought his body back to Campania and arranged for it to be buried at Naples.

When Virgil was about to set out for Greece, Quintus had written a poem in which he prayed to the gods to keep Virgil safe. He invoked the ship which was carrying him:

Ship, which owe (me) Virgil who has been entrusted to you, deliver him safe, I pray, to the shores of Attica, and keep safe half of my soul.

Virgil had arrived safe at the shores of Attica, but Quintus' prayers had been in vain. He mourned the death of his dearest friend without cease.

Exercise 51.1

1 Maecenas called together his friends to listen to the poets.
2 Amongst others Propertius came to recite a poem.
3 By reciting his poem very well he earned the greatest applause.
4 Tibullus had retired to the country to compose poems.
5 Horace tried to console Tibullus by writing a letter to him.
6 Horace used to go to the palace to greet Livia.
7 Livia provided an example of a Roman lady in carrying out her duties.
8 Augustus asked Horace to help him in writing his letters.
9 Horace said, 'If I were to obey the emperor, I should not have enough leisure to compose poems.'
10 Maecenas replied, 'Tell the emperor that you are not strong enough to undertake so great a work.'

Exercise 51.2

quondam prīnceps Quīntum ad palātium arcessīvit. cum eō advēnisset, Līviam in tablīnō invēnit lānam facientem. eam rogāvit cūr Augustus sē arcessīvisset; illa autem negāvit sē scīre. ille ad prīncipem festīnāvit, quī eum benignē accēpit.

'Quīnte,' inquit, 'tē rogō ut mē adiuvēs. tot negōtiīs occupātus sum ut omnēs epistolās scrībere nōn possim. vīsne tu ad palātium cotīdiē venīre ut mē adiuvēs in epistolīs scrībendīs?'

Quīntus attonitus est sed nōn timēbat vēra dīcere. 'prīnceps,' inquit, 'gaudeō tē mihi tantum/adeō cōnfīdere. mē oportet tē adiuvāre. sed tantō honōre nōn dignus sum, et timeō nē sī hoc faciam nōn satis ōtiī habeam ad carmina compōnenda.'

prīnceps Quīntum nōn coēgit sibi pārēre sed excūsātiōnem eius aequō animō accēpit.

P.S.

1 Andragoras took a bath with us, he dined cheerfully, and yet (literally: the same man) was found dead in the morning. You ask the reason for so sudden a death, Faustinus? In his sleep he had seen Dr Hermocrates.

2 What have you to do with us, you wicked schoolmaster, creature hateful to boys and girls? The crested cocks have not yet broken the silence: already you are thundering away with savage murmurs and beatings. We neighbours do not ask for sleep all night: for to lie awake is a light matter, (but) to lie awake throughout (the night) is serious. Dismiss your pupils. Will you, chatterbox, take as much to keep quiet as you receive to shout?

Chapter 52

Peace and emperor

Since all wars were ended at last, the gates of the temple of Janus were closed, which meant that there was peace throughout the whole Roman empire. And so Augustus decided to consecrate a new age by celebrating the secular games. He called Quintus to him and said, 'Quintus, as you know, we are preparing the most holy games to usher in a new age. We must do everything to carry this out with the utmost reverence. I shall see that a magnificent altar is built, on which sculptors will illustrate the gifts of Peace. The new age must also be celebrated in sacred song. This song, dearest friend, you must write.' Quintus was delighted

that the emperor had such confidence in his genius and hurried home to think out a poem.

Carmen Saeculare

At last the time came for the games. For three days the whole Roman people kept holiday. The games were celebrated with the greatest reverence and the greatest sanctity. On the first day Augustus with Agrippa made sacrifices on the Capitol hill to Jupiter best and greatest and to queen Juno. On the third day sacrifices were made to Apollo and Diana on the Palatine; that night, when the priests had duly performed the sacrifices, a chorus of boys and girls sang Horace's song:

Phoebus Apollo and Diana, queen of the woods, shining glory of the sky, O ever to be worshipped and ever worshipped, grant what we pray for at this sacred time, when the Sibylline verses have advised us that chosen girls and pure boys should sing a song to the gods whom the seven hills delighted ... now Loyalty and Peace and Honour and old-fashioned Shame and Virtue, long neglected, dare to return, and blessed Plenty appears with her overflowing horn ...

So Horace celebrates the new age, not only celebrating peace but recalling all those ancient virtues, relying on which the Romans had advanced their city from small beginnings to so great an empire. Wars were now over and the republic was about to start a golden age. This had to be celebrated by the whole Roman people.

Exercise 52.1

1 The games must be celebrated with the greatest piety.
2 The whole people must keep holiday.
3 Augustus had to perform sacrifices on the Capitoline hill.
4 On the third day all the citizens had to come together to the Palatine.
5 A chorus of boys and girls will have to sing Horace's poem.
6 Hurry, friends; we must set out at once.
7 Night is at hand; if we delay, we shall have to stay the whole night on the mountains.
8 We shall not be able to get home today; we must wait here for the sun to rise.
9 We must look for a shepherd who will receive us into his cottage.
10 If we don't find a shepherd, we shall have to sleep in the wood; so we will be safe.

Exercise 52.2

1 Maecenas handed the letter to his runner to be carried to Quintus.
2 Maecenas arranged for many friends to be called

together to hear the recitation.

3 When all the wars were finished Augustus arranged for the Secular Games to be celebrated.

4 Horace composed a song to be sung in honour of (for) Apollo and Diana.

Exercise 52.3

1 omnibus bellīs cōnfectīs, portae Iānī templī claudendae sunt.

2 pāx quā nunc fruimur semper servanda est.

3 novum saeculum nōbīs lūdīs celebrandum est.

4 Horātius carmen optimum scrīpsit chorō cantandum.

5 omnibus cīvibus ad montem Palātīnum festīnandum est.

6 ibi carmen nōbīs audiendum erit quod scrīpsit Horātius.

Exercise 52.4

Quīntus dīcēbat/dīxit sē in fundō suō ōtiō fruī posse carminibus compōnendīs. eum iūvit librōs veterum legere ōtiōsumque in umbrā iacēre. sed rē vērā cum ad fundum revēnerat, semper eī dīligenter labōrandum erat. vīlicum vocāvit cūrāvitque/vīlicō vocātō cūrāvit agrōs arandōs; puerōs ēmīsit quī ovēs custōdīrent; ipse suīs manibus saxa ex agrīs removēbat. ūvae carpendae erant vīnumque faciendum. cum vesper adesset, saepe vīcīnōs ad cēnam vocābat; postquam modestē cēnāvērunt, in hortō sedēbant vīnum bibentēs atque dē philosophiā colloquentēs. vix dīcere possēs Quīntum ignāvum esse, sed hāc vītā contentus erat semperque trīstis cum Rōmam redeundum erat.

P.S.

1 Love conquers all things; let us too yield to Love.

2 Happy the man who could find out the causes of things!

3 Fortunate too is he who knows the gods of the country.

4 So great a task it was to found the Roman race.

5 Do not trust the horse, Trojans! Whatever it is I fear the Greeks even when they bring gifts.

6 Recall your courage and put aside sad fear; perhaps some day you will delight to remember even this.

7 I have lived, and completed the course which Fortune had given me.

8 Trojan son of Anchises, the descent to Hell is easy; night and day the door of black Dis (king of the underworld) is open; but to recall your steps and to escape to the upper air, this is the task, this is the toil.

9 They stood praying to be the first to cross the stream and held out their hands in longing for the further shore.

Chapter 53

Cartoon captions

1 The smoke and noise of the city were hateful to Quintus.

2 Whenever he had retired to his farm, he used to move the rocks from the fields with his own hand.

3 If it rained a lot, he was very anxious about his vines.

4 He himself used to pick the grapes with his farm manager, who was a great help to him.

Quintus the countryman

As Quintus became older, he stayed longer on his farm. For he was tired of business and the din and smoke of the city were still hateful to him. When he was staying in the city, he often used to say to himself:

O country, when shall I see you? And when shall I be allowed to enjoy sweet forgetfulness of the anxious life, now with the books of the ancients, now in sleep and laziness?

He preferred to live in the hills throughout the summer, afraid that he might fall ill, if he stayed in Rome. For very many were attacked by fever, if they endured the heat of summer in the city.

And so Quintus, after spending the summer on his farm, when winter came, used to go down to the sea and spend the winter near Naples. For the temperate climate of the place was very useful to his health. At the beginning of spring, when the west winds were blowing and the first swallow had returned to Italy, he sent a message to Maecenas to say that he would soon return to Rome.

One summer, when he was about to leave Rome for his farm, he promised Maecenas that he would stay in the country for only five days; then he would return to Rome and visit Maecenas. But when he arrived at the farm, he was so content that he did not want to go back to Rome but stayed in the country the whole of August. And so he had to write a letter to Maecenas, to confess that he had proved a liar; he begs his friend to forgive him:

After promising that I would be in the country for five days, I've been missed for the whole of August; what a liar I am! And yet, if you want me to live sound and in good health, you will grant me (the same) pardon when I'm afraid to fall ill, as you grant me when I actually am ill, Maecenas ... But when winter spreads the snows on the Alban fields, your bard will go down to the sea and spare himself and read books all huddled up; he will revisit you, dear friend, together with the Zephyrs, if you allow him to, and the first swallow.

When Quintus was staying on his Sabine farm, he really did become a countryman. He sent out the slaves to reap the crops. He appointed boys to guard the sheep. With his own hands he moved stones from the fields, he picked the grapes and made the wine himself. The wine he had made on his own farm, he offered to his guests; so, when he was inviting Maecenas to dinner, he said:

You will drink cheap Sabine wine from modest cups, wine which I myself stored and sealed in a Greek wine jar.

If it seldom rained, Quintus was anxious about the crops; if hailstones poured down on the vineyard, he was afraid for the grapes. For he so loved his farm that he always revisited it with joy, and was always sad when he had to return to Rome.

The country mouse and the town mouse

With such a life he was completely content and did not envy others who were richer than he. He told a story to warn us not to wish for too much. In this story a country mouse is persuaded to visit a city friend and taste the joys of the city:

Once a country mouse is said to have entertained a city mouse in his poor hole, an old host (entertaining) an old friend.

The country mouse brought out the best things from his poor store to delight his proud guest; he accepted them disdainfully and scarcely tasted them.

At length the town mouse said to him, 'Why do you choose, friend, to live in misery (suffering) on the ridge of a steep wood? Wouldn't you prefer men and the city to wild woods? Get going with me, trust me. Since earthly creatures live with mortal souls, and there is no escape from death for great or small, therefore, good friend, while you may, live happily in pleasure; live remembering how short your life is.' When these words had struck the country mouse, he leapt lightly from his home; then they both complete their intended journey, longing to creep under the walls of the city at night.

Midnight had already come when they entered a wealthy house. The town mouse placed his guest on a couch and put before him a magnificent feast:

He, reclining (on his couch), rejoiced in his change of fortune ... when suddenly a tremendous banging of doors shook them both from their couches.

They ran through the whole dining-room, terrified; at the same time the house echoed with (the barking of) dogs.

Then the country mouse said, 'I've no use for this life; goodbye: my wood and my hole, safe from traps, will comfort me with a little vetch.'

Exercise 53.1

1 The crops were a great anxiety to Quintus.
2 Hailstones sometimes destroyed the grapes.
3 The farm was always dear to Quintus.
4 Livia was an example to the Roman ladies.
5 Licentious women were hateful to her.
6 Livia was a great help to Augustus.
7 'Don't you want to buy this dog? He will be very useful to you.'
8 'I already have a dog which is dear to me and which guards the sheep well.'
9 'But your dog is weak; without doubt this dog will be a help to you.'
10 'That dog seems savage to me; I am afraid that it may destroy the sheep.'

Exercise 53.2

1 saying (participle)
2 you said
3 (having been) said (participle)
4 saying (gerund)
5 about to say (participle)
6 to be said (gerundive)
7 say! (imperative)
8 to have said (infinitive)
9 we shall say
10 let us say/we may say
11 having spoken (participle)
12 to speak (infinitive)
13 speaking (gerund)
14 speaking (participle)
15 to be about to speak (infinitive)
16 he might speak
17 speak! (imperative)
18 they might have spoken
19 let us speak
20 you were speaking

Exercise 53.3

1 Augustus left five legions in the East to guard the borders of the provinces.
2 He equipped four fleets to destroy pirates and keep merchants safe.
3 In the city of Rome he instituted watches to protect the citizens from robbers and fires.
4 He guarded the public roads throughout Italy so that travellers might journey more safely.
5 Quintus sent a messenger to Maecenas to tell him that he would soon return to Rome.

Exercise 53.4

1 hic canis pāstōrī magnō auxiliō erat.
2 nam magnō ūsuī erat in ovibus dēfendendīs.

3 itaque pāstōrī cordī erat.

4 cum ā lupō vulnerātus esset, pāstōrī magnae cūrae erat.

5 pāstōris uxor canem summā cūrā fovēbat sed nihil prōfēcit.

6 pāstor medicum arcessīvit quī eum cūrāret, sed medicus eum servāre nōn potuit.

7 uxor pāstōris dīxit alium canem emendum esse.

8 sed novus canis pāstōrī nōn ūsuī erat in ovibus custōdiendīs.

9 pāstor dominum rogāvit ut sibi bonum canem daret quī ovēs custōdīret.

10 dominus nūntium ad pāstōrem mīsit quī dīceret sē canem optimum eī mox datūrum esse.

Exercise 53.5

Quīntus Maecēnātī suō salūtem plūrimam dat. cum Rōmā discēderem, prōmīsī/pollicitus sum mē quīnque diēbus reditūrum esse. adhūc tamen fundō meō adsum. tē rogō ut mihi ignōscās. calōrem enim aestātis in urbe ferre nōn possum; in collibus mihi manendum est dum vēnerit autumnus. sī nunc Rōmam redeam, sine dubiō aegrōtem; tū autem trīstis sīs, sī audiās mē febre mortuum esse. praetereā valdē occupātus sum. poēma scrībō dē arte poēticā, quod et longissimum est et difficillimum. cum aestas praeterierit, Neāpolim dēscendam brūmamque ibi peragam. sed simul ac redierit vēr prīmamque vīderō hirundinem, Rōmam festīnābō spērōque mē tē ibi vīsūrum esse.

P.S.

1 You may drive out Nature with a pitchfork, but she will always come running back.

2 Those who run across the sea change the sky, not their minds.

3 While we speak, jealous time will have/has fled; pluck (the flowers of) today, trusting as little as possible in tomorrow.

4 He died wept by many good men.

5 Remember in trouble to keep a level mind.

6 We are all hurried the same way.

7 If the world were broken and fell upon him, the ruins will strike him unafraid.

Chapter 54

Cartoon caption

To the departed spirits. To Quintus Horatius Flaccus. He lived for fifty-seven years. He died lamented by many good men.

Invincible death

As Quintus became older, he was often sad; now death seemed to threaten both himself and his friends. In a poem which he wrote to a friend called Postumus, he said this:

Alas, Postumus, Postumus, the years glide flying by and your piety will bring no delay to wrinkles and the attack of old age (old age pressing on) and invincible death ...

One day, sitting under the ilex tree above the spring of Bandusia, he had begun to turn over past times in his mind. He recalled to mind old friends; he remembered the living, of whom Maecenas was now ill and Pompeius was growing old in a villa near the sea; nor indeed did he forget the dead, Marcus Cicero, who had become consul and proconsul of Asia, Virgil, who had died with the *Aeneid* unfinished, his sister and parents, whom he missed even now, and the many friends who had perished in the civil wars.

Spring was drawing near; the sun was shining; a light breeze shook the trees; cool water was flowing from the spring with a gentle murmur. Everything was beautiful, everything fostered quiet and tranquillity. But Quintus was sad. He was trying to complete that poem which he had written many years ago about the return of spring and about the joys which spring brings with it. Now he had become both older and wiser. He had learnt that all things beautiful quickly pass, that life is short, that death awaits all, that no one comes back from the dead:

The snows have fled away; now grass returns to the fields and leaves to the trees. Earth changes its seasons, and the rivers growing smaller flow between their banks. Grace with the Nymphs and her two sisters dares to lead the dance unclothed. The (passing) year and the hour which snatches away the kindly day warn you not to hope for immortality. The cold (of winter) grows mild before the west winds (of spring), summer presses on spring, summer which will perish itself as soon as fruitful autumn has poured out its harvest, and soon winter comes running back to numb us.* But the swift(ly passing) moons make good the losses in heaven: we, when we die and go down where father

---

iners = inactive, sluggish; it is untranslatable and we have lifted a phrase from the translation of James Michie.

Aeneas, where rich Tullus and Ancus have gone, are dust and a shadow. Who knows whether the gods above will add tomorrow's times to the sum of today? Everything which you give to your dear self will escape the greedy hands of your heir. When once you die and Minos has given his majestic judgement on you, neither your birth, Torquatus, nor your eloquence, nor your piety will bring you back. Diana cannot free Hippolytus from the darkness of the underworld for all his chastity, and Theseus cannot break the chains of Lethe for his dear Perithous.

He had finished his poem; he got up and returned slowly to the house. He had scarcely crossed the threshold when his farm manager with tears falling down his cheeks ran up to him. 'Master,' he said, 'I have received the saddest news: Maecenas is dead.' Although Quintus had long known that Maecenas was seriously ill, he was struck by anguish. He went silently into his study and for a long time he mourned alone for his closest friend, who had so often helped him, who had always been kind, always generous. Afterwards he learnt that Maecenas had written this to Augustus in his will: 'Remember Horatius Flaccus as you remember me.' Quintus had now lost all his dearest friends; he was tired of life. A few months later he himself died; he was buried on the Esquiline hill near the tomb of Maecenas.

Exercise 54.1

1 When the civil wars were finished Augustus gave peace back to the Roman people. (ablative absolute)
2 But the Roman empire would never have been safe, unless he had extended the boundaries to the rivers Rhine and Danube. (contrary to fact conditional clause)
3 To do this, either he himself or his generals campaigned for many years and added many foreign nations to the empire. (purpose clause)
4 The poets sang that he would lead his forces against the Parthians, lest he should leave the disaster received by Crassus unavenged. (indirect statement; negative purpose clause)
5 But they did not know what Augustus had in mind; for he undertook no war, unless it was necessary to fight. (indirect question; open conditional clause)
6 He received one disaster, by which Varus was destroyed in Germany with three legions. Augustus never forgot this disaster. (connecting relative; genitive after **obliviscor**)
7 At length, when peace was restored throughout the empire, he decided to celebrate the secular games. (ablative absolute; impersonal verb)
8 Quintus had to write a song, which a chorus of boys and girls sang at the games. (gerundive of obligation; relative clause)
9 When Maecenas had died, Quintus was tired of life. (**cum** = when (past); impersonal verb)
10 For he was afraid that with all his friends dead he might be left alone. (clause of fearing)

P.S.

1 I drove into exile those who had murdered my father and afterwards, when they were bringing war against the republic, I twice conquered them in battle.
2 I often waged wars, both civil and foreign, by land and sea over the whole globe, and in victory I spared all citizens who asked for pardon. I preferred to preserve rather than destroy foreign nations which I could safely pardon.
3 The senate voted that the temple of Janus, which our ancestors wished to be closed when peace had been won by land and sea throughout the whole Roman empire, should be closed three times when I was leader.
4 I extended the boundaries of all the provinces of the Roman people on which there were neighbouring peoples that did not obey our rule. I added Egypt to the empire of the Roman people. For this service I was called Augustus by decree of the senate.
5 In my sixth and seventh consulships after I had put an end to civil wars, (though) through the agreement of all I had absolute power (controlled all things), I transferred the republic from my power to the control of the senate and the Roman people.
6 From that time on I exceeded all in influence, but had no more power than the others who were my colleagues in each magistracy.
7 When I wrote this, I was in my seventy-sixth year.

Tacitus *Annals* 1.2

When he had seduced the soldiers by gifts, the people by the corn dole, all by the attractions of peace, he increased his powers little by little and drew to himself the functions of the senate, magistrates, and laws, with no opposition, since (all) the boldest men had fallen through war or proscriptions, and (as for) the rest of the nobles, the readier any of them was for slavery, the higher they were raised in wealth and honours, and, grown great from the new dispensation, they preferred their present safety to the old dangers ... And so the state of the nation was turned upside down and nowhere was found any of the old, honest (Roman) character: all looked to the orders of the emperor.

P.P.S.

The violence then burst out more fiercely; there were more leaders of the mutiny. And a certain Vibulenus, a common soldier, lifted up on the shoulders of bystanders before the tribunal of Blaesus, said, 'You (the mutineers) have given back light and life to these innocent and unhappy men: but who is giving back life to my brother, who is giving back my brother to me? Last night Blaesus murdered him through the gladiators, whom he keeps and arms to destroy his soldiers. Answer, Blaesus; where have you thrown his corpse? Not even enemies begrudge burial (to the dead). When I have sated my grief with kisses and tears, then order me too to be slaughtered.'

He inflamed these words by tears and beating his breast and face with his hands. In this way he roused such a tumult that the soldiers came near to killing their commander (Blaesus). But they did drive out the tribunes and the prefect of the camp; their baggage was plundered as they fled, and the centurion Lucilius was killed, to whom they had given the nickname 'Give me another', because when he had broken his staff on the back of a soldier in a loud voice he used to demand another and then yet another.

Appendix I

Do you, Roman, remember to rule the peoples by your authority (these shall be your arts), and to make peace the norm, to spare the conquered and war down the proud.

1 Augustus

I pacified the sea of pirates ... I extended the boundaries of all the provinces of the Roman people which bordered on nations which did not obey our empire. I brought peace to the provinces of Gaul and Spain, and also Germany, where the Ocean forms the boundary from Cadiz to the mouth of the river Elbe. I brought peace to the Alps from the district which is nearest to the Adriatic sea to the Tuscan sea, without waging war on any people unjustly ... I added Egypt to the Roman empire ... The peoples of Pannonia, which no army of the Roman people had ever approached before I was leading citizen, I brought under the empire of the Roman people, and I extended the boundaries of Illyricum to the river Danube.

2 Virgil

Aeneid 1.276–96
Romulus shall take over the (Trojan) race and found the walls of Mars and call (his people) Romans after his own name. For these I set no bounds of space or limits of time: I have given them dominion without end. Even savage Juno will change her plans for the better, and together with me will cherish the Romans, lords of the world and the togaed race ... There shall be born a Trojan of fair origin, Caesar, to bound his empire at the Ocean, his glory at the stars. Then wars shall end and the generations of violence will grow gentle: grey haired Faith and Vesta, and Romulus together with his brother Remus shall make the laws; the gates of War, grim with their close-knit fastenings of iron, shall be closed; wicked Madness, sitting inside on top of his savage arms and bound by a hundred knots of bronze behind his back, shall roar horribly from his bloody mouth.

Aeneid 6.788–853
Now turn your two eyes this way, look on this race, your Romans. Here is Caesar and all the descendants of Iulus destined to come beneath the great vault of heaven. This is the man, this is he whom you have often heard promised to you, Augustus Caesar, son of a god, who will found again in Latium a golden age throughout the fields once ruled by Saturn. He shall extend the empire beyond the Garamantes and the Indians; their land lies beyond the stars, beyond the annual path of the sun, where Atlas who bears the heavens turns on his shoulder the axle-tree (of the sphere of heaven) studded with burning stars ...

Others will beat out bronzes which breathe more softly (I can believe it) and coax living faces out of marble, they will plead cases better, they will plot the wanderings (of the stars) of heaven with the (astronomer's) rod and foretell the rising of the constellations: but you, Roman, must remember to rule the peoples by your authority (these shall be your arts) and to make peace the norm, to spare the conquered and war down the proud.

3 Tacitus

The Britons, quite unbroken by the outcome of the earlier battle and awaiting either vengeance or slavery, and taught at last that their common danger must be averted by unity, roused the powers of all their states by embassies and treaties. And now over thirty thousand armed men could be seen, and still the warrior youth was streaming in when Calgacus is said to have spoken as follows before a vast crowd assembled and shouting for battle:

'Whenever I consider the causes of the war and our

own peril, I have great confidence that the union you have formed today will be the beginning of freedom for the whole of Britain: for you have all united and you are untouched by slavery, and there are no lands beyond this, and not even the sea is free from danger, since the Roman fleet threatens us. And so battle and arms, which are the honourable course for the brave, are also the safest for cowards ... There is no people beyond us, nothing but waves and rocks, and the Romans are more hostile (than these), whose pride you would try in vain to escape by obedience and restraint. Plunderers of the whole world, when there is no more land for their universal pillage (when land has failed them laying waste everything), they set their eyes on the sea: if an enemy is rich, they are greedy, if he is poor, they are eager for glory; neither East nor West will have sated them: of all the world they alone lust after wealth and want with equal eagerness. Using false names, they call plundering, murdering, raping 'empire' and where they create a desert, they call it peace.

'Nature willed that each man's children and relations should be his dearest: these are carried off by conscription to serve elsewhere; even if wives and sisters escape the lust of the enemy, they are defiled by those who call themselves (in the name of) friends and hosts. Our goods and fortunes are worn away by tribute, the annual produce of our fields by the corn tax, our very bodies and hands in making roads through woods and marshes while subject to beatings and insults. Slaves born into servitude are sold once and then are even fed by their masters: but Britain buys its servitude every day and feeds it every day ... And so since all hope of mercy is gone, at last take heart ... The Brigantes, led by a woman, could burn a colony, storm a camp and throw off the yoke: we are untouched (by the Romans) and unsubdued and brought up for liberty; let us show at the very first clash what sort of men Scotland has kept (for herself) in reserve.

'Here is your general, here your army: there is tribute, the mines and the other penalties suffered by slaves, penalties which according to the outcome of this battle (it depends on this field) you must either endure for ever or avenge at once. And so as you are about to enter battle think of both your ancestors and your posterity.'

Appendix: The metres of the poems in Part III

Teaching scansion

Latin poetry was written to be read aloud. Its publication was usually at a *recitātiō* and the ancients attached prime importance to the sound of verse. The purpose of teaching scansion is simply to help your students to feel the rhythms of the poems and read them rhythmically. Any lesson on metre should begin with one or more readings aloud by the teacher. If from the start your students have learnt correct pronunciation, they may well feel the rhythm of metres they have never studied, before they know anything about scansion.

It would be wise to start the study of metre not with dactylic hexameters but with a very simple metre such as iambics; Horace: *Epode* 2 (chapter 41) is not only the first verse quoted in our book but also the right starting point for a study of metre.

Quantity

The scansion of Latin verse of the classical period is quantitative, not accentual as in English. Syllables are either light or heavy, regardless of where the accent falls on any given word.

(a) All syllables are heavy which contain a long vowel or diphthong, e.g. **laetī, sōlēs, Rōmānī**. For the purposes of scansion heavy syllables are marked with a macron ‾, light syllables with the symbol ˘. This convention sometimes results in a syllable containing a short vowel being marked with a macron; see below.

(b) If a short vowel is followed by two consonants, whether in the same or in different words, the syllable is heavy, e.g.

tāntāe | mōlĭs ĕ|rāt Rōmā̄nām | cōndĕrĕ | gēntĕm.

In this line the syllables underlined are heavy although in each case the vowel is short.

(c) Exceptions to rule (b): if a short vowel is followed by a combination of mute (**p, t, c, b, d, g**) and

liquid (**r** and less commonly **l**), the syllable may be scanned either light or heavy, e.g. **pă̆tris, volŭcris, latĕbrae**. This is really a question of pronunciation; such syllables can be pronounced either **pāt-ris** or **pă-tris** (**tr** making one sound).

Elision

A final open vowel followed by a vowel in the next word is elided, as in the French *c'est*, but in Latin the elision is not written, e.g.

cōntĭcū̆|ēr(e) ōm|nēs īn|tēntīqu(e) | ōră tĕ|nēbānt

The final **e** of **conticuēre** elides before the following **o** of **omnia** and the final **e** of **que** elides before the following **ō** of **ōra**.

hūc sē | prōvēc|tī dē|sērt(ō) īn | lītŏrĕ | cōndūnt

The final **ō** of **dēsertō** elides before the following **i** of **in**.

More surprisingly, a final syllable ending **-m** elides before a following vowel, e.g.

pārs stŭpĕt | īnnūp|tāē dōn(um) | ēxĭtĭālĕ Mĭ|nērvāē

The **-um** of **dōnum** elides before the **e** of **exitiāle**.

In reading Latin verse the elided vowel or syllable should be lightly sounded.

The metres

Iambics

An iambic metron (measure) consists of two iambic feet: ˘ ‾ ˘ ‾ . A spondee (‾ ‾) may be substituted for an iamb in the first foot of each metron:

˘ ‾ ˘ ‾

The last syllable in the line in all types of metre may be long or short (anceps).

The commonest iambic line is the iambic trimeter; this scans, counting in feet, as follows:

$$\overset{1}{\smile}\ \overline{}\ \Big|\ \overset{2}{\smile}\ -\ \Big|\ \overset{3}{\smile}\ \overline{}_{\wedge}\ \Big|\ \overset{4}{\smile}\ -_{\wedge}\ \Big|\ \overset{5}{\smile}\ \overline{}\ \Big|\ \overset{6}{\smile}\ \breve{}$$

There is a caesura, i.e. a rhythmical pause between words, half way through the third or fourth foot, marked ∧. The only example of iambics in Part III is Horace: *Epode* 2 (chapter 41), where iambic trimeters alternate with iambic dimeters:

bĕā|tŭs īl|lĕ ∧ quī | prŏcūl | nĕgōtĭīs

ūt prīs|că gēns mōrtā|lĭūm

Dactylic hexameters

The dactylic hexameter consists of six dactylic metra (-‿‿). A spondee (- -) may be substituted for a dactyl in any of the first four feet; the fifth foot is nearly always a dactyl and the sixth is always a spondee or -‿ . There is usually a strong caesura (a break between words after the first long syllable of the foot) in the middle of the third foot:

ārmă vĭ|rūmquĕ că|nō, ∧ Trōĭ|ae quī | prīmŭs ăb | ōrīs

(3rd foot strong caesura)

If there is a weak caesura (a break between words after -‿) or no caesura in the third foot there are usually strong caesuras in the second and fourth feet:

quīdvĕ dŏ|lēns ∧ rē|gīnă dĕ|ūm ∧ tōt | vōlvĕrĕ | cāsūs

(3rd foot weak caesura;
strong caesuras in 2nd and 4th feet)

īndĕ tŏ|rō ∧ pătĕr | Aenēās ∧ sīc | ōrsŭs ăb | āltō

(no 3rd foot caesura;
strong caesuras in 2nd and 4th feet)

This is the metre used by Homer and all subsequent epic poets. Virgil uses it in his *Eclogues*, *Georgics* and *Aeneid*. Horace uses it in all the *Satires* and *Epistles*.

Elegiac couplets

These consist of a dactylic hexameter followed by the first half of the same (up to the third foot strong caesura) repeated. In this book they are only used in the lines of Propertius quoted in chapter 51:

mīrā|bār quīd|nām ∧ vīs|īssēnt | mānĕ Că|mēnae,

āntĕ mĕ|ūm stān|tēs ∧sōlĕ rŭ|bēntĕ tŏ|rŭm.

Lyric metres

There is a wide variety of lyric metres which first appear in the poems of Sappho and Alcaeus, who wrote in the Aeolic dialect about 600 BC. Horace claims to have been the first to adapt these metres to Latin poetry (*Odes* 3.30.13–14):

dīcār ...
prīnceps Aeolium carmen ad Italōs
dēdūxisse modōs.

But Catullus had in fact led the way in the previous generation.

In these metres, which are dance rhythms, we cannot speak of feet or metra; the unit is the line and many systems are constructed in four-line stanzas. Most Aeolic metres contain a unit called the choriamb (-‿‿-) and the lines are built up round one or more of these. They usually consist of a base (e.g. - -, ‿-), choriamb(s), clausula (a closing cadence which can take various forms). Thus the line quoted above scans:

prīncēps | Aeŏlĭūm | cārmĕn ăd Ī|tălōs

i.e. base (- -), two choriambs (-‿‿- -‿‿-) and clausula (‿-).

The lyric metres illustrated in this book are:

Asclepiads
All Asclepiad metres, of which there are several forms, consist of base (- -), one or more choriambs, clausula. Horace: *Odes* 3.13 (chapter 46) is the only example in this book:

ō fōns | Bāndŭsĭae, | splēndĭdĭŏr | vĭtrō

dūlcī | dīgnĕ mĕrō | nōn sĭnĕ flō|rĭbŭs,

crās dŏ|nābĕrĭs hae|dō

cuī frōns | tūrgĭdă cōr|nĭbŭs

Sapphics
This is the favourite metre of Sappho. It is composed in four-line stanzas, of which the first three are the same:

-‿-᷉ (extended base), -‿‿- (choriamb), ‿-᷉ (clausula)

The fourth line consists of:

-‿‿- (choriamb), ᷉ (clausula).

In this book the *Carmen Saeculare* (chapter 52) is in Sapphics and the lines quoted in chapter 53 (**vīle potābis ...**) form the beginning of a Sapphic stanza (*Odes* 1.20).

Phōebĕ sīlvā|rūmquĕ pŏtēns | Dĭānă

lūcĭdūm cāe|lī dĕcŭs, ō | cŏlēndī

sēmpĕr ēt cūl|tī, dătĕ quāe | prĕcāmŭr

    tēmpŏrĕ sāc|rō.

Alcaics

This is the favourite metre of both Alcaeus and Horace. In this book *Odes* 2.7 (chapter 42) and 3.26 (chapter 50) are written in Alcaics. They consist of four-line stanzas in which lines 1 and 2 are the same:

⏒ – ⏑ – – ∧ | – ⏑ ⏑ – | ⏑ ⏒

⏒ – ⏑ – – ∧ | – ⏑ ⏑ – | ⏑ ⏒

    ⏒ – ⏑ – – – ⏑ ⏒

   – ⏑ ⏑ – ⏑ – | ⏑ – ⏒

vīxī pŭēllīs ∧| nūpĕr ĭdō|nĕŭs

ēt mīlĭtāvī ∧| nōn sĭnĕ glō|rĭā;

    nūnc ārmă dēfūnctūmquĕ bēllō

      bārbĭtŏn hīc părĭēs | hăbēbĭt.

There is a caesura after the fifth syllable of the first two lines; the second half of the line consists of a choriamb + clausula. The third line starts like the first two but there is no caesura and no choriamb in the second half; it is a very heavy line. The last line moves fast; it consists of an expanded choriamb
(– ⏑ ⏑ – ⏑ ⏑ –) followed by a clausula (⏑ – ⏒).

When the principles of scansion have been learnt, it is important to emphasize that Latin verse should be read with attention not only to scansion but also to the natural pronunciation of the Latin words; the stress accent natural to every word of two or more syllables should not be distorted. There are two rhythms being sounded at once, and the reader has to acknowledge both.

    In the hexameters of Virgil there is usually a clash between the the stress of the scansion and that of the word accent (marked ´) which is usually resolved in the last two feet of the line, where they coincide, e.g.

ā́rmă vĭ́|rūmquĕ cắ|nō, Trōiāe quī | prī́|mŭs ăb | ṓrīs

   Ītắlĭ|ām fā́|tō prŏfŭ́|gŭs Lāvī́nĭăquĕ | vḗnĭt

Attainment test 7 **to be taken after chapter 40 (one hour)**

Read the following passage carefully and then answer the questions below:

A ghost story in which justice triumphs

cum duo quīdam amīcī iter ūnā facerent et ad oppidum quoddam
vēnissent, alter in caupōnā pernoctābat, apud hospitem alter. quī
cum cēnāvissent et dormīrent, vīsus est in somnīs eī quī erat apud
hospitem ille alter ōrāre ut sibi subvenīret, quod sibi mors ā
5 caupōne parārētur. is prīmum somniō perterritus surrēxit; deinde
cum sē collēgisset somniumque vānum esse cōnstituisset,
recubuit.
    tum eī dormientī īdem ille vīsus est rogāre, quoniam sibi vīvō
nōn subvēnisset, nē mortem suam inultam relinqueret;
10 'interfectus' inquit 'in plaustrum ā caupōne coniectus sum et
stercus suprā iniectum est. tē ōrō ut māne ad portam adsīs,
antequam plaustrum ex oppidō exeat.' ille hōc somniō commōtus
prīmā hōrā bubulcō ad portam obviam iit; eum rogāvit quid esset
in plaustrō. ille perterritus fūgit, mortuus ērutus est, caupō rē
15 patefactā poenās dedit.

ūnā together
caupōnā inn; *pernoctābat* stayed the night
apud hospitem with a friend (host)
subvenīret (+ dat.) come to help
caupōne innkeeper
somnium vānum esse cōnstituisset had decided that
    the dream was meaningless

inultam unavenged
plaustrum wagon
stercus (n.) dung

bibulcō carter; *obviam iit* (+ dat.) went to meet
ērutus est was dug out
patefactā revealed

Cicero: De Divinatione 1.56

1 Translate the first paragraph.   (30)

2 What does the dream figure in the second dream ask his friend to do? Why does he have to
    ask this? (*ll.* 8–9)   (2+2)

3 What does the dream figure say has happened to him (*ll.* 10–11)?   (4)

4 What request does the dream figure now make of his friend (*ll.* 11–12)?   (4)

5 What did the dreamer do as a result of the second dream?   (3)

6 What did the carter do?   (1)

7 What happened to the innkeeper?   (2)

8 From the second paragraph, write out an example of (a) an indirect command,
    (b) an indirect question, (c) an ablative absolute.   (6)

9 In what cases are the following, and why are these cases used:
    dormientī (*l.* 8), **vīvō** (*l.* 8), **prīmā hōrā** (*l.* 13)?   (6)

                                                                        TOTAL: (60)

© Oxford University Press: this may be reproduced for use solely by the purchaser's institution.

Attainment test 8 **to be taken after chapter 47 (one hour)**

Read the following passage carefully and then answer the questions below:

One of the guests at the freedman Trimalchio's dinner party has just told a story about a werewolf

attonitīs admīrātiōne omnibus, Trimalchiō, 'tibi crēdō,' inquit; 'sciō
enim tē vēra semper dīcere. sed ego ipse vōbīs rem horribilem nārrāre
possim. cum adhūc puer essem, cōnservus quīdam mortuus est. cum
igitur illum māter misera plōrāret et nōs dolērēmus, subitō strigae
5   strīdēre coepērunt. nōs adeō territī sumus ut immōtī sedērēmus. sed
servōrum quīdam, homō fortis et validus, gladiō strictō, ē iānuā
prōcurrit et strigam mediam trāiēcit. audīvimus gemitum sed – mihi
crēdite; vērē enim dīcam – strigās ipsās nōn vīdimus.
   homō autem noster reversus sē prōiēcit in lectum et corpus
10   līvidum habēbat. sī eum vīdissētis, putāvissētis eum flagellīs caesum
esse. nōs clausā iānuā rediimus iterum ut officia perficerēmus. sed
dum māter corpus amplectitur suī fīliī, tangit et videt manuciolum
esse dē strāmentīs factum; nōn cor habēbat, nōn intestīna, nōn
quicquam. nam strigae puerum ēripuerant et supposuerant
15   strāmentīcium vavatōnem. mihi crēdite, sunt mulierēs quae plūs
sciunt, sunt nocturnae quae omnia ēvertere possunt. sed homō ille
fortis post hoc factum numquam recreātus est sed paucōs post diēs
phrenēticus periit.

Petronius: Satyricon 63 (adapted)

cōnservus	fellow slave
plōrāret	was weeping over
strigae	witches; **strīdēre** to hiss
coepērunt	began
strictō	(lit.) having been drawn
gemitum	groaning
corpus	body
līvidum	black and blue
eum flagellīs caesum esse	that he had been beaten with whips; **amplectitur** embraces
manuciolum	small bundle; **strāmentīs** straw
cor	heart
supposuerant	they had substituted
strāmentīcium vavatōnem	straw doll
plūs	too much; **recreātus** made well
phrenēticus	mad

1   Translate the first paragraph.   (30)

2   When the slave came back into the house, what did he do? What did he look like?   (2+2)

3   How did the narrator and his companions react? **clausā iānuā** (*l.* 11): why do you suppose
    they did this?   (2+2)

4   What did the mother discover had happened to her son? What had the witches done?   (6)

5   What does the narrator say about certain **mulierēs** in the sentence beginning **mihi crēdite** (*l.* 15)?   (4)

6   What happened to the **homō fortis** in the end?   (3)

7   What modern stories of this kind can you think of?   (2)

8   What tense of the subjunctive are **putāvissētis** (*l.* 10) and **perficerēmus** (*l.* 11), and why are they
    in the subjunctive?   (4)

9   From paragraph two, write out an example of (a) an ablative absolute; (b) a purpose clause;
    (c) an indirect statement.   (3)

                                                            TOTAL: (60)

© Oxford University Press: this may be reproduced for use solely by the purchaser's institution.

Attainment test 9   to be taken after chapter 54 (one hour)

Read the following passage carefully and then answer the questions below:

The Roman legions' successes in Germany seem to be a cause for rejoicing, but Quintilius Varus' false sense of security leads to disaster

breve fuit id gaudium: Germānī victī magis quam domitī erant,
mōrēsque nostrōs magis quam arma suspiciēbant. postquam Drūsus
mortuus est, Quīntilius Vārus imperātor factus est, cuius superbiam
barbarī ōdisse coepērunt. duce Arminiō arma corripiunt; sed tanta
5   erat Vārō pācis fīdūcia ut, quamquam dē coniūrātiōne ā prīncipe
quōdam Germānōrum monitus erat, nōn commovērētur. itaque
imprōvidum eum et nihil timentem undique aggrediuntur. castra
rapiunt, trēs legiōnēs opprimunt. summā ferōcitāte pugnātum est.
    nihil illā caede quae per palūdēs perque silvās facta est fuit
10   cruentius, nihil crūdēlitāte barbarōrum saevius, praecipuē in lēgātōs.
aliīs oculōs, aliīs manūs amputābant: ūnius excīsa est lingua, quam in
manū tenēns barbarus quīdam, 'tandem,' inquit, 'vīpera, sībilāre
dēsine!' ipsius quoque Vārī corpus, quod mīlitēs in terrā cēlāverant,
effossum est. signa nostra barbarī adhūc tenent iamque sunt nōbīs
15   recipienda. hāc clāde factum est ut imperium Rōmānōrum in rīpā
Rhēnī flūminis stāret.

id gaudium i.e. the rejoicing over the apparent conquest of the Germans
domitī erant had been tamed
suspiciēbant respected
fīdūcia (+gen.) confidence in

imprōvidum off his guard
opprimunt overwhelm
caede massacre; **palūdēs** marshes
cruentius more bloody; **praecipuē** especially
excīsa est was cut out; **lingua** tongue
sībilāre to hiss

effossum est was dug up; **signa** standards

Florus: 4.12 (adapted)

1 Translate the first paragraph.   (30)

2 What do we find out about the terrain where the massacre took place?   (2)

3 Who especially suffered from the brutality of the barbarians?   (1)

4 Give three examples of the barbarians' brutality.   (3)

5 Who is the **vīpera** (*l.* 12)? What case is the word in? What does the barbarian mean by his exclamation? And how does the sound of this exclamation reflect its meaning?   (1+1+2+2)

6 What two things are we told happened to Varus after his death?   (2)

7 What happened to the Roman standards and what now remains to be done about them?   (3)

8 What are we told in the last sentence was the consequence of the disaster?   (2)

9 **stāret** (*l.* 16): what subjunctive of what verb is this? What is the first person singular of the perfect indicative active of this verb?   (2)

10 Explain the following case usages: <u>**duce Arminiō**</u> (*l.* 4); <u>**aliīs**</u> oculōs, <u>**aliīs**</u> manūs (*l.* 11).   (4)

11 Explain the following constructions: **pugnātum est** (*l.* 8); **signa ... sunt nōbīs recipienda** (*ll.* 14–15).   (2+3)

TOTAL: (60)

© Oxford University Press: this may be reproduced for use solely by the purchaser's institution.

Answers to the attainment tests

Attainment test 7, to be taken after chapter 40

1 When (a certain) two friends were making a journey together and had come to a certain town, one stayed the night in an inn, the other with a friend/host. When they had had dinner/dined and were sleeping, there appeared in his sleep to the one who was with the friend that other one, begging him (lit. appeared to beg him) to come to his help because death was being prepared for him by the innkeeper. He (i.e. the former) at first got up, (thoroughly) terrified by the dream; then when he had pulled himself together and had decided that the dream was meaningless, he went back to sleep (30).

2 Not to leave his death unavenged (2); his friend had not come to his help (1) when he was alive (1).

3 He has been killed (1), thrown into a wagon by the innkeeper (2) and covered with dung (1).

4 To be at the gate in the morning (2) before the wagon can get out of the town (2).

5 He went to meet the carter at the gate at the first hour (3).

6 He ran off (1).

7 He paid the penalty (2).

8 (a) **nē mortem suam inultam relinqueret/ut māne ad portam adsīs**; (b) **quid esset in plaustrō**; (c) **rē patefactā** (6).

9 Dative – it appeared *to* him as he slept; dative – agreeing with **sibi**; ablative – time when (6).

Attainment test 8, to be taken after chapter 47

1 When all were astonished with wonder, Trimalchio said, 'I believe you; for I know that you always speak the truth. But I myself could tell you a horrible thing. When I was still a boy, a certain fellow slave died. And so when his wretched mother was weeping over him and we were grieving, suddenly the witches began to hiss. We were so terrified that we sat without moving. But one of the slaves, a brave and strong man, drew his sword (lit. his sword having been drawn), ran out of the door and transfixed a witch through/in the middle. We heard a groaning but – believe me; for I shall speak the truth – we did not see the witches themselves' (30).

2 He flung himself on the bed (2); his body was black and blue (2).

3 They went back to finish their jobs (2); they closed the door to keep the witches out (2).

4 That he had been replaced by a small bundle made of straw (2), without a heart (1) or intestines (1); the witches had substituted a straw doll (2).

5 They know too much (1); they are nocturnal/work at night (1); they can overturn everything/turn everything upside down (2).

6 He died (2) a madman (1).

7 Award marks for appropriate answers (2).

8 **putāvissētis**: pluperfect (1); contrary to fact conditional clause (1); **perficerēmus**: imperfect (1); purpose clause (1).

9 (a) **clausā iānuā**; (b) **ut officia perficerēmus**; (c) **eum flagellīs caesum esse/manuciolum esse dē strāmentīs factum** (3).

Attainment test 9, to be taken after chapter 54

1   That rejoicing was short-lived: the Germans had been conquered rather than tamed (i.e. the Romans had beaten the Germans but not tamed them), and they respected our customs/civilization rather than our arms. After Drusus had died, Quintilius Varus became/was made general, whose pride the barbarians began to hate. Under the leadership of Arminius, they seize(d) arms; but so great was Varus' confidence in peace that, although he had been warned about the conspiracy by a certain chief of the Germans, he was not disturbed. And so they attack(ed) him from all sides when he is/was off his guard and fearing nothing. They seize(d) the camp, they overwhelm(ed) three legions. The battle was fought with the greatest ferocity (30).

2   It was marshy and wooded (2).

3   The officers (1).

4   They tore out eyes (1), hands (1), a tongue (1).

5   A Roman (1); vocative (1); the Roman can no longer talk/threaten/bite (2); hissing sound (2).

6   He was buried and dug up (2).

7   They were taken by the barbarians (1) and they need to be recaptured (2).

8   The border of the Roman empire (1) was at the Rhine (1).

9   Imperfect (active) of **stō** (1); **stetī** (1).

10 Ablative absolute (2) (there being no present participle of **sum**); dative of the person concerned or dative of disadvantage (2).

11 Impersonal use of the passive (2); gerundive to express 'must', 'should' or 'ought'; **nōbīs** = by us: 'the standards must be taken back by us'/'we must take back the standards' (3).